THE COMPLETE CAR MODELLER
1

THE COMPLETE CAR MODELLER

1

Gerald A. Wingrove

Dedication

To Phyllis, a true partner in all things

First published in 1978 by G. T. Foulis & Company

New edition 1993

This edition published in 2003 by
The Crowood Press Ltd
Ramsbury, Marlborough
Wiltshire SN8 2HR

www.crowood.com

British Library Cataloguing-in-Publication Data
A catalogue record for this book is available from the
British Library.

ISBN 1 86126 644 8

Printed and bound in Great Britain by The Cromwell
Press, Trowbridge

The author expresses his sincere thanks to:

Bryan Beddows, Maidenhead, Berks.
Elliott Machine Equipment Ltd, London
Nixon & Whittick Ltd, Windsor, Berks.
The National Motor Museum, Beaulieu, Hants.
Automobile Quarterly – USA.
Harrah's Automobile Collection – USA.
The many owners of cars and collectors of miniatures
for making this work possible.

Colour photography – Rob Inglis
Additional material and line drawings –
G. A. Wingrove.

Author's Notes
The methods and techniques described in this book
necessarily involve the use of machine and hand tools
which are sharp, heat sources which burn, and a
number of chemicals, such as resins and paint, which
are poisonous. It cannot be over-emphasised that the
greatest care must always be taken when working with
all tools and materials, or injury can result. I have
endeavoured to bring this to the notice of my readers
from time to time, throughout this book. This is
something of which one should not be frightened, just
aware, as, in most cases, accidents can be prevented if
one knows what to expect, and the necessary
precautions are taken.

Dimensions are given primarily in Imperial units
because even now most modelling material, metal and
wire stock is available in these sizes.

Contents

Introduction to First Edition

The car as a subject for modelling has for too long been neglected, especially when one considers the wealth of books, articles and plans that cover model aircraft, ships, railways and traction engines. Could it be that the motor car is an uninteresting subject? The answer to this, of course, is positively, NO! Could it be that as a subject it just does not appeal to the model maker? Again the answer, I feel, must be 'NO' if only from the number of plastic kits of cars that can be seen in every model shop. Could it then be that the motor car presents more than its fair share of problems to the aspiring modeller? This, I think, must be the reason why so few have hitherto been prepared to scratch build the model car. Wire wheels, and more particularly rubber tyres, have until now, presented the modeller with almost insurmountable problems.

My aim in this book is to show that with modern materials and one or two new techniques, it is now as simple to produce an accurate scale and fully detailed model of a motor car, in a scale of your choice, as it is of a ship or an aircraft.

Of the materials used in this context, cold curing silicone rubber is the most important. This material not only makes it possible for the modeller to produce accurate scale and fully detailed rubber tyres, but also gives him a most versatile tool for moulding all manner of intricate parts. Of the techniques, the method of producing accurate scale wire wheels is probably the most important. We will see, that with this method, the modeller can make a relatively simple jig that will produce any number of correctly spoked wire wheels, in both sequence and number. The wheels and tyres are to a model car, as shapely legs are to a woman, a poorly made wheel will distract more than anything else from the charm of the whole model. Consider, for example, that there will be between four and six per car, all of which must look identical and that from whatever angle the car is viewed, one is bound to see at least two of them.

I feel that the word 'CAR' is a most unsatisfactory general description because of the very wide differences, of design, use, shape and size of the vehicles that are lumped together under this heading. We only have to consider the difference between the ordinary family saloon of today with the formula I Grand Prix car and then with the stately formal town carriage of the 1920's and 30's and again with the cars of the 1890's, to see just how inappropriate this word is.

However, in considering this question you will, perhaps, have realised what a vast and fascinating subject the car can be as a subject for modelling. To cover this subject as a whole, would need a library of books and to deal with just a single car would, I feel, greatly restrict the amount of useful information that could be given. So I have chosen to describe the building of a very small part of one family of cars, namely, the sports car. By treating the subject in this way I will try to show two things. Firstly, some of the details that are peculiar to individual cars, particularly with reference to wheels again, and secondly, the methods and techniques that can be applied to any make or type of car of any period. I will also endeavour, where possible, to give alternative methods of approach to some of the problems presented in modelling these cars, bearing in mind that most of my readers may not have such a sophisticated workshop as myself.

It should always be borne in mind that the motor car is a machine made by machines and the approach by the modelmaker should be along similar lines. Whereas the character of some subjects is enhanced by the slight discrepancies of hand-worked materials, this is not so with the car. The wheels again are the prime example of this, they must all be identical and look as though they have all been made with the same tools. The finish of the bodywork is another example. No other subject that I can think of demands, by virtue of its character, such a perfect finish. This may well have been applied by hand by a craftsman on the original cars, but the perfectly smooth high gloss finish is today associated more with spraying, a mechanical method as distinct from the brush. I feel the approach to finishing the model, should be along similar lines if at all possible. I hope to show that this can be achieved in most cases without employing expensive equipment. In this age of 'instant everything' it is not now necessary to purchase a spray gun and air compressor at great expense in order to spray a model motor car. For a few new pence it is possible to buy a spray can from a very wide range of colours, that will produce just the right finish along with the imperfections that will also be required on some parts of our models. Although the majority of the models described hereafter are in private collections throughout the world, several may be viewed amongst the collection of some 25 cars I have built for the National Motor Museum at Beaulieu in Hampshire.

6

G.A. Wingrove

Introduction to the New Edition

It is now more than a quarter of a century since I started automobile modelling, and over a decade since I wrote the first edition of this book. The techniques that I developed in the early years to produce a Wingrove miniature, as originally set out here, were of such good standing that they still serve me just as well today. However, this is not to imply that advances and improvements have not been made over the years. They have, but with the exception of two major ones, most have been of a minor nature, and many of these are in the field of technology by way of improved paints and adhesives.

The two major improvements to the quality of my work over the past decade have been in developing skills to manipulate very thin gauge sheet metal to conform to the intricate and delicate shapes of my chosen subjects, and the designing and building of the louvre press. The former prompted the writing of *Complete Car Modeller 2* (CCM2), while the latter could be more fittingly dealt with in this book (CCM1).

As is my practice, I have not provided a cutting list of sized material from which to build one of these machines. Doing this can provide more problems than answers, for it has always been harder to find a supplier of materials willing to sell one and a half inches of something, rather than 20 feet of it. One does not have to be making things for very long to start accumulating an ever-larger box of odds and ends. It is to this 'scraps' box that I invariably look to first, when consideration is being given to designing a new jig or tool. In most cases there will be just one or two set sizes that will need to be incorporated into a new tool for it to perform the particular task for which it is being made. The outside parameters can be almost anything, and more often than not, can be adjusted to accommodate whatever material is available.

Half of the joy of creating is in producing from your own plans rather than building from someone else's numbers. The most difficult part is coming up with an original idea. If my accumulated experience can assist you in your endeavours, then my time spent with pen and paper has been worthwhile.

Gerald A. Wingrove
Digby, Lincoln.
England.

First Steps

As with an earlier book of mine (The Techniques of Ship Modelling) which dealt with the tools and techniques used in Ship Modelling, and to which I will refer from time to time, I feel that the place to start this subject is again with the work bench and basic tools. Unlike the ship modeller, some form of machinery is essential if my reader intends to go the 'whole hog' and build his models from basic materials. However, with the many standard parts that are now available with the growing interest in radio control model cars, to say nothing of the useful pieces that can be 'borrowed' from innumerable plastic and metal kits, the ardent modeller should still be able to turn out some really first class work with the minimum of tools. I would suggest, though, that this is not a subject for the kitchen table.

The first essential requirement in our work, is good lighting, particularly if you are intending to produce wire wheels. I cannot overstress this point, as the most valuable tools of the craftsman are his eyes, and they are also the most vulnerable to damage.

The heart of the model makers' workshop is the lathe. In my case this has always been an Emco machine. With ship modelling and the early car miniatures, I made use of the most versatile of all miniature lathes the Emco Unimat SL. This one machine tool, with all its attachments, will cater for almost all of the needs of this book. Emco now produce a slightly larger version called Unimat 3, having a cast iron bed for those with a little more money looking for something a bit more solid than the original Unimat.

For the really dedicated, including myself, there is nothing to compare with the Emcomat range. My present workshop is equipped with an Emcomat 7 complete with its milling attachment and it is as good as a second right arm. If I had to design a machine to undertake the work discussed in these pages, it would look like an Emco machine tool.

The next essential in the work area, for the production of first class models, is a place for all the tools. These should preferably be off the bench but within reach of the working position, a little thought and planning here will show in your work for ever after. Of the other tools, the most important is some form of dividing head. The marking out of the three or four spokes of a steering wheel is one thing but the

drilling of between twenty and thirty holes on a diameter of about a quarter of an inch or less, is quite another. However, among the accessories for the Unimat is a small dividing head that would be quite adequate for most of the work that we will be discussing.

The art of modelling the sports cars illustrated in this volume — and I happen to believe it is an art — is not so much in the tools and methods discussed as in the techniques that the modeller will need to teach himself. With silver solder, silicone rubber, the resins and with aluminium, the results obtained will depend much more on how they are used than on the tools or even the materials themselves. As an example, take rope-making for model 'Ships'. Obtain the materials and tools, some fine thread and a rope walk and 'hey presto!' we have our rope. To silver solder two small pieces of brass together is very complex even when we have the solder, flux and a burner. It took me very many months of patient trial and error to master this technique as well as the techniques involved with some of the other materials to be discussed here.

I am not pressing this point to try and discourage my reader from making a start on this subject, but I am trying to indicate, that if the results are not perfect the first time, the answer will, in all probability, lie in the lack of mastery of this or that technique. I can explain my methods with any number of words, but in the end it is the hand of the craftsman that has to learn by experience.

Most of the materials and their use and working will be dealt with as and when they are required during the building of a model. However, as silver soldering is one technique used on and off throughout this work, I feel it would be better to deal with it here.

As you will no doubt know, a car is made up of innumerable complicated shaped pieces of metal. These can be basically divided into three types i.e., those that are round and can be turned, those which are of sheet and can be formed, and those which are cast. The parts that can be turned on the lathe and the parts that can be hammered or pressed from sheet metal present few problems. Castings however are quite a different matter. I feel it would be a waste of time to consider casting single pieces for a 'one off' model, as apart from expensive equipment, one would also need a pattern. There are, however, two other alternatives, the pieces can be milled or carved from the solid whether in metal or wood — or they can be built up from small pieces. I use the former method as a foundation for some of these larger items, such as engine blocks and certain radiators, and the latter for most of the complicated parts and it is the properties of silver solder that make this possible. One of these properties is that a single soldered joint requires a slightly higher temperature to re-melt it than it did to form it in the first instance, so even with a single melting point solder, it is possible to build up complicated assemblies with several solderings without necessarily disturbing the previous joints. I should perhaps point out that this is not possible with soft solder, for although similar assemblies can be built up with this, they are never as strong, nor in my opinion as satisfactory. As the various silver solders have a melting range of between 600 and 800 degrees centigrade, they require the use of a flame as against a soldering iron for the soft solder. There are very many appliances on the market to suit all pockets, from the small methylated spirit burners to bottled gas torches of all sizes and prices.

In the work to be discussed I make use of two types of flames, one is pencil thin for very fine work and the other broad for heating heavier work and for heating aluminium.

Silver solders can be purchased in a variety of shapes, sizes and melting temperatures. The sizes and shapes that I find most useful are 1/16" diameter and the .025" diameter wires and I use both of these with a melting range of 608° centigrade to 617° centigrade. These, as with all solders, require the use of a special Flux. For very fine work, I also make use of a silver solder paste, this is a mixture of metal powder and flux paste which is painted on to the parts to be joined. The differing melting points can greatly facilitate the building up of very complicated assemblies. For example, the first joints can be made with a solder melting at a temperature of 740° to 780° centigrade. The next joint with a solder melting at 630° to 690° centigrade. Thus on working the last joint, there is no possibility of the first two joints coming apart because the required temperature is well below their melting points. The one drawback with this method of working is the necessity to keep a stock of many solders and fluxes. As I mentioned earlier, a silver soldered joint

requires a slightly higher temperature to melt it a second time and it is this technique that I use for all of my soldering, so eliminating the need for using more than one grade of solder and flux. However, there is a great deal of technique involved in being able to build up an assembly with perhaps 40 or 50 separate silver soldered joints. The illustrations throughout this volume though should be proof enough that it is possible and I would hope, by the conclusion, to show that it is within the average model makers abilities. Actual examples and their sequence of building will be discussed at the appropriate time, but I will give the basic points here.

It is in the use of the flame and the flux that the art of silver soldering lies. It is important to always use the correct flux with a particular grade of solder, as one of its properties is to indicate by its fluidity, when heated, that the correct soldering temperature has been reached. This is the vital point as the difference between the first melt and the re-melt are only a few degrees. Another property of the flux is to lower the melting temperature of the solder even on a re-soldered joint. This means, that if we have a piece of brass that already has two soldered joints on it, and we wish to add another piece of metal to the assembly, if this new piece is to be located close to one of the old silver soldered joints, then all that is required is a spot of flux on the new piece bringing it up to the soldering temperature while in contact with the old joint. This method will re-melt and secure the new piece of metal, while the second adjacent unfluxed joint will lie undisturbed. Although the second unfluxed joint will not appear to have melted, it will have become very weak and should this particular piece have much weight, there would be a tendency for the second joint to break. To avoid this I make use of small pins or dowels. These are of brass or nickel silver wire of between .012" to .060" diameter, depending on the size and nature of the assembly. Another advantage of always fitting items together with small pins is that the most complicated assemblies can be built up and dismantled at will and not until the separate items are satisfactory is it necessary to permanently bond the lot together with silver solder. In some cases as we will see, if the assembly is of a really complex nature, then it might be simpler to solder together the pieces into several set assemblies and to build these into the final part. This method of holding pieces together with small dowels or pins is not only used for the parts for soldering, it is, in fact, the key to my method of building models.

When I build a model car I build from the ground up as it were. First the wheels, then axles, chassis, mud-guards, body and the various fittings and accessories. However, I do not paint or have chromed any of these parts until the model is complete. By the use of small pins to hold all these parts together I am able to build and take apart each, or all of the parts, as many times as I wish. When all the parts have been made, the model is completely stripped and the individual parts are given the final finish, whether it be paint, polish or plating and then they are rebuilt for the last time with screws and resins.

Let us now consider how we can treat our subjects. The motor car is not only a most versatile subject by way of the innumerable and vastly differing styles, but it also offers a number of very interesting possibilities on how the subject is modelled. The following types or classes are offered as food for thought.

The difference between one class and the next is in the detail shown and not in the quality of the craftsmanship required. In other words one can reach the same standard in each class.

1) A solid model with only external detail shown. This would show the car as it is seen at the kerbside — with seats, dash, controls and all external body fittings, but no engine or underbody detail. 2) As above but with opening bonnet and doors and engine detail, but no transmission or underbody fittings. 3) Full chassis details complete with or without body, everything to scale but non-working. 4) As (3) but fully working. 5) Fully detailed externally as (1) but fitted with some form of power and radio control.

Each of these classes may be sub-divided into those models that are completely hand-built and those which make use of proprietary parts. It will be seen from this that there are possibilities in each of these classes for varying degrees of talent, mainly depending on how much of the model the builder is able to produce himself. By viewing the subject in this way we can, for example, in any of the classes, start with a basic commercial kit and perhaps just change the body style. The next stage could be to improve some of the detailing, the wheels perhaps, and the final stage being to make every part oneself.

The classes offer three distinct aims. Classes 1 and 2 provide the modeller with the opportunity of capturing the character of his subject without having to concern himself too much with the mechanical side. Classes 3 and 4 offer the opportunity of infinite mechanical detail and classes 4 and 5 provide for the modellers who like to see their masterpiece working.

This work deals mainly with the first type of model, although a chapter is devoted to the second. However, it is my aim while dealing primarily with one class of model, to give sufficient information for my reader to try his hand at the others. I will not, however, touch upon radio control; there are plenty of specialist books on the subject and it is also one of those systems that can be bought off the shelf in kit and component form, so it need not present any problems for those interested in this aspect of modelling cars.

Although I have made quite a point of the technique of silver soldering, there are, of course, several other techniques which will be touched upon later. I have also endeavoured to show, that although the motor car is a sophisticated mechanical subject it is still one that can be approached by someone with little more than the knowledge gained in building plastic kits. This, of course, is not meant to infer that the beginner should expect to be able to build the models discussed in this book from scratch as these were, however, it does mean, that having gained some experience from kit building, the modeller should now be able to progress from modifying kits to building every part himself and this, in stages, as large or small as his abilities and tools will allow. It may be some consolation to my readers to learn that I have had no training in any of the occupations to be discussed, all the methods and techniques have evolved by trial and error over a number of years. I felt, many years ago, that if one could use a saw, a file, glue and a pencil it would be possible to make a start on almost anything and once a start has been made the problems solve themselves.

Let us now have a look at the work to be undertaken and the problems and answers involved. Each of these will be dealt with in the order in which they would be encountered during the building of a typical model.

The first requirement is that of a plan. There are many on the market of a wide variety of cars and of varying degrees of accuracy and detail. If you already have your plans, but they are not to the scale that you wish to work in, I would refer you to the summary preceding the plans at the end of this work. The question of scale is an important one in the context of this volume, as some of the results obtained with the methods described, notably wire wheels, would not necessarily be acceptable in other than the scale used here. This scale is one to twenty or .050 inch to one inch. Though the scale may be enlarged to some extent, it is not really practicable to reduce it, mainly because of the problems associated with getting all the required spokes into a wheel hub on a smaller scale. If there is no plan available for the subject to be modelled, then there is a problem and, as problems and the methods of overcoming them are the themes of my book, we can now get down to work.

A car is a familiar everyday sight for all of us, though in these days of mass-production and all alike styling there is precious little character in so many of the modern ones. However, without delving too deeply it is possible to find some of the more interesting vehicles and in particular, the sports car. Throughout the Summer months there are gatherings of enthusiasts and owners of vintage, veteran, classic and thorough-bred cars. Almost all the great names in cars now have a following that has formed itself into a club or register and most of these hold at least one specialist meeting with their cars annually. These meetings are usually listed, with dates and places, in the 'Veteran and Vintage Magazine' and most, if not all, are of course open to the general public. So if you are looking for a particular car to model, or just one with character, then it is not too difficult to locate it.

Having found the subject, the first thing to do is approach the owner. Always remember here, that if he allows you to make the necessary notes and photographs of his car, he is doing you a great favour. The owners of these cars do a commendable service to us all in spending their time and money in preserving and showing these splendid cars and we should not forget, that but for them, most of the cars of more than about twenty years old would by now, have been lost forever. I have found, almost without exception, that these people are of a very friendly disposition and provided you do not expect them to turn their cars inside out, they are most co-operative towards the model maker. As a token of appreciation, I always make a point of sending the owners of the cars that I have used as subjects, a copy of the completed plans and a photograph or two of the completed model. Another way of showing your gratitude, and one that is always appreciated, is to let the owners have a copy of the photographs you have taken of their cars. It is vital that the model maker should present himself well and maintain the utmost respect towards all those with whom he comes into contact.

Having found our sports car, vintage or otherwise, the first problem is, where to start? Well, we have two tasks ahead of us. One is to record some dimensions and the second is to record, photographically, the shape and proportions. Assuming that we will only have a limited amount of time with the car, that we do not already have any data on it and that we are not particularly familiar with its technicalities, we will be starting from square one. In this case, I start by taking the photographs and these are shot with a camera that will take a sharp negative that will enlarge to about half-plate size (6" x 4"), in a set order. (FIG. 1.) Get to know the subject, her shape and what special features she has. On the way round also make a mental note of the parts to be dimensioned. The actual number of photographs and dimensions that should be taken depends on a number of factors:- The complexity of the subject, the amount of detail to be shown in the model and not least with regard to photographs, the amount of expense that you can afford.

FIG. 1 shows the first eight positions that I use, no matter what vintage the subject is. Plates 1, 2 and 3, illustrate three of these first shots. Note that the second is taken from a low angle, the other two positions, to go with plates 1 and 3, would also be taken from this low position while the shot of the other side of the car, to go with plate 2, would be taken from a medium height. In this way the maximum amount of data can be shown up from quite a small number of basic shots. These will, in any case, give enough data of any subject for a simple model. For the sort of model that we will be building though, an additional number of photographs will be called for. These will be close-ups of individual details, such as brake drums, axles, brake linkage, dash fittings etc., and some of the detailed items, such as steering arms and brake linkage, will require several shots from different angles to illustrate everything.

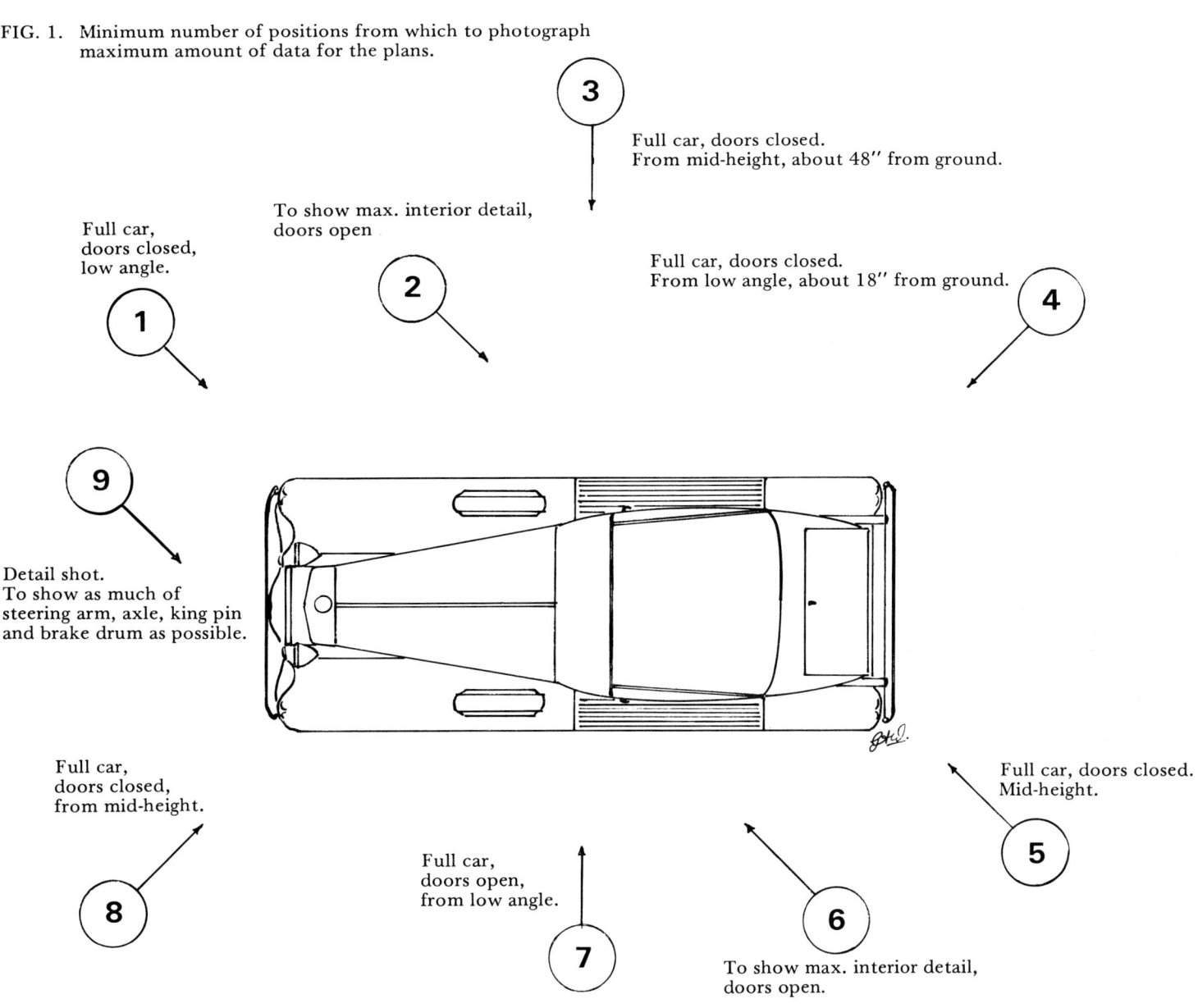

FIG. 1. Minimum number of positions from which to photograph maximum amount of data for the plans.

3 — Full car, doors closed. From mid-height, about 48″ from ground.

Full car, doors closed, low angle.

To show max. interior detail, doors open

2

Full car, doors closed. From low angle, about 18″ from ground. **4**

1

9

Detail shot. To show as much of steering arm, axle, king pin and brake drum as possible.

Full car, doors closed, from mid-height.

Full car, doors closed. Mid-height.

8

Full car, doors open, from low angle.

7

6

5

To show max. interior detail, doors open.

Plates 4 to 12 illustrate the type of close-up detail photography. I have used some of my collection of photographs of the Blower Bentley, as they give a good idea of the complex detail that can be found and requires to be shown even on a model without engine or underbody detail. Having successfully built a scale front end of this car there should be little difficulty with a fully detailed engine on the same scale. Plate 4 is the type of shot that should always be taken as this not only shows plenty of petrol tank pipework and fittings, but the angle from which it was taken also clearly shows the profile shape of the tank. Note that only the bottom is straight, the top, back and front form a slight radius. However, from plate 5 we can see that the flat part at the bottom of the tank is only a cut-out portion to clear the exhaust pipe. The tank does, in fact, have a radiused undersurface as well, other than this small portion. Plate 6 not only shows us the spring shackle — the reason for the photograph — but also clearly shows the relative position of the upward turn of the chassis to clear the back axle. Note also that the body is almost flush with the chassis at this point. Plates 7 to 10 illustrate the need to take several shots of the more complex material. In this case the blower and carburettors. Even with these, several more shots were required to record where some of the pipework disappeared to. Note, in plate 9 a clear indication of the lower axle shape. Note also in these prints, the relative position of the friction-type shock absorbers and the front spring shackle. Plate 11

Plate 1.

Plate 2.

Plate 3.

shows nothing in particular and yet when used in conjunction with some of the other shots may well answer quite a few problems. Several of these should be taken. Plate 12 is intended as a reminder not to forget the floor of your subject. There may be several characteristic features there which would otherwise be missed. Shots of the dashboard and the pedals may, on inspection, reveal in the bottom of one corner some unexpected and unaccountable handle disappearing off the edge of the photograph. Remember, you may not have another chance of seeing the car, so it is better to take more pictures rather than less. You will inevitably find that you have still missed out something however many you take — I usually do. Most often it is some part of the brake linkage which disappears behind something or other and then comes out from under another part of the car at a different angle. Although these can be niggling little things, they will appear, at first sight, to be much more important than they really need to be, particularly if we always bear in mind what we are attempting to achieve with our completed model. In this case the model is to show the car as we would expect to see it at the kerb-side, so if some part disappears out of sight, then that is all we really need to show. If you wish to fill in these missing parts and cannot have access to the car to find out what they are, then a very close inspection of the collection of detailed photographs and a little imagination, will usually provide a satisfactory solution to the problem.

If, for instance, the blank spot is at the change of direction of a brake cable, then it would be safe to assume that there would be a pulley there for the cable to go around. If a number of detail or close-up shots have been taken of the car, then a close inspection, with a magnifying glass if necessary, should reveal similar pulleys and their mountings in another part of the system which will give enough information to fill in the blank spot. This procedure should, however, be used only when there is no alternative, as a model of a 1929 Blower Bentley should only be called that, if that is what it is seen to be. Variations should not be accepted unless they are described as non-original.

This, however, is not to say that licence cannot be employed in portraying the subject as it can sometimes distract from the character of the car to show everything. The best example I can find to illustrate this

Plate 4.

Plate 5.

Plate 6.

Plate 7.

Plate 8.

Plate 9.

Plate 10.

Plate 11.

Plate 12.

point is the art of the caricaturist and the cartoonist — the depiction of as little as possible to convey as much as possible. Who has not seen those cartoons in the Daily Newspapers of prominent people, drawn with, maybe a dozen lines, but instantly recognisable as the particular personality — with a convincing expression as well! We have a similar task with the treatment of a subject as a class 1 or 2 type of model, except that we will be building our caricature in three dimensions and we cannot like the cartoonist, enlarge out of scale, the characteristic features, but must achieve our goal by paying particular attention to how we detail the model. I will have more to say on this point later, when we discuss what detail to show in the model.

Like the photo's, the number of dimensions required depends as much on the subject, as on the sort of model to be made. As a guide though I recorded about two hundred per car to draft the plans for each of the models illustrated in this volume. FIG. 2 shows my method of taking down this information. The vital factor here, and one that I learnt the hard way, is to tie all the dimensions together taking enough of them to be able to cross check the vital ones. I used three primary points from which to take most of the main dimensions. These being, the two axles and the ground. However, it is not practicable to relate all the dimensions to these three points, so a number of secondary points are established, which are double-checked against the one or more of the first three.

To illustrate this, consider the following points in FIG. 2: The wheel base 'A' is the first dimension to be established (wheel centres). Next, the spring shackles 'B' dimensioned fore and aft from the wheel centres and from the ground. 'C' Most of the chassis fittings, brakes, shock absorbers, lamp supports etc., can now be checked relative to the nearest one or more of these. For the body dimensions, however, a higher point or points is required from which to relate the measurements other than the wheel centres. For this I start with the firewall 'D' as it is in the centre and, therefore, offers the best point from which to relate the body measurements with those of the chassis, I also try and relate the rear door post 'E' with the rear axle. The body dimensions can then be related to one or other of these points so that when drafting the plans, we can at least have the body correctly placed on the chassis, a most vital point with regard to showing off

FIG. 2. Sample of noting dimensions from actual car.

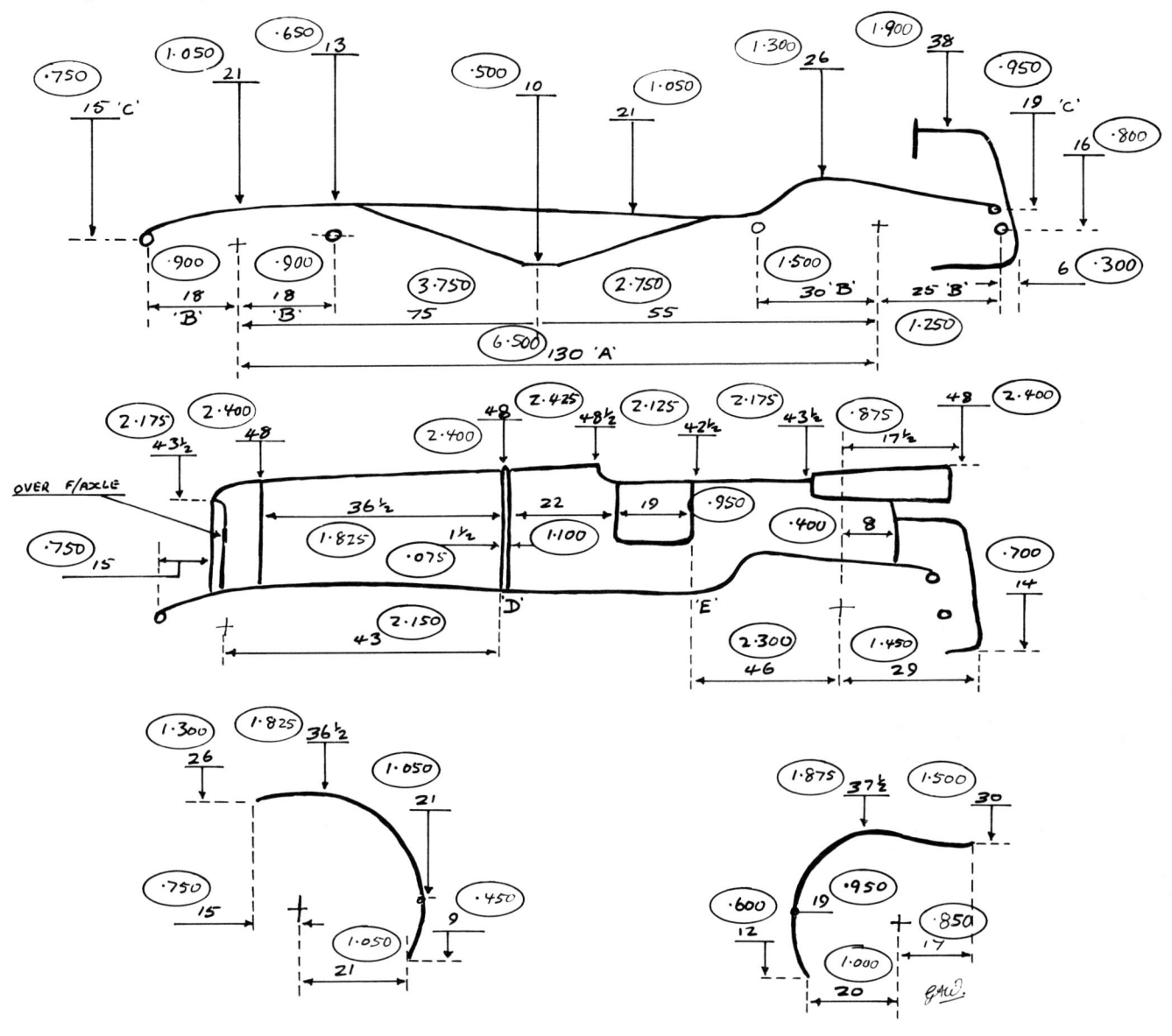

the individual character of the cars of the inter-war years. It will be noted that the wing or fender dimensions are also related to the wheel centres. With these six dimensions per wing, plus a good profile photograph of the particular wing, it is difficult to draft the part incorrectly on the final plans. The measurements so far discussed have dealt with lengths. With regard to widths, these should, in the first instance, be taken across the car at the main longitudinal reference point. Hub caps, spring shackles, radiator etc. If we are dealing with a shapely body, such as the type 43 Bugatti, then as many body widths as possible should be noted, to capture the correct curvature for the plan. However, do remember to relate the points at which each of these measurements are taken with one or more of the main primary points either on the body or chassis and also relate them to the ground.

If, as for instance with the Blower Bentley, we find a rather complicated item to deal with, say, the blower up front, then aim to note only the sizes of the major components and relate one or more of these to a primary point on the chassis. In this case, it is quite easy to relate it to the forward spring shackle, the radiator and the ground. By a short but careful study of even the most complicated parts it is usually possible to find one or more major items in the centre or close enough, to relate by proportion to nearly all the smaller pipes and fittings.

The relative proportions of the smaller components is an important aspect of interpreting the collection of data into a model, as it will be most unlikely that the average modeller would have access to the car long enough to sketch and dimension every single item.

17

The only alternative is to obtain a full and complete set of blue prints of the car and all its fittings, which in most instances is out of the question, as many of the older and more interesting ones have been destroyed, or are otherwise unobtainable.

One should not worry too much about the apparent inaccuracies of the preliminary rough sketches for dimensioning, as these merely serve as a diagram on which to indicate measurements. Before we can start the plan it is necessary to convert all the dimensions into the chosen scale sizes. At one to twenty this is .050 ins. to 1 inch. This is very convenient as it is only a case of multiplying the dimension expressed in inches by five, add noughts and a decimal point to the appropriate place, and we have the new size i.e., 12 ins. times .050 equals .600 ins. In FIG. 2 I have shown the 1/20 scale sizes (in rings) as well as the actual ones, and it is these that are used to lay out the plans and working drawings.

For converting to other scales a slide rule or better still a small electronic calculator can be very useful. FIG. 3 is an indication of the completed side drawing of the 1929 Blower Bentley, drawn up from data collected as above. Further on in this book there is a photograph of the complete model, built from these plans. In FIG. 4 we have the plans for the Bentley Blower. Note that it shows only the main components. I draft all of my plans in this way, as it is these parts that have to be made first and if all the pipework and guards were included, one would have difficulty in finding the basic parts.

With these main components made, it is a simple matter to fill in the accessories from the photographs, checking all the time the proportions of them in relation to the adjacent parts in the photographs and with the scale parts that we have made. We will see a little later in the proceedings, that there is yet another stage with regard to drawings. We have so far seen only the first two. The main use of this second stage is to relate all the data, both dimensional and photographic, to a recognisable whole, with everything drawn together in a single scale. In doing this, we can not only build up shapes from the basic dimensions of the actual car, but we can also add, from photographs, those smaller items that we did not measure, again making use of relative proportions. It is possible (although I seldom make use of the method myself) to calculate dimensions from a photograph provided,

that you already have a measurement of at least one item included in the photo. Say, for example, we have a photograph of the side of a car and the dimensions of one of the doors, and we want to know the dimensions and relative location of the door handles. In this case, it is possible to take the door measurements directly off the photograph and relate them to the known dimensions. When the difference between the two has been calculated the answer can be used to find the missing dimensions of the door handles and any other parts in the vicinity. However, it must be borne in mind that this can only work out satisfactorily if the photograph was taken square on to the particular part being worked and if the parts are within a few inches (actual) of being on the same plane otherwise the answers will be greatly distorted, through the parallax of the lens.

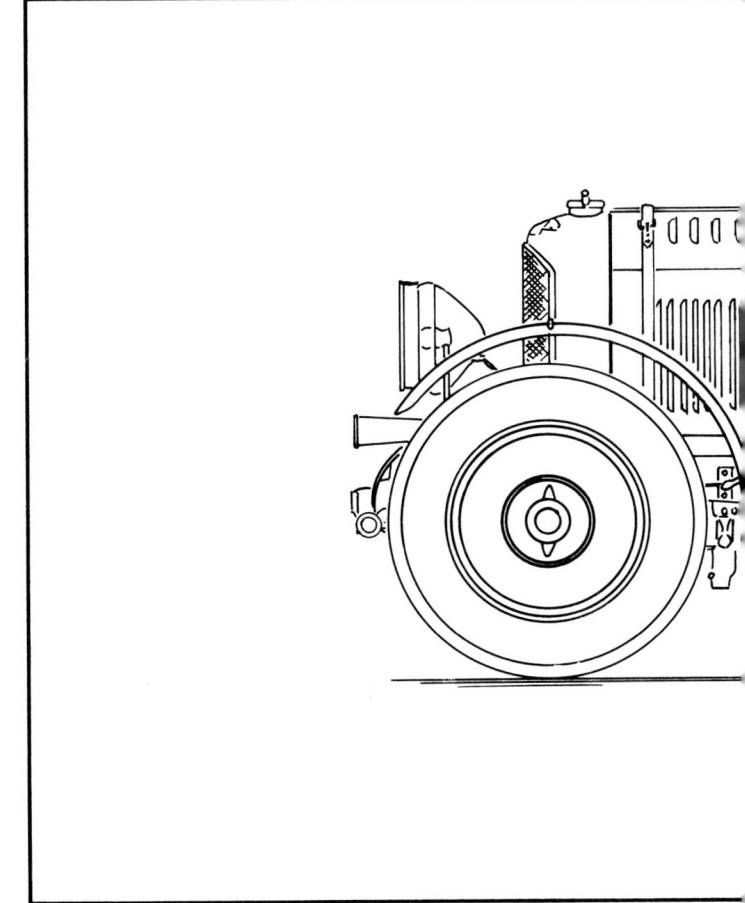

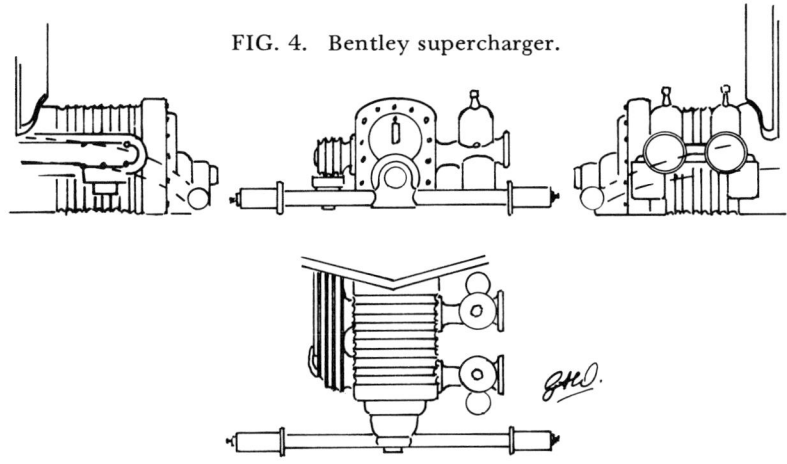

FIG. 4. Bentley supercharger.

Having arrived at a complete plan for our subject FIG. 5, showing all the significant items in their correct positions, I then proceed to rough out a third set of dimensional sketches (FIG. 6). These are the most fully dimensioned, though they are not drawn to scale, the use of this third stage, as may be imagined, is to provide me with turning or cutting sizes. They do, however, also provide me with a breakdown of the more complex parts that on the actual car might well have been castings. FIG 6 illustrates both these points, in this case the Bentley wheel parts. Readers may feel, up till now, that I appear to be drawing the same parts over and over again without any apparent gain. However, if we compare FIG. 2, 4 and 6 the progress is more clearly seen.

To recap briefly, the first stage is to record enough dimensions to cover the outside shapes of the basic part of the subject. The next stage is to put these on paper, all to the same scale, and fill in the missing and smaller details in proportion, to form the plans. The third stage is to take off from the plans, one at a time, the individual components of the car. To dissect each of these into workable parts and to measure them for making up in either wood or metal. The dimensions for this last stage come in the first place from the original measurements, taken from the car and secondly by vernier or rule from the plans. We will come back to FIG. 6 and discuss the parts in detail, when we start building the model chassis and fittings in a later chapter.

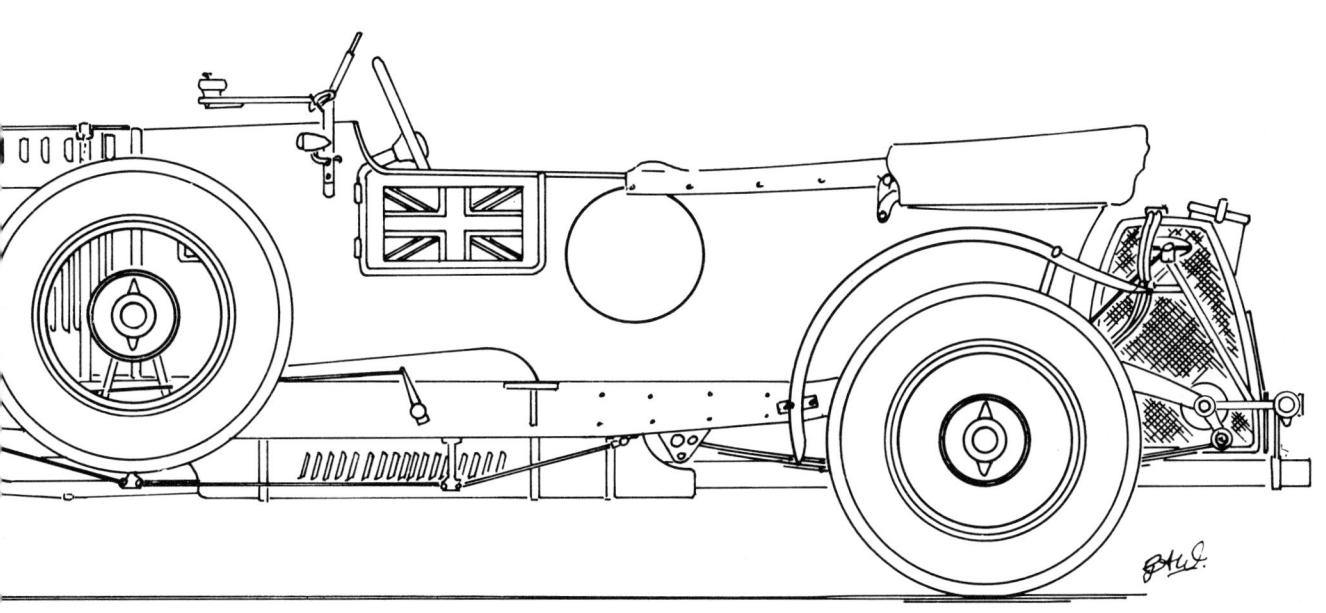

FIG. 3. 4½ Litre Blower Bentley

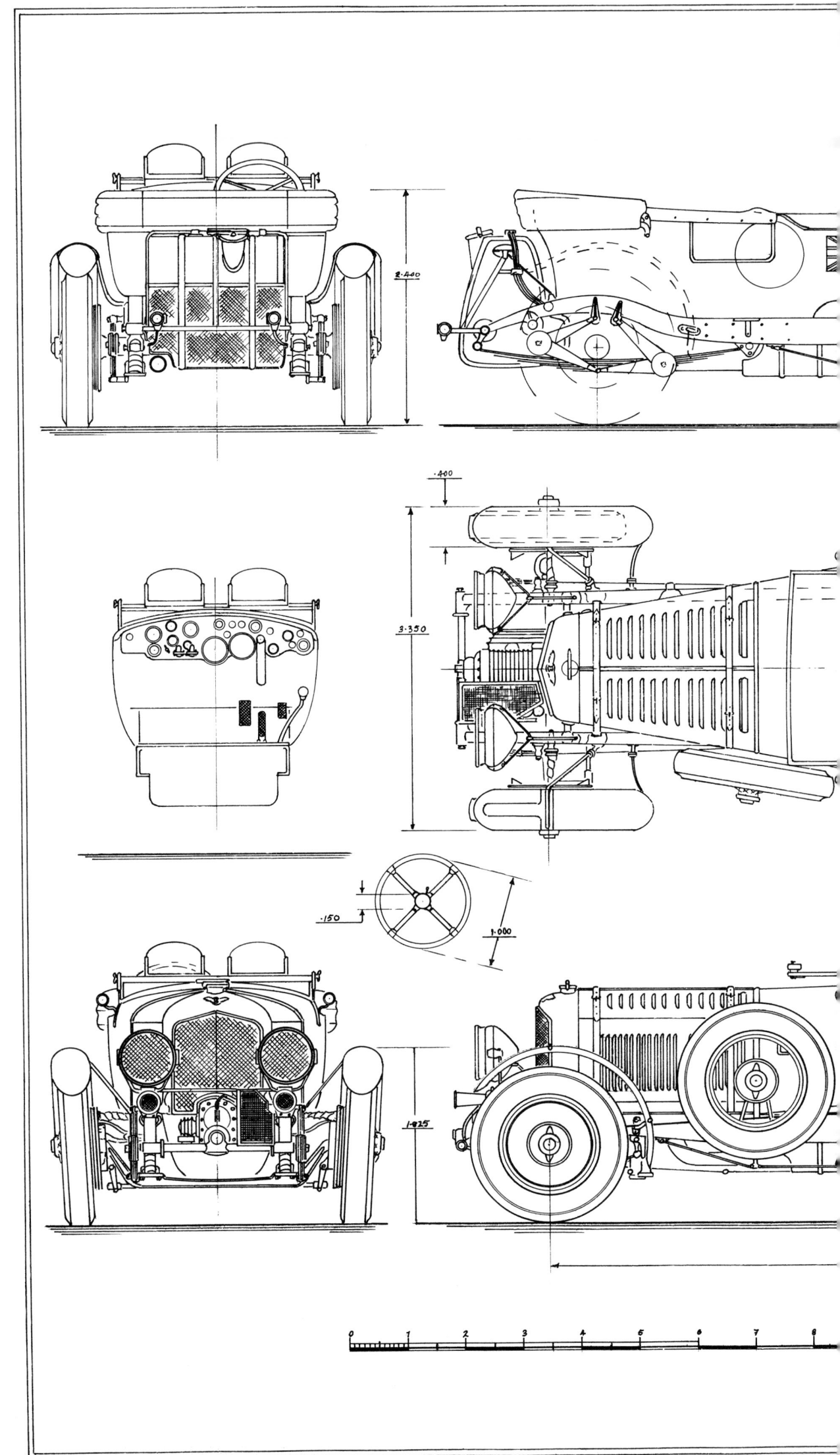

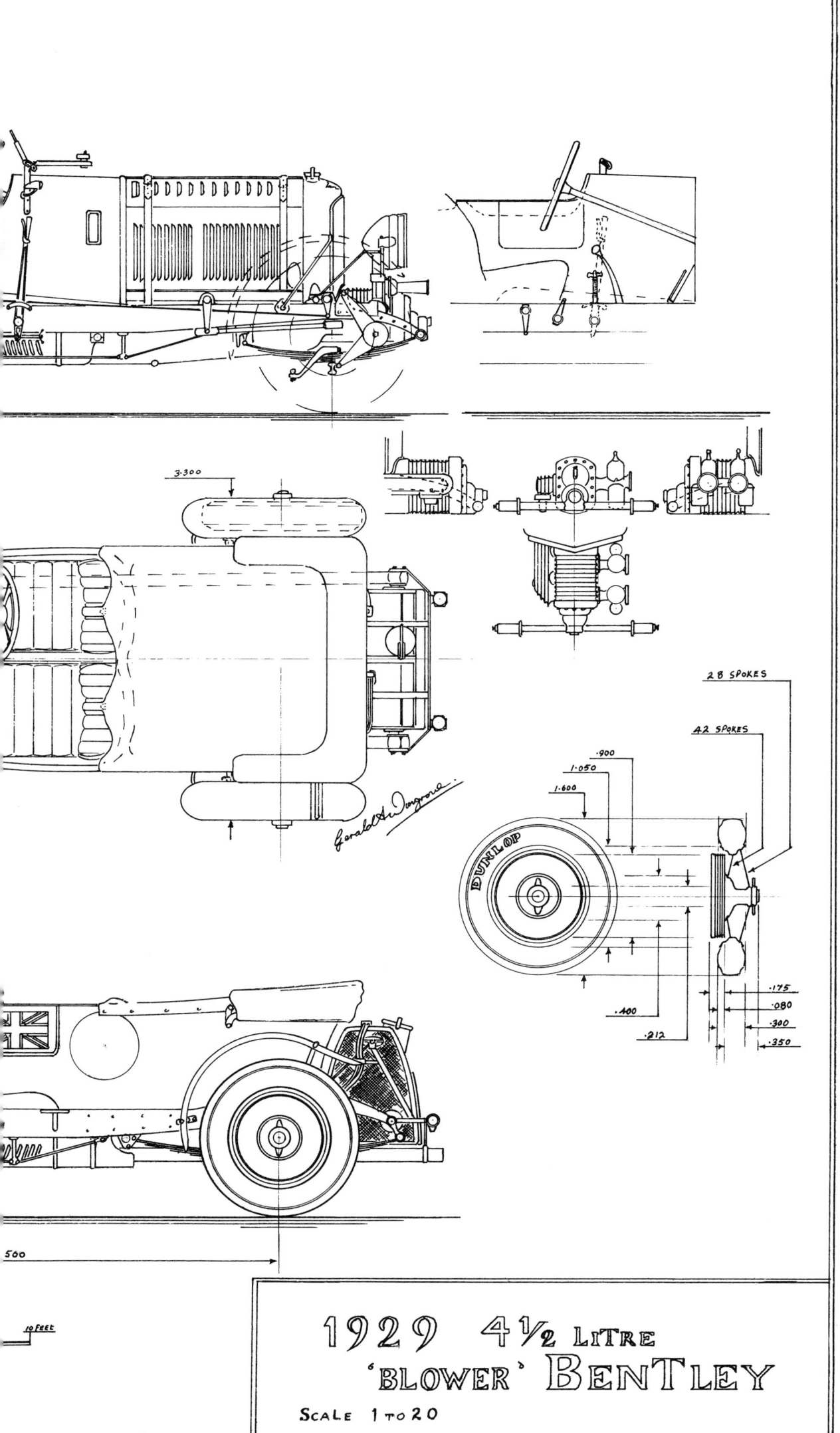

FIG. 5.
Full 3 view
Blower Bentley
plans.

3·300

28 SPOKES

42 SPOKES

·900
1·050
1·600

DUNLOP

·175
·080
·300
·350
·400
·212

Gerald A. Wingrove

500

10 FEET

1929 4½ LITRE
'BLOWER' BENTLEY

SCALE 1 TO 20

21

Chapter 2

Tyres & Wheels

Having collected the data and drafted the plans, we are now ready to start building and as this proceeds from the ground up, we will commence with the tyres. By so doing we will also be dealing with techniques and materials new to many model makers.

Let us consider the material first. It is a cold setting silicone rubber used in the electronic industry for incapsulating delicate equipment and as a flexible sealing material, it is also used as a flexible moulding and mould-making material. Its advantages over natural rubber are many. Not least and particularly for the model maker, its ease of handling. The only equipment required is a cup or small container, a small thin flat piece of wood, for mixing, and a set of household scales.

There are several manufacturers of these rubbers. The products of Dow Corning Corp., have given satisfactory results in the context of our particular requirements. Various manufacturers, however, produce several different types of silicone rubber, each with its own particular curing system. It is therefore, far better for the reader to contact one or other of these manufacturers to obtain copies of their very useful leaflets on current materials and curing systems, than for me to go into detail on the proportions of catalyst etc., applicable to the particular rubbers on the market at the time of writing. However, I think some broad hints, based on my experience with this medium, might prove useful. The material to be looked for should have a viscosity equivalent to double cream. It should be black in colour or at least be able to take a black pigment and have a catalyst curing system able to start setting the material off in about ten to fifteen minutes. The Dow Corning silicone rubber at the time of writing, is white in colour. It will, however accept enough black pigment (lamp black) to produce a very acceptable tyre. When the material is to be used for mould making, it is also useful to be able to extend the curing time (hot life) to several hours.

When the materials and leaflets have been obtained, it may well be found that most of the data contained in the leaflets refers to applications and properties concerning the rubber which are not particularly relevant for our purpose. The reason for this is that we are dealing with a comparatively new material that has been designed to answer the needs of some specific problems in industry. We however are adapting it for

FIG. 6. Sample of working drawing.

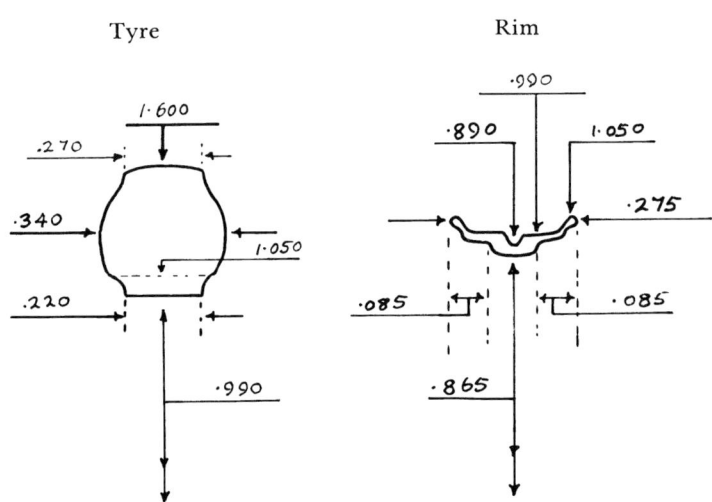

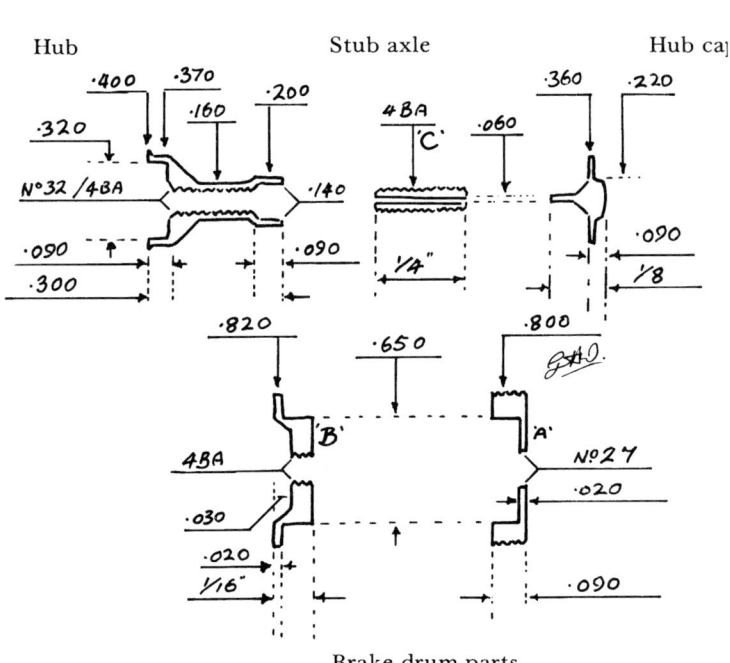

Brake drum parts

our own use. The information required from the current data sheets, will be the proportions of catalyst to rubber and perhaps the addition of an accelerator to shorten the hot life down to the required time for the tyres.

It is advisable to make some trial runs with various combinations of catalyst and rubber etc., based on the data supplied, and before starting actual work with the rubber and noting the setting times and proportions as in the data sheet (they usually deal in terms of mixing up pounds at a time, whereas the quantities required for making single tyres is in the order of from about ¼ ounce up to 1 ounce at a time). In terms of catalyst, this will in all probability be a matter of counting the drops from an eye dropper.

Having discussed our material let us now give some thought on how we can make use of it. Because rubber is a flexible material it is far simpler to mould than it is to machine. So the making of a mould is our first consideration. This can be approached from two directions. The mould can be either machined i.e., turned and bored on a lathe from a suitable material or it can itself be moulded with the aid of a pattern. Because the former method requires more skill in the use of tools and rather more expensive machinery than the average modeller is likely to have, I will confine myself to the latter method, which is, incidentally, essentially that by which I produce my own tyres.

In making patterns and moulds one of the most important points to consider is the possibility of undercuts. On a tyre these will present themselves in the form of the tread pattern around the circumference FIG. 7 'X'. It is sometimes possible to use a little licence in the preliminary design of parts to be moulded to eliminate difficult undercuts. However, in this case, the resultant tread FIG. 7 'Y' would be undesirable as part of a highly detailed and accurate scale model.

The answer to this problem, lies in the use of a flexible pattern. This must, however, be made in a flexible mould taken from a machine pattern. The sequence of events is as follows:—

First a pattern for the tyre is turned up on the lathe. Two rubber half-moulds are taken off of this. A rubber tyre is then made using the rubber moulds. This tyre is finally used as a flexible pattern to produce two hard resin half-moulds in which the set of tyres are made.

Before we take each of these stages in detail, there are one or two points worth mentioning. The first is that the whole process is very much less complicated to undertake than it is to describe, so do not be put off by words. Secondly, one might ask that as a tyre can be produced using the flexible moulds, why bother with hard resin moulds. The answer lies in the fact that with a flexible mould a perfect tyre may not be produced every time and that as some form of release agent is required when moulding rubber in rubber to stop sticking, should this occur, there is a tendency to damage the moulds. The third point worth mentioning is that should the modeller already possess one very nicely detailed tyre in rubber or soft plastic, then he can dispense with the first two stages and use this as a pattern for the resin moulds.

Now to the sequence of events in detail. The tyre pattern is essentially a perfect tyre in every detail,

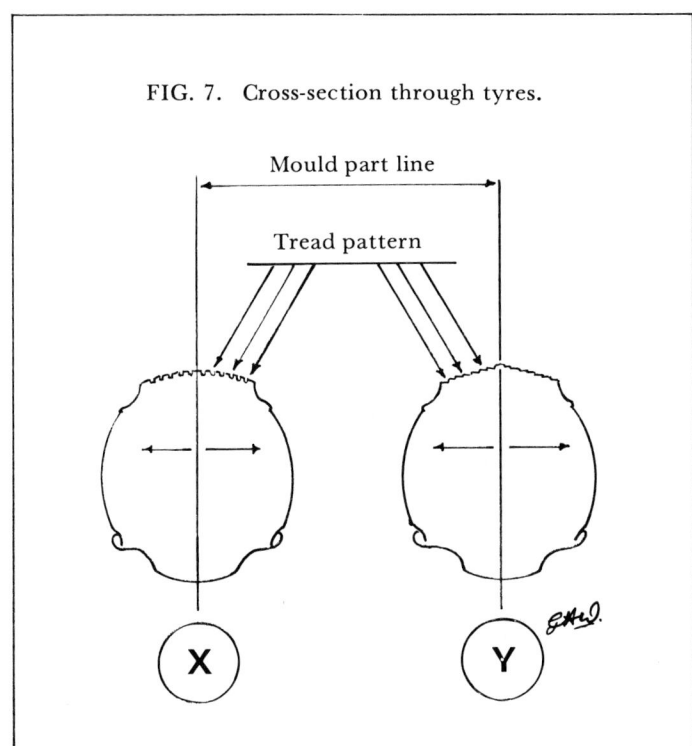

FIG. 7. Cross-section through tyres.

Mould part line

Tread pattern

X   Y

23

but made in a material suitable for machining. My own patterns are machined from perspex, but metal would be equally suitable.

The tyres are, of course, treated as though they were solid so the first turning operation consists of forming the tyre wall on one side complete with any rings, boring the centre out to size and turning the grooves for the tread. The second operation would be to reverse the pattern in the lathe chuck and form the opposite tyre wall. The next operation, should it be required, is to mount the tyre on a suitable spigot or mandrel in a dividing head and mill the small nicks representing the tread around the two edges of the tyre. The final task is to add the wall markings, tyre size and makers name etc.

FIG. 8.   Tyre mould making.

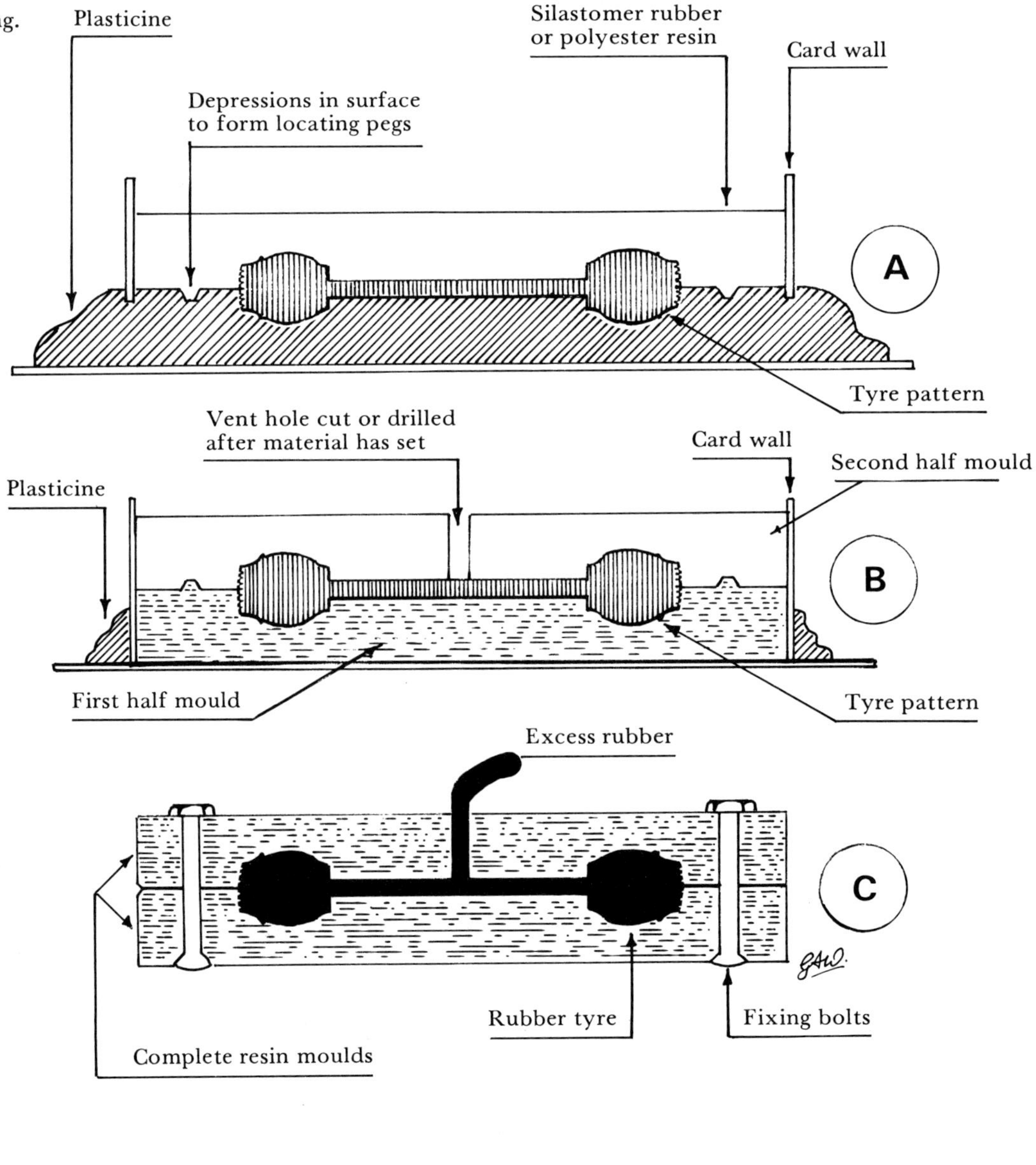

FIG. 9.
Bugatti wheel assembly.

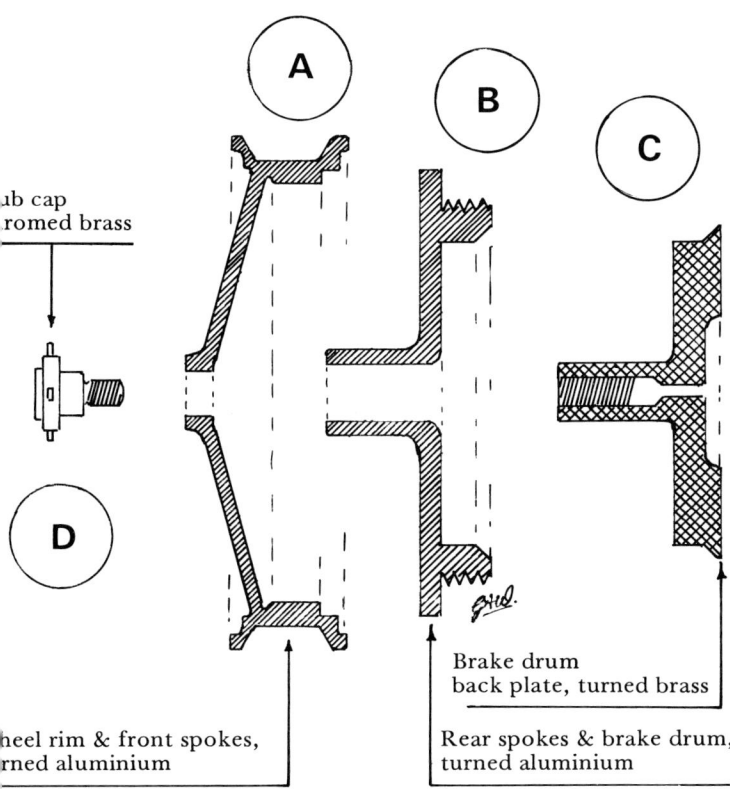

ub cap
romed brass

heel rim & front spokes,
rned aluminium

Brake drum
back plate, turned brass

Rear spokes & brake drum,
turned aluminium

Had we been machining the moulds and not the tyre pattern, then this final touch would have been very difficult, as all the lettering would have to be engraved in reverse! Because we are working with the pattern the only requirement is a pot of thickish paint, a fine painting brush and a steady hand.

The paint that I use for this is cellulose because it dries quickly and can be built up in thickness. The operation consists of painting in on the pattern all the necessary details that are required on the final tyre walls. The silicone rubber is able to reproduce the minutist detail; even a single layer of paint for the wall markings, will appear in the mould as very fine engravings and will reappear on the final rubber tyres.

The completed pattern is now pressed into a bed of plasticine so that one side is masked (FIG. 8A). The plasticine being finally modelled so that it forms an even flat surface, with a sharp crisp edge, where it meets the pattern. It is worth while spending a little time on this last point, as if any complications arise at a later date, they will as likely as not, be along this edge or parting line.

A small tool is now turned up to form several shallow tapered dimples in the plasticine, making sure not to place them too near to the pattern. These will appear on the first half-mould as small pegs and will assist in the correct location of the two complete parts of the mould. A strip of card is then curled and taped to

form a ring and this is pressed into the plasticine to make a wall to contain the moulding material.
The silicone rubber, is then mixed and poured in. This is another of the stages where a little extra care will be amply rewarded. The biggest nuisance in using any of these moulding materials is the creation of small air bubbles. These show themselves in two ways. First there are those produced in the mixing and secondly there are those that have been formed between the material and the pattern either because of some fine recess detail or simply as a result of pouring the material over the pattern.

The answer to the first problem, is to subject the mixed moulding material to a vacuum, which will extricate all the air bubbles formed during the mixing operation. However, this entails more expenditure for specialised equipment and in order to avoid this, much care should be taken in the mixing. On no account must the mixing of catalyst and the basic materials be skimped, as the result will be a mass of partly cured material.

The answer to the second problem is in the technique of using the material. When the material has been mixed and is ready for pouring, a small stiffish brush (hog hair as used for oil painting) is inserted with the material and used with a stippling action to coat the pattern. This procedure is continued until quite a heavy layer of moulding material has been built up on the pattern, ensuring that it is forced into the fine detail and corners. Only when the pattern has been so treated should the remainder of the materials be poured in and then not directly onto the pattern, but into one corner of the container so that the material can flow out and over the part being moulded.

The longer the curing time chosen for the moulding material, the more time there is for the air bubbles that have been mixed in, to find their way to the surface. This can be helped, to some extent, by prodding the surface with a small piece of wood. It will be found that when this is almost withdrawn from the rubber the bubbles stretch and burst and other bubbles, further down, are drawn to the surface.

When the first half-mould has set, the card wall and plasticine are peeled off and any small particles of the plasticine removed from the surface of the mould. The rubber part of the mould surface is then given a light coating of vaseline as a parting agent. Silicone rubber will not normally bond to anything without

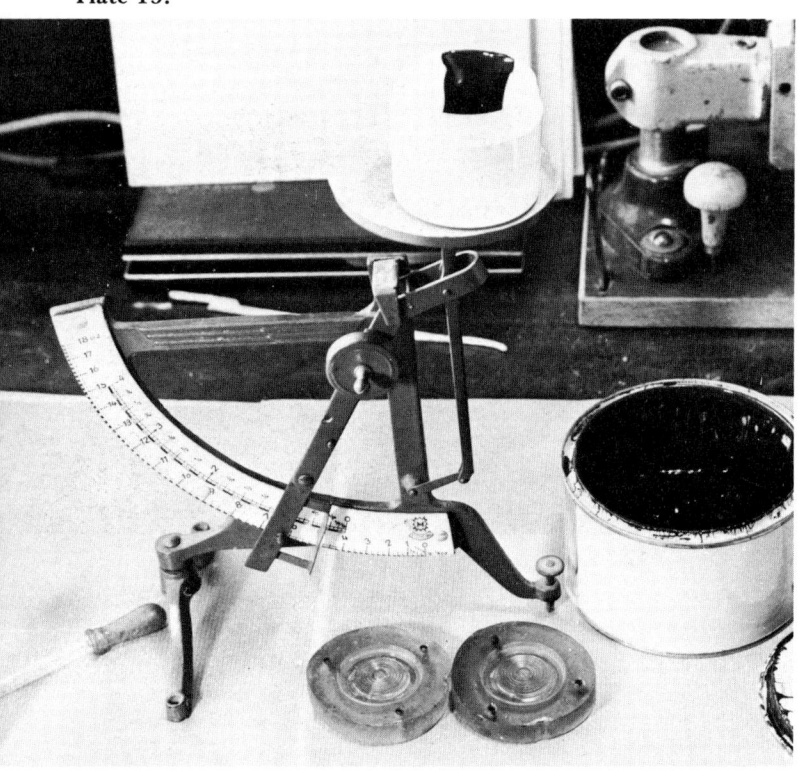

Plate 13.

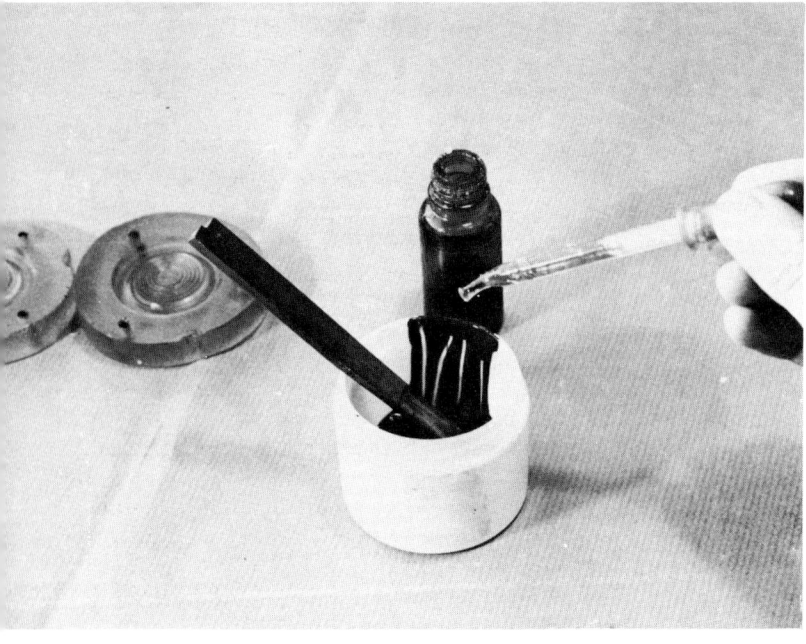

Plate 14.

a special primer. However, there is sometimes a tendency, where fine detail is in use, for the rubber to stick in places. Vaseline or talcum powder, will prevent this.

Another wall of card is now formed and taped to the half-mould still containing the pattern. An amount of moulding material is mixed and the process of stippling and pouring repeated. When this has set and the mould halves are separated, the pattern is removed and a small vent hole (FIG. 8B), about 1/8th diameter, is drilled or cut through the centre of one half. This is to allow surplus rubber to escape when making the tyre.

With all the surfaces treated with a release agent, the mould is now ready to receive the rubber for the first tyre or rather flexible tyre pattern. This should be stippled into both halves of the mould, making sure that no air bubbles are allowed to form in the tread pattern. The tyre cavities are finally filled with rubber, surface bubbles disposed of and the two parts of the mould brought together.

When the mould is opened and the tyre removed, any flash is removed from the mould parting line so that it can be made ready to produce the working moulds. The process to make these is exactly the same as that just described except that plain polyester resin or a similar material is used in place of silicone rubber for the two mould halves. When these have been made, they are matched together and drilled to take three or four small bolts to hold them tightly together in use, in order to eliminate most of the flash that may form on the parting line (FIG. 8C).

It is an advantage to use a short setting time when mixing the rubber for the actual tyres, so that any bubbles that are produced in the mixing, and there will inevitably be some, are contained in the centre of the tyre. If the setting time is an hour or more it will be found that all the air bubbles will have come to the upper surface of the mould and the tyre will be useless.

As there is a very slight shrinkage in the rubber after setting, the time factor is important, if one side of the tyre is not to be slightly smaller than the other. The first two half-moulds in rubber should be made as soon after one another as possible and then left for a day or two to harden before being used to produce the flexible pattern. The same procedure is also advisable when producing resin moulds.

Plate 15.

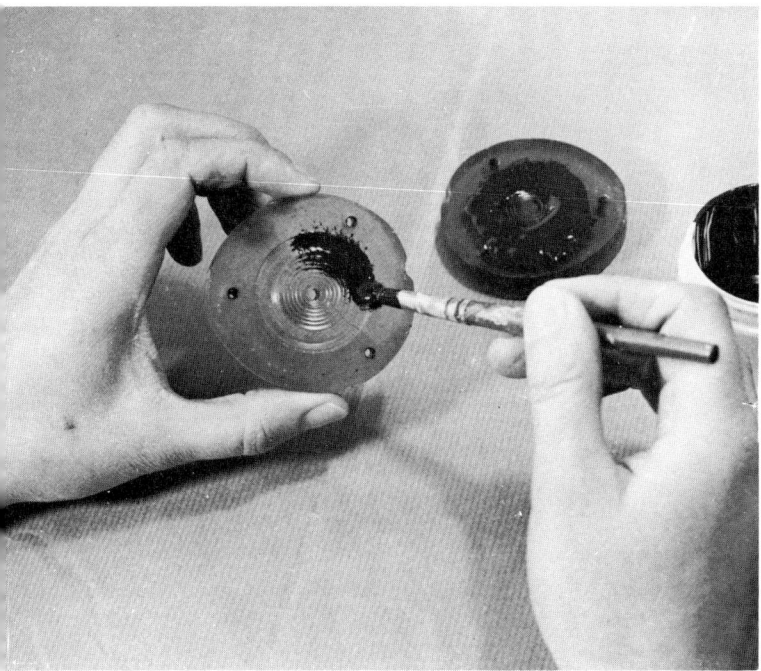

Plate 16.

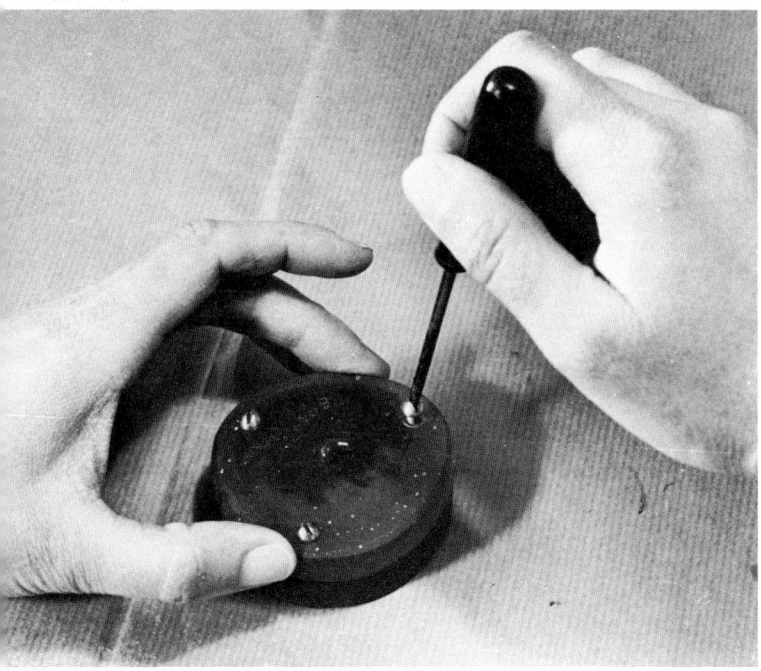

Plate 17.

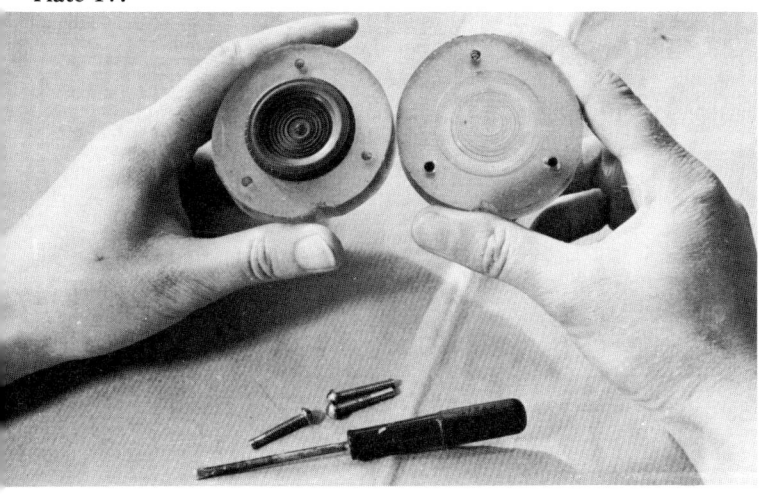

Plate 18.

We are now ready to make our first proper tyres. Plates 14 to 18 show the various processes. The tyre being made is one of a set for the 1927 type 43 Bugatti. Plates 13 and 14 illustrate the simple tools and techniques required in using silicone rubber. First the quantity of the rubber is weighed and the necessary amount of catalyst added with an eye dropper. These are then thoroughly mixed together and stippled into the tyre mould. (Plate 15.)

In plate 16 we see the two parts of the now filled mould being bolted together, with the excess rubber just starting to worm out of the vent hole in the centre. In plate 17 we see the mould open with the newly moulded tyre in the left-hand side. Plate 18 shows the new tyre fitted to its rim and on the right, the waste portion removed from the centre.

Before we progress to the wheels, there are two further points worth mentioning in connection with silicone rubber. Temperature can have a considerable affect on the setting time. The higher the temperature, the faster the setting time. This can be of particular use when making the tyres in that the mixing of the rubber and its application to the mould can be undertaken in the coolest part of the room to be sure of the maximum hot life. When the mould has been closed and screwed home, it can be placed near a radiator or similar moderate heat source in order to set it off as quickly as possible thus preventing the inevitable air bubbles surfacing on one side of the tyre.

Plate 19.

Plate 20.

Before we deal in detail with various wheel styles and
how to make them it might be worth taking a closer
look at FIG. 6, for this not only shows my method of
sorting out turning sizes, but also shows an example
of breaking down the parts into manageable pieces.
The main parts of the wheel are straightforward
enough, but the brake drum is worth specific mention.
It will become apparant as we progress, that some
thought in the early stages can make life much easier
later on. For example, the centre finned part 'A'
requires to be completed in aluminium so it was
turned as a separate item. 'B' and 'C' are to be painted
and 'B' also has to have several pieces soldered to it,
so it is turned from brass. I will have more to say on
splitting parts for painting later. Note also that the
stub axle is threaded for the wheel hub. None of my
models need to be working so the wheels are fixed.
When I have fitted bearings to the wheel hubs, the
models are invariably pushed about and even played
with, which is something that should not be
encouraged for finely detailed miniature. (For the
absolute purist even a finger print can permanently
affect exhibition-class paintwork.)

There are literally hundreds of different wheel designs,
in fact, almost every motor manufacturer appears to
use a different one each time he presents a new model
to the public. However, most of these wheels can be
grouped under one or other of the following headings:
Pressed, cast, artillery, and wire spoked. This order
reflects the relative complexity of each type, com-
mencing with the basic form. Let us therefore
consider each in turn.

The Pressed Steel wheel is a comparatively modern
invention, associated more with the mass produced
family type and so-called modern sports car.
The production of this type presents the minimum
amount of work. The rim would be turned as for a
wire spoked wheel (to be dealt with shortly), the disc
and hub would be turned off a single piece, so that
the outside diameter of the disc is a press fit to the
inside of the rim. Finally these are silver soldered
together after the necessary detailing has been
completed. Alternatively, the wheel could be made in
three parts by separating the hub from the disc. This
would offer an advantage where the detailing of the
wheel disc is an angular pattern rather than one that
could be reproduced on a lathe. The disc with ribs,
rather than rings, could then be cut from thin brass

Plate 21.

FIG. 10. Method of producing Bugatti wheel parts.

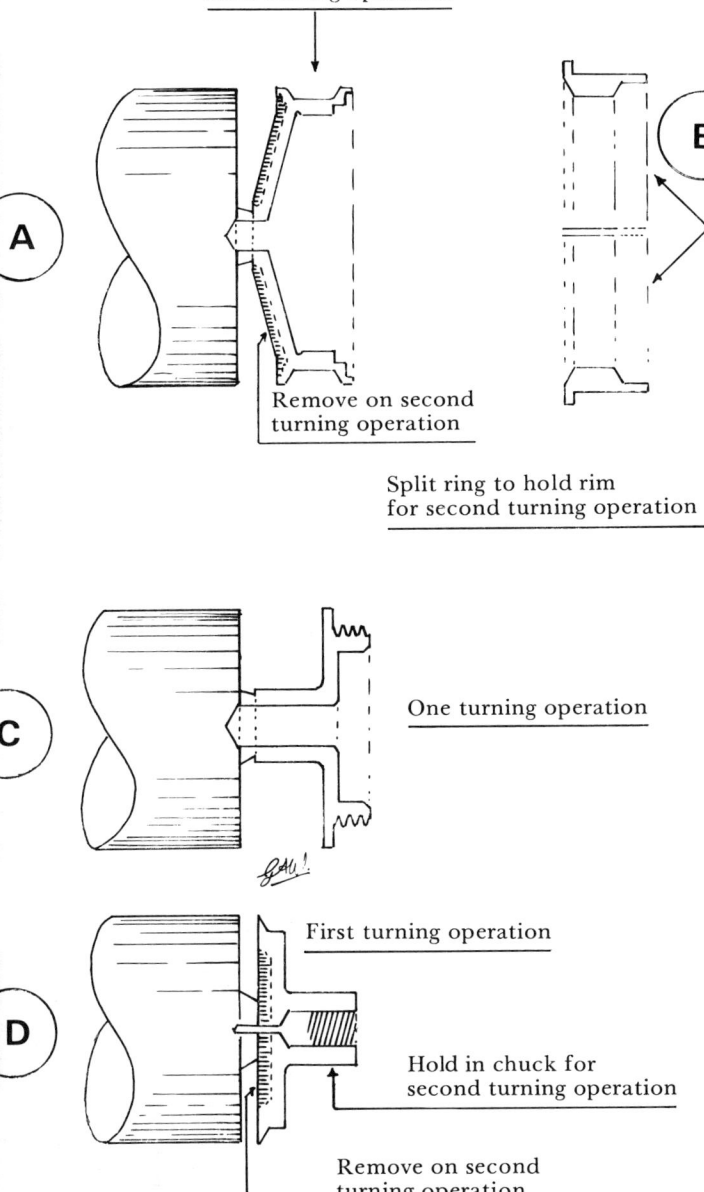

First turning operation

Remove on second
turning operation

Split ring to hold rim
for second turning operation

One turning operation

First turning operation

Hold in chuck for
second turning operation

Remove on second
turning operation

sheet and subjected to the attentions of punch and
die for the detailing, before being silver soldered to
the hub and rim.

For the Cast Wheel (which is enjoying a revival at this
time), I have chosen an example from a type 43
Bugatti. Plates 19, 20 and 21 illustrate the size of the
problem, in that the wheel and brake drum were cast
in one piece. For our purposes this would be
impractical, if not almost impossible. The answer
therefore, lies in machining the wheels from aluminium
bar. Because the wheel is hollow, it has spokes at the
back and front, and it is necessary to make it in at
least two parts. FIG. 9 shows my own breakdown of
the actual wheel into its component parts. ('A' and
'B' FIG. 9). Though there may be several ways of
doing this, the aim should be to make the joints of
the two parts as inconspicuous as possible. Part 'A'
and 'B' are, of course, turned from aluminium and
should form together as a good press fit. The backing
plate 'C' was made from brass, so that it could be
silver soldered to the axles back and front. 'D' was
also turned from brass and was chrome plated and
used to hold the assembly together.

In FIG. 10 the various operations necessary to produce
the Bugatti wheels illustrated in this volume are shown.
At 'A' we see that almost the whole of the rim, inside
and out, and the front spokes and hub, can be
machined in one operation, it only being necessary to
mount it a second time in order to thin the spokes
down and recess the front rim. This second operation
presents a recurring problem when making wheel rims:
how to hold it in a chuck without damaging the very
thin edges. At 'B' we see a possible answer in the form
of a split ring. This is turned from brass bar or tube,
however, before the bar is turned to size, it first has a
section cut off with a fret saw. This, and the place
from which it was cut, is now squared up with a file,
and the two parts are then soft soldered together.
When the turnings and boring are complete and
exactly match the outside diameter and groove of the
rim, they are parted from the bar and heated to
remelt the soft solder, so that the two halves can be
separated. I have found this a much more satisfactory
method of producing split rings, than by utilising
the hack saw after the ring has been turned.

In 'C' FIG. 10, we see that all the work can be
completed to produce the remainder of the hub, the
rear spokes and the brake drum inside and out in a

single operation. In 'D' we see the necessary operations to complete the backing plate and stub axle.

The above events, of course, only refer to the turning operation. To complete the wheels, the spokes will need to be milled and plates 22 and 23 show this in progress. Plate 24 showing both the component parts and a complete Bugatti wheel. For those without a mill and dividing head, a fine metal-work fret saw and a set of needle files, will also do the job.

There is one small feature peculiar to these wheels and apparent in plates 19 and 20, which I did not include in mine and this is, the slight angle that each spoke sets with the rim, it allows the spokes to act as a sort of fan to assist in the cooling of the brake drums. To add this feature to the spokes, one could either mill it in or make up a punch and die. The latter could be made up to modify all the spokes in a single operation, or made to twist each individually. However, I do not feel that the character of the wheel is necessarily lost without this small detail.

The aluminium Bugatti wheel is not a typical example of a cast wheel. I have, however, discussed it in detail because of the very interesting family of cars fitted with it.

The more usual cast wheel, that we would expect to find associated with the sports car, would probably be the modern Magnesium type. These, if made from brass in two parts, present few problems. First the rim is turned and then the hub and spoke diameter

Plate 22.

Plate 23.

Plate 24.

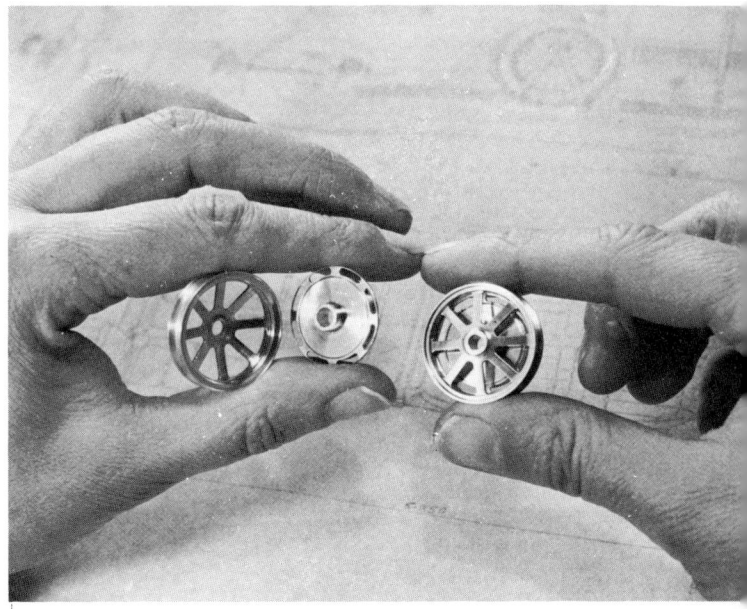

FIG. 11. Artillery wheel parts.

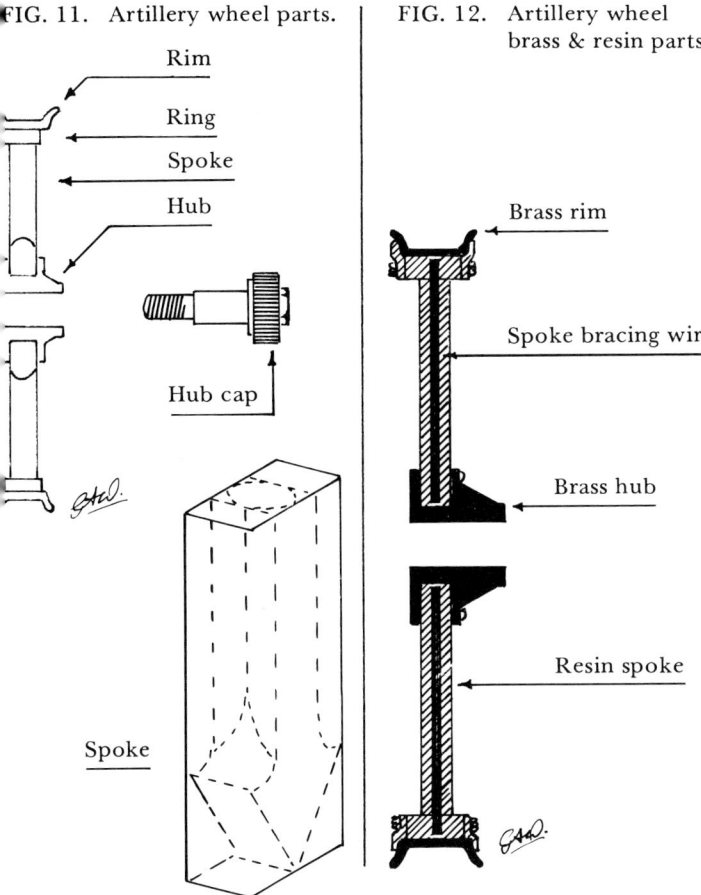

Rim

Ring

Spoke

Hub

Hub cap

Spoke

FIG. 12. Artillery wheel brass & resin parts.

Brass rim

Spoke bracing wire

Brass hub

Resin spoke

FIG. 13. Wire wheel turned parts.

Rim turned from brass tube

First turning operation

Second turning operation
Split bush

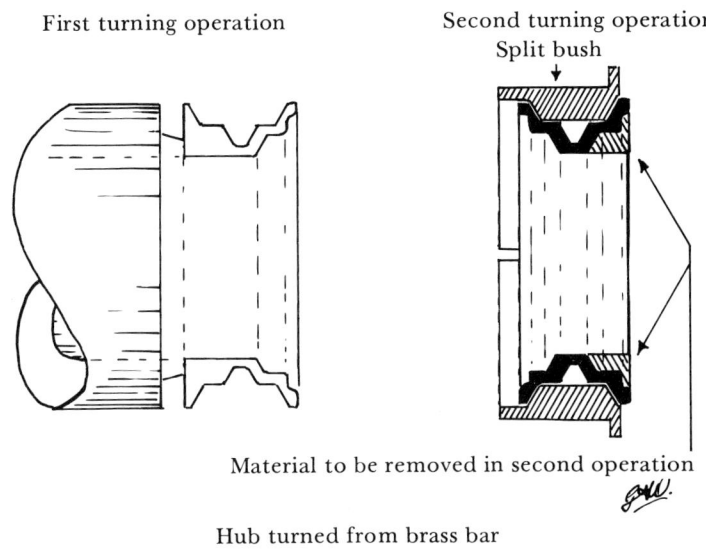

Material to be removed in second operation

Hub turned from brass bar

First turning operation

Second turning operation

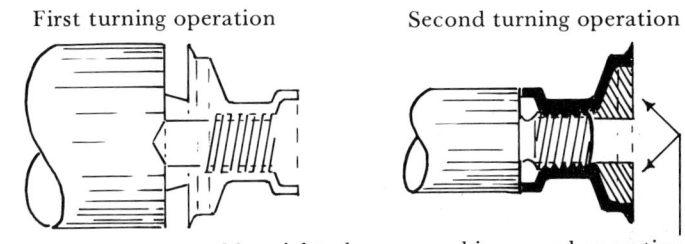

Material to be removed in second operation

Plate 25.

Plate 26.

are turned. The outside diameter of the latter being a press fit in the former. With the hub and spoke diameter separate from the rim, it is an easy matter to file or mill the most complicated spoke form. When the detailing is completed, the two parts are silver soldered together. If the original was dull metal then an unpolished nickel plate would be a satisfactory finish. If the original was polished, however, a full chrome would be required to transform the brass wheels, into presentable replicas.

The next wheel style to consider, is the Artillery Wheel. These were usually made of wood. If the original was finished as polished wood on the actual car, then the model wheel will also need to be made in a similar material. This, however, was not always the case, as many of these wheels were painted and lined. In this case we can approach the subject from a slightly different angle.

Our model utilising this type of wheel is of a 1913 Mercer Raceabout and although the actual car had wooden spokes those on the model were moulded.

First a pattern is made and this is accomplished in exactly the same way as if it were a wheel for fitting to the model. It is however an advantage (to avoid the necessity of dulling the detail with paint or grain filler) to make the pattern from brass or other metal rather than wood.

In FIG. 11 we see the parts required. Rim, ring, spoke and hub. Attached to the ring will also be a number of bolts and plates, which on the full size wheel, held the actual tyre rim to the wheel. The spokes for this type of wheel are best made individually. In this way it is easier to attend to the chamfers and radii on the sides of the spokes. When all is complete, the whole is assembled with silver solder.

The pattern is then set in a bed of plasticine and a half-mould is made of one side, with silicone rubber, in the same way as with the tyre pattern. The plasticine is then removed, release agent applied and the second half-mould is made. Plate 25 shows the pattern, moulds and first moulded wheels for the back and front Mercer wheels, the brass patterns are on the right.

The wheels are moulded in resin, either polyester or epoxy. However, these would not be suitable materials from which to make the entire wheel as they are far too brittle. The answer, therefore, as shown in FIG. 12, is to make the rim and hub from brass. These are set into the mould before the resin is poured, as also are the short pieces of piano wire used to brace the spokes. By thinking in terms of combinations of differing materials in answering some of these problems, we can very often use the good points of each, without having to trouble ourselves with the disadvantages. In this case we are using metal where strength is required and resin for moulding the fine details. In plate 26 we see a back and front Mercer wheel made in this way.

Now we come to the most beautiful wheel style, the Spoked Wheel. These, when modelled neatly and accurately, can make an otherwise indifferent model look immensely appealing, but if poorly made will ruin the most perfect model car.

As may be expected, there is more work involved in producing this type than the previous examples. The work is less involved with tooling, although more patience is required for fitting the spokes. In my experience, about three hours are needed to spoke an average wheel. Before we can get to this stage, however, the wheel parts need to be made and a jig is also required, so let us start at the beginning.

FIG. 13 illustrates the procedure necessary to produce the rims and hubs. Two turning operations are called for to produce each, the most appropriate material, being brass. I purchase brass for the rims in the form of extruded brass tube or hollow rod, which saves on machining and material cost. The brass for the hubs, is, of course, bought as bar. A split bush is again employed in the second turning operation for the rim. For the hub, a small threaded spigot is used, with a strip of fine emery paper wrapped around the outside being all that is required to unscrew the hub from the spigot.

FIG. 14. Spoking jig.

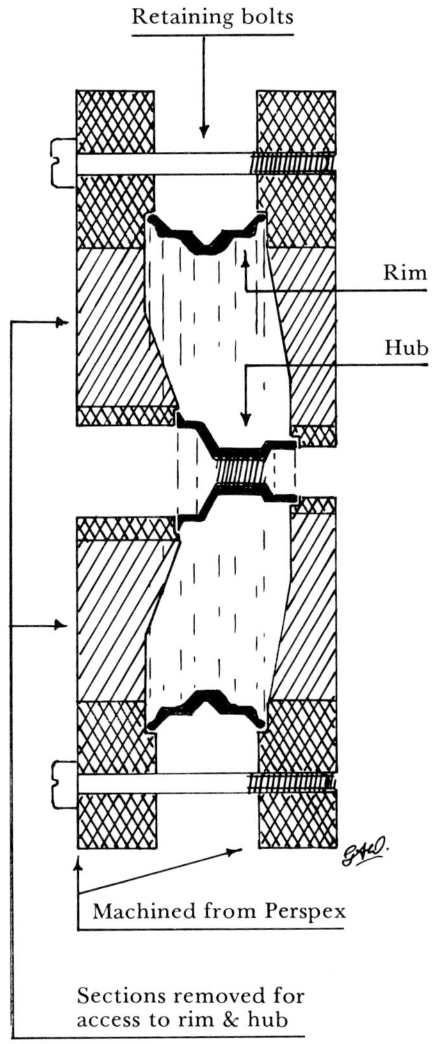

Retaining bolts

Rim

Hub

Machined from Perspex

Sections removed for access to rim & hub

Plate 27.

Plate 28.

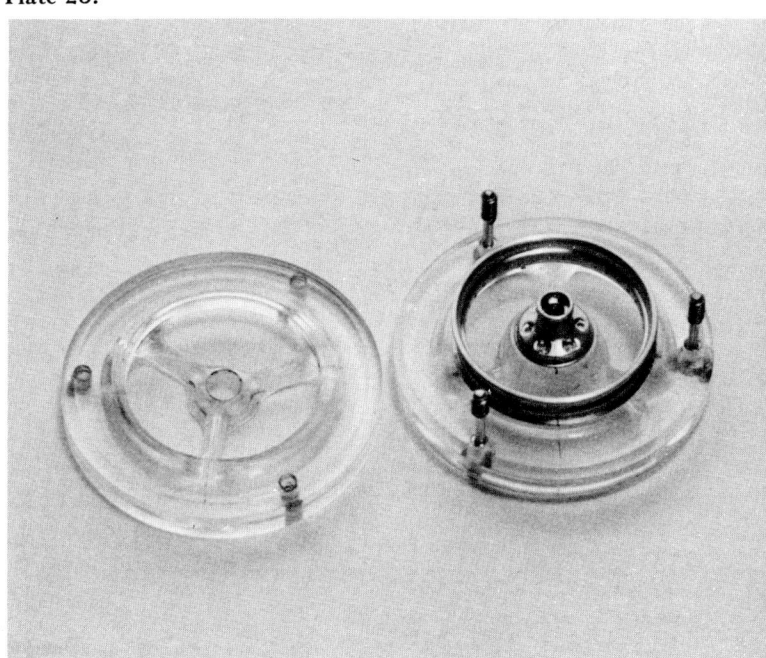

Having turned the component parts, we still have one operation to perform before they can be wired together. This is to drill the spoke holes, and is best performed with the aid of a dividing head. (Plate 27.) Although a ring, accurately marked out and previously drilled, could be slipped over the rim or hub and used as a jig to drill these holes, the drilling of the rim presents few problems, which is more than can be said for the small diameter of the hub. Here great care is needed, as even with a drill of only .012" diameter, there is only about this amount of metal left between the holes when they have all been drilled. It will be seen from this that it is a very easy matter to run the holes into one another if caution is not exercised. Should two holes run into one in the drilling operation, then the hub need not necessarily be scrapped, for a spot of silver solder, deposited in the offending holes, will often allow them to be redrilled in the correct place.

FIG. 14 illustrates how the spoking jig holds the rim and hub in relation to each other, for the spoking operation. The essence of the spoking jig is that it holds the parts in such a way that one can work on the inside and outside of each part without hindrance. The rim and hub should be held as firmly as possible and concentric with one another.

The material that I use for my own jigs is clear perspex (acrylic), this is because it does not impede the light, a vital point when one has to fit seventy or more spokes into a wheel of less than one inch diameter. Perspex also has sufficient flexibility to act as a clamp in holding the hub in place. The main point in the design of the jig is the placing of the spokes on each side. These should be staggered, so that there is no area of the assembled wheel parts that cannot be freely approached from at least one side. These jig spokes, three per side, can be clearly seen in the opened jig in plate 28.

The manufacture of the jig is straightforward, the sizes being determined from the wheel parts and the data taken from the actual car wheel. These should all be settled before the work is commenced and should be worked to as closely as possible.

The actual spoking is accomplished with stainless steel wire of about 36 s.w.g. (.008 inch diameter), and curved tweezers, plate 29, plus a small pair of pliers. The spokes are threaded from hole to hole with the tweezers, and the pliers are used to pull each spoke taut every time the wire is passed out of the hub or rim. It is theoretically possible to fit all the spokes in with a single length of wire although in practice there

Plate 29.

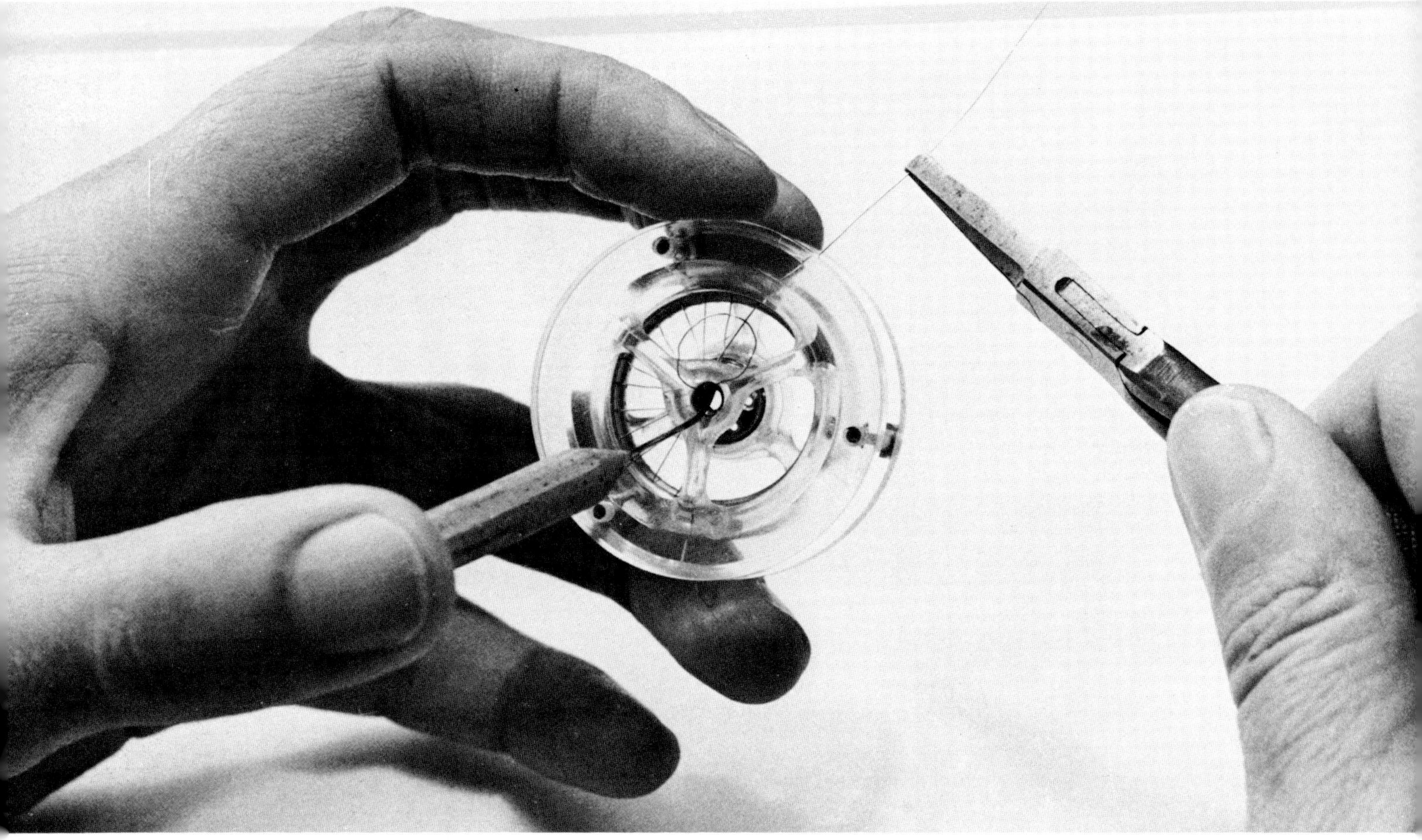

Plate 30.

Plate 31.

are difficulties owing to the contortions it has to go through which result in kinking and metal fatigue. I find the most convenient length is about 12", two or three lengths being necessary to complete a wheel, depending on the number of spokes. Where to start and the sequence in which the spokes are fitted, will depend, to some extent, on the actual wheel being modelled. I was surprised to discover just how many varieties of spoking arrangements there were. I had somewhat innocently believed that all spoked wheels were wired together in the same way. In the first ten cars completed in the Montague Motor Museum collection, only two had the same spoke pattern.

As a general rule, the order of spoking is to complete the front row first i.e. front hub to front rim and then the back row, back hub to back rim. Should there be three rows of spokes then the extra row would probably be a cross over from the front rim to the back hub. If this arrangement is encountered it is an advantage to fit it first, with the front row next and the back row last.

Plate 32.

Apart from the variation of two or three rows of spokes crossing each other in their individual rows, it is sometimes necessary to circle the rim one, two or even three times per row, to achieve the correct sequence. In plate 30 we see a completed wire wheel, in this case for a Brooklands Riley. Note the one on the left which clearly shows the stitching of the wire spokes from one hole to the next.

It may be gathered from this explanation that the wire wheels of your car need more than a passing glance, if they are going to be faithfully reproduced. Plates 31 and 32 illustrate the minimum photographic requirements. In this case they illustrate the detail on a Blower Bentley. This has two rows of spokes. Had there been three, then several more shots would have been useful if all the data of sequence and pattern had not been taken down on paper when the car was being viewed. When collecting data for plans, I usually find time is at a premium, so I invariably leave spoking data to the camera except, of course, for computing the actual number of spokes in each row. I then sort out the pattern and sequence problems from these when more time is available.

For an example of sequence and pattern with regard to wire wheels, we will take the Bentley wheel, plates

31 and 32, which incidentally, is the same size and has the same spoking arrangement as that on the Invicta and M45 Lagonda. FIG. 15 illustrates the simplest way that I have found, so far, to lay out the necessary data for a wire wheel. The first thing to note is the number of spokes and spoke holes required. In this case, twenty-eight for the front row and forty-two for the back row. The datum line 'X' is the key to converting this data into practice with the rim and hub assembled in the spoking jig. In plate 28, the datum line can clearly be seen scribed on both halves of the jig. With some of the more complicated spoking arrangements, particularly those with three rows, it is often an advantage when drilling the rims and hubs to make some mark as to the datum point for fitting these in their correct positions in the jig. In our example, because every third hole in the forty-two-hole row is directly opposite one in the twenty-eight-hole row, (X1, X2

and X3) it is comparatively simple to adjust the parts in the jig so that a row of holes, in line with the jig datum marks can be seen. Having assembled the parts in the jig, we now come to the actual spoking. For this, one should always remember, the first few holes to be stitched are the vital ones. If a mistake is made at this stage it may not be discovered until the last spoke is about to be fitted and the unfortunate result for those who find themselves in this position, is to take some snips, cut all the spokes out and start again.

Starting with the rim FIG. 15 'A' the wire is threaded through the hole opposite the datum line on the jig. It is then passed to 'A1' on the hub and pulled taut. Note: this is the fourth hole on the hub from the datum line. The wire now passes via 'A2', 'A3' on the rim, leaving four empty holes from where you

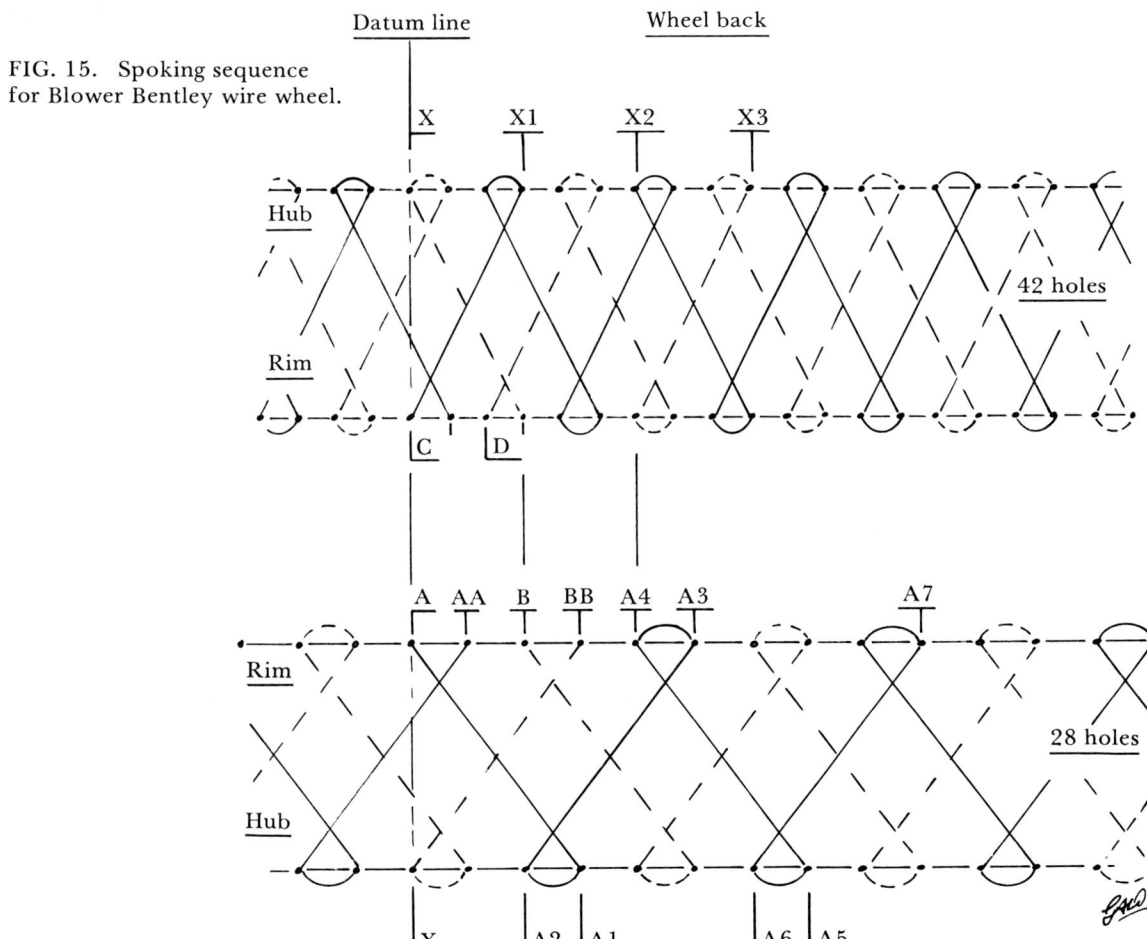

FIG. 15. Spoking sequence for Blower Bentley wire wheel.

Chapter 3

Chassis

started. This first pair of spokes are the most important as all the remainder will be placed relative to these.

The wire from 'A3' is now passed via 'A4' to 'A5' on the hub. It will be seen that this operation will leave only three empty holes from the last one and it is this figure 3, that we must bear in mind, for the remainder of this circle of spokes. As we pass the wire out of the hub and rim we must have three empty holes from the last wired one (A7 via A6). We use one of these holes to turn the wire back to either rim or hub, the remaining two that are empty are used to form the second circle of spokes to make up the front row.

We started our first row at 'A' and it will finish at 'AA'. The second row in order to complete the front is started at 'B' and is somewhat simpler than the first, in that it is only a matter of threading up the alternate pairs of holes in the rim and hub ending at 'B'. The wire ends are twisted together and laid flat in the rim to be hidden under the tyre. The back row of spokes is accomplished in exactly the same manner as the front with the first row starting at 'C' and the second at 'D'.

To complete the wheel, we need one more fitting, a tyre inflater. I mention this item last as it is very easy to fit in the wrong place. It is only after the spokes are in place that the error can be discovered. On inspection of plates 31 and 32 we will see that it is placed between two spokes of the front row. However, if we turn to FIG. 15 we see the sort of problems that a little forethought can prevent. If the hole for the inflater had been drilled between 'A' and 'AA' then, in practice, it would be impossible to make use of it. It should, of course, be placed between holes 'AA' and 'B' where the spokes cross over nearer to the hub. Having constructed our wheel it only remains to be painted and this aspect will be covered in a later chapter, dealing with painting in general. There is, however, one point that I should make here with regard to the finish for wire wheels. Should chrome plating be necessary, it is advisable to have the rims and the hubs plated, before the parts are assembled with spokes. This is essential as the combination of such fine detail as wire spoking, with the comparatively large areas of plain rim and hub, and their close proximity, would make for complications in the plating bath.

With the wheels finished we have completed the most repetitive components of a model car, and for me the one that taxes my enthusiasm the most. I find that to work at my best I must see something growing, as it were, in front of me. When you have spent several months with moulds, patterns, jigs and tools etc., and have come up with a mere set of four, five or six wheels and tyres, they can in no way be made to look like the start of a car. However, put them together on axles and a chassis frame, and everything we do thereafter to the miniature, starts to take on a life of its own.

First, the chassis frame, which if you glance through plates 33 to 43 will indicate exactly what I meant by the model growing before your very eyes. The first stage in making a frame, is to cut out the side members, but before we can do this we must transfer the shape of these from the drawing to the material from which they are going to be made. The material, incidentally, is 1/8" thick brass sheet.

To transfer the shape from the drawing we use a template, which can either be cut from thick card or thin sheet metal, preferably the latter. To overcome the almost impossible task of transferring the data from the plan to the metal via carbon paper, I first glue a sheet of paper to the thin metal, aluminium or brass, and then, with the aid of the carbon, trace the required shape off the plan. It is also worthwhile to trace off such points as rivet heads and fixings for radiator, fire wall, fender stays, etc., as it is important to see that they are in exactly the same place on each side of the frame. With all these points marked out and drilled through the template, it is a much simpler method to use this to mark out the two pieces of metal for the side members than it would be to try marking them out directly from the drawing.

With the template drilled it can be cut from the sheet with snips and trimmed with files to exactly match the drawing. We now arrive at the stage illustrated in plate 33, with the two pieces of 1/8" brass sheet for the frames and the thin aluminium template in the centre. To assist in marking these pieces, I first go over them with a black or blue felt tip pen, when this has dried the template is laid on each and outlined with a sharp scriber, so that a definite impression is left on each, giving the precise shape of the template, not forgetting also to transfer the additional data from the drawing. The waste material is now removed by

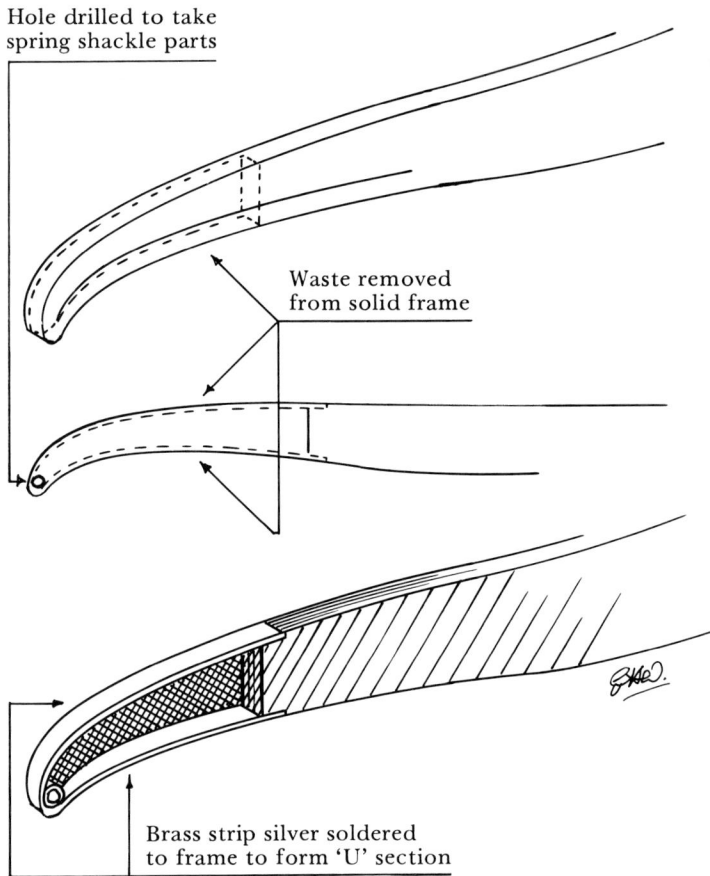

FIG. 16. Chassis frame 'U' section.

Hole drilled to take spring shackle parts

Waste removed from solid frame

Brass strip silver soldered to frame to form 'U' section

either file or milling machine until the actual side frames also match the drawing. My way of doing this is first to drill all the necessary holes, for rivets and fixing points etc., in each piece, with the aid of the template, and then fix the two pieces together with two or three 1/32" rivets using these holes. After this I mill off all the waste material from both pieces together, and the two sides of the frame then match exactly.

It may have been noted that my frame is being built up from two solid side members which on the real thing would each be of a 'U' section. As the particular miniature we are discussing at this stage is to be detailed as a 'kerb side' model, i.e. one showing only that detail that can be seen from the outside, I do not feel it is necessary to go to all the trouble to produce a full 'U' section frame only to hide it from view. With engine and full underbody detail, it is another matter, and we will be covering this aspect in a later chapter. For this type of model I feel it is only necessary to show the 'U' section at each end of the frame, which not only saves a substantial amount of work, but also makes for a sturdy platform on which to build the body.

To make the 'U' section, the four ends of the frame, from the back of the radiator forward, and from the rear of the body back, are cut out on the inside to leave about 1/32" of metal (FIG. 16 plate 34). About .012" is also removed from the top and bottom of each end with a file, so that a brass strip .012" thick x 1/8" wide can be silver soldered in its place, so transforming the ends to the correct cross section.

With the introduction of thin sheet metal into the proceedings it would, I feel, be appropriate to mention a very simple, but invaluable tool for cutting. As anyone will know who has used snips to cut thin sheet, they invariably curl one or both pieces. There are some new cutting tools on the market for sheet metal, that get over this problem, but they nibble a strip 1/16" to 1/8" wide to give a flat surface on each side of the cut, which in our case would mean wasting as much metal as we are using, not a good idea with brass the price it is these days. My cutting tool (FIG. 17) is ground from a piece of broken hacksaw blade, and if shaped, as shown, is really two tools in one. At 'A' we have a sharp 'V' which when pulled across a sheet of metal with the aid of a steel rule, in the direction shown, will cut a thin groove in the sheet. With several

sweeps of this tool, a deep enough cut can be made in the sheet so that when the pieces on either side of the cut are bent several times they will separate on a very clean line. I use this tool for all cutting of sheet metal up to 1/16" thick. A second operation for which this tool is most useful, is to aid the bending of sheet, by putting a 90° groove or crease across the sheet before

FIG. 17. Tool for cutting sheet metal

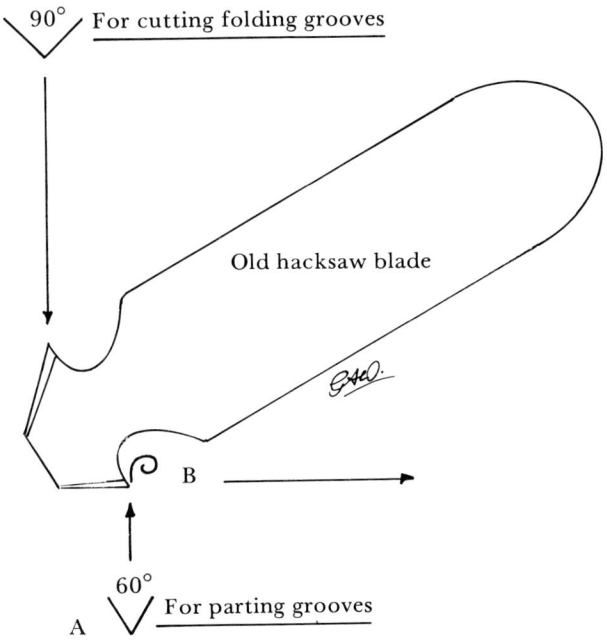

90° For cutting folding grooves

Old hacksaw blade

B

60° For parting grooves

A

Plate 33.

Plate 34.

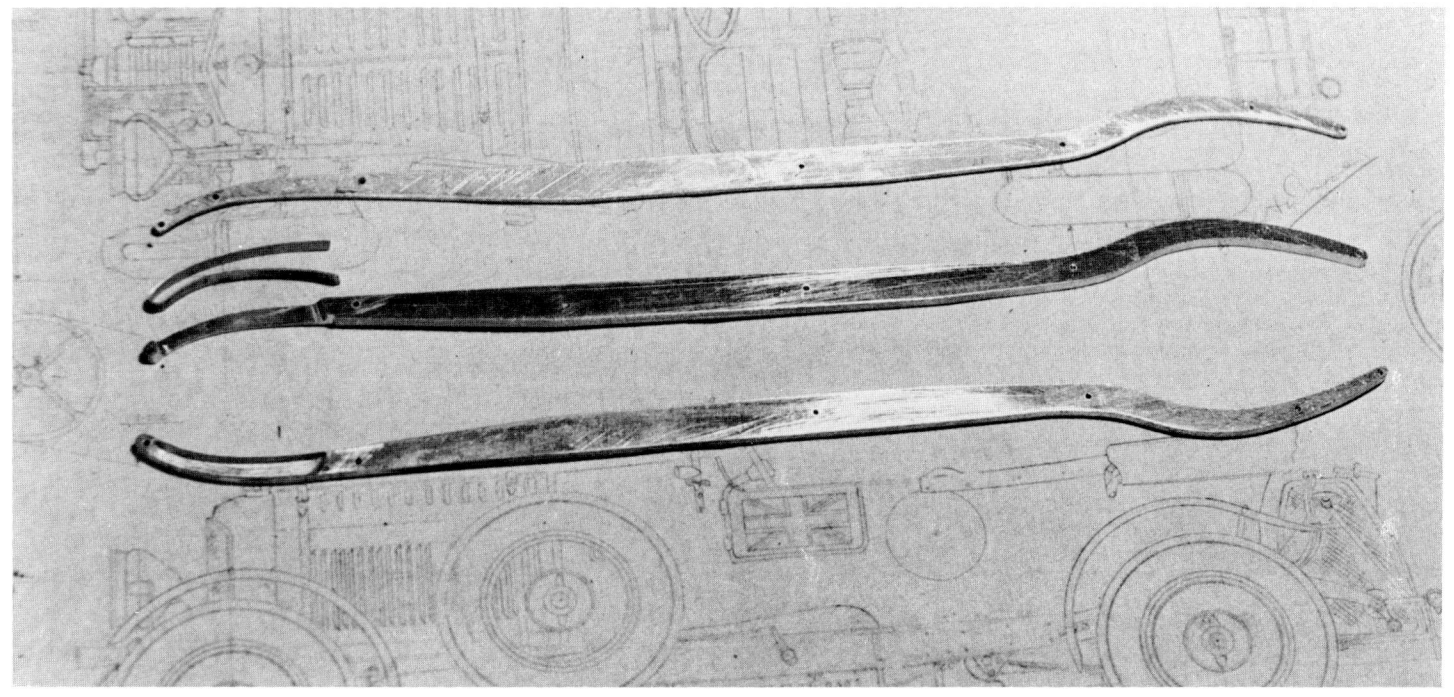

Plate 35.

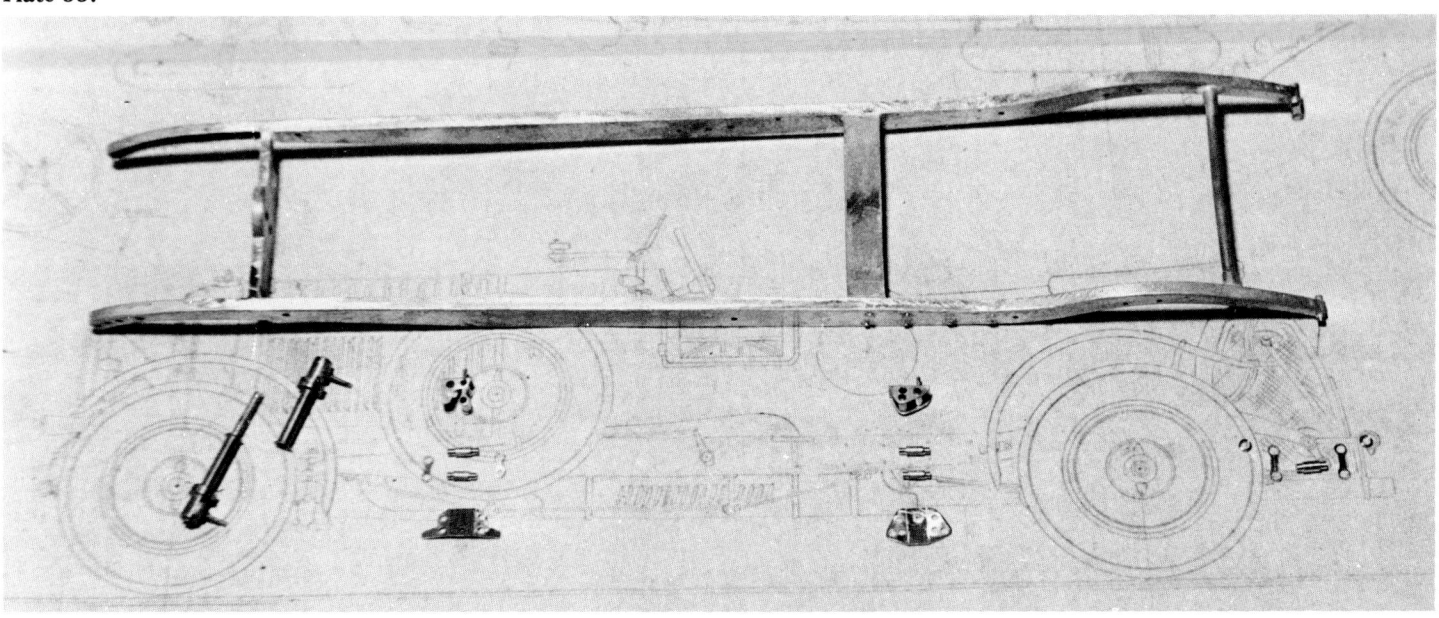

Plate 36.

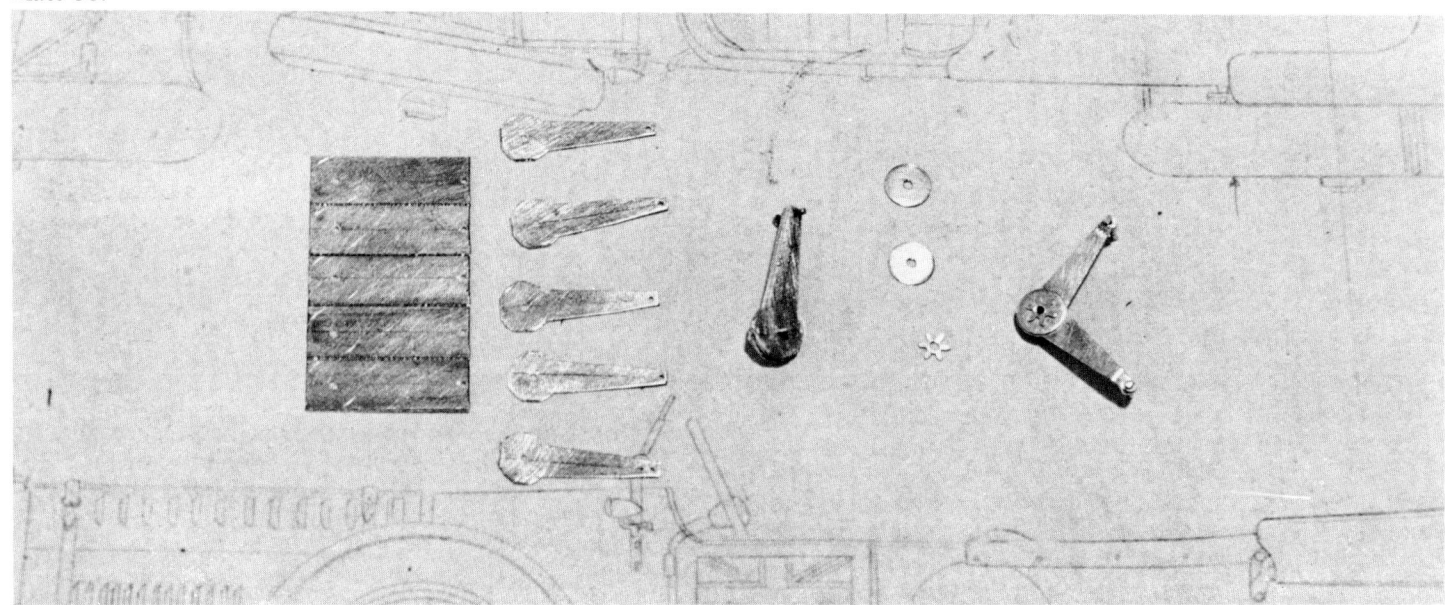

Plate 37.

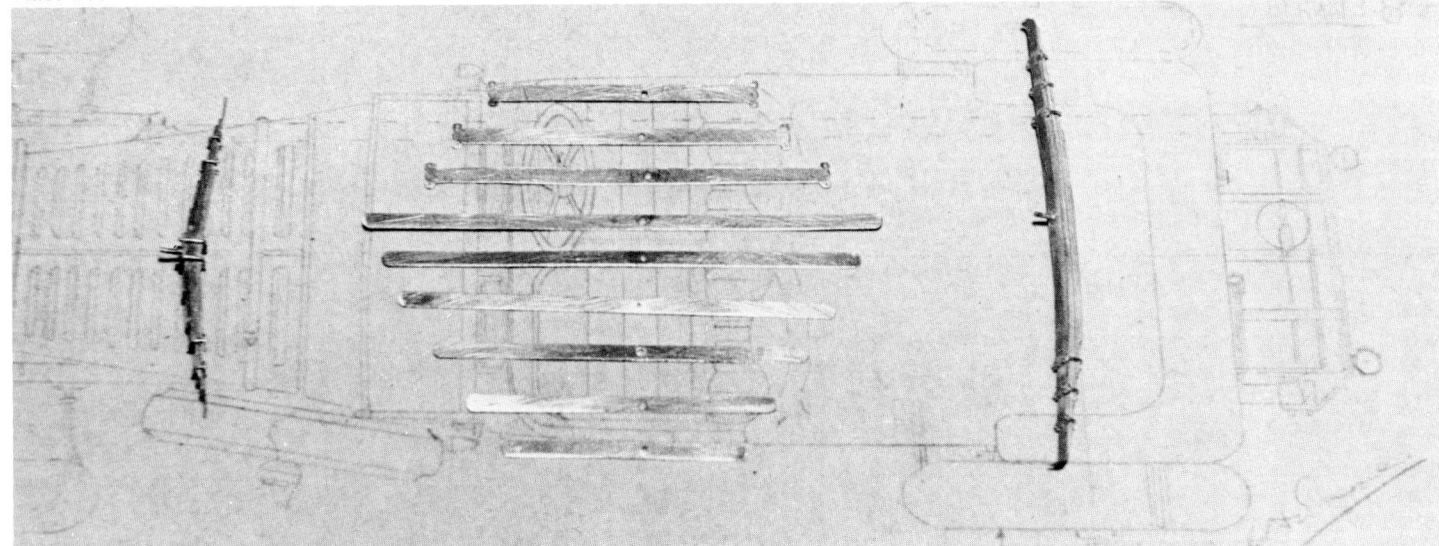

folding. This gives a nice sharp finish to the outside of the corner. The only point to remember when sharpening the tool is to try to get a smooth radius at 'B', as this will greatly assist the ease of working and cleaness of cut.

To return to the chassis frame, our next task is to connect the two side members. As the centre part of the frame is not going to be visable on this particular model, it is not too important what goes there, so, as can be seen from plate 35, I have done this as simply as possible. Note also in this plate the first of the fittings, from left to right below the frame. The front cross member — made in two pieces as it is required to pass through, and support the front end, of the super charger. It will also be noted that both parts are provided with dowel pins for fixing to the front of the frame; this is because it will need to be chrome-plated before final assembly. The second item is the rear shackel for the front spring. This, as can be seen from the lower separated parts, is made up from a small piece of thin sheet, two even smaller flat brass pieces drilled and filed to form a figure of eight and two turned pieces with steps on each end, which fit between the last two parts. The front and rear shackels for the rear spring, are also built up from similar parts, although they are of a different form.

My method of marking these items — those from sheet that is — is to select a piece of suitable thickness, mark it out for all the points necessary for a complete set of shackel, spring and shock absorbers. I then drill all the holes, and split the sheet up with the cutting tool, so that I am left with a separate pile of flats for each item. If we look on the left of plate 36, one of these is marked out and drilled for shock absorber parts. It should be observed that all the parts being discussed have at least two holes in them. This is an easy matter to thread them onto soft wires of suitable size, rivetting the ends over lightly, so that each set of parts can then be filed to shape as a single block (as we did with the two sides of the chassis frame). This not only saves considerable time, but also ensures that each set of parts is identical. The turned parts for the above do not, I think, require any comment.

Plate 37 shows the spring parts. Note, a hole is drilled through the centre of each leaf, as it is necessary, with the aid of a rivet, to hold each leaf in its correct place in the spring. I have made several references to rivets since we got onto the chassis and also to dowel pins.

In ninety-nine cases out of a hundred these refer to 1/32" diameter brass rivets of varying lengths, a supply of which I always have to hand. I find them one of the most versatile of the few stock items that I purchase, not only for use as rivets, but also those with the round heads serve as bolts. There are many instances where we need to show hexagon nuts or bolts on a motor car and if we had to turn to hexagon bar for these and turn each one on the lathe, then we would find ourselves working on them for a month of Sundays. I found quite early on that the best answer was to take a round-head rivet and grip the head lightly in three separate places with a set of smooth jawed pliers, thus converting it to six small neat flats. It will be found that dozens can be adapted in no time at all and, most important, they all look alike.

From the springs we move to the axles and the front one in particular. If we look at FIG. 18 we will get an idea of the sort of work involved. What I have shown here is the average sort of assembly, and it should be noted that apart from the axle beam itself, all the items are made up by simple turning operations. The king pin, which is not required to do any work, is a short round bar with two grooves, dowelled and silver soldered at the top and bottom segments to the brake drum and at the centre section to the axle beam. The brake drum is shown in two pieces. Many of the sports cars I have built in miniature show aluminium finned drums through the wheel, and are also fitted with painted back plates. If we separate these parts, as shown, we can turn the finned drum from aluminium and polish it and it is finished, whereas the back plate really needs to be turned from brass, as it not only has the king pin to be soldered to it, but also the brake linkage and maybe, small inspection covers as well. It is much easier to solder these to brass than aluminium. It is also a much simpler matter to polish one item paint the other and then fit them together, than to try and make them as one, masking the finned part in order that the remainder can be painted.

As can be seen, the wheel is threaded onto the stub axle, which is not only a very convenient way of locking wheels in place, but also holds the brake drum parts together. The hub cap can also be held in place with a thread of its own, or, if of very small size, with a spot of resin.

For the axle beam itself I use one of two methods. If it is of small section and the grooves are of equal

FIG. 18. Front axle parts.

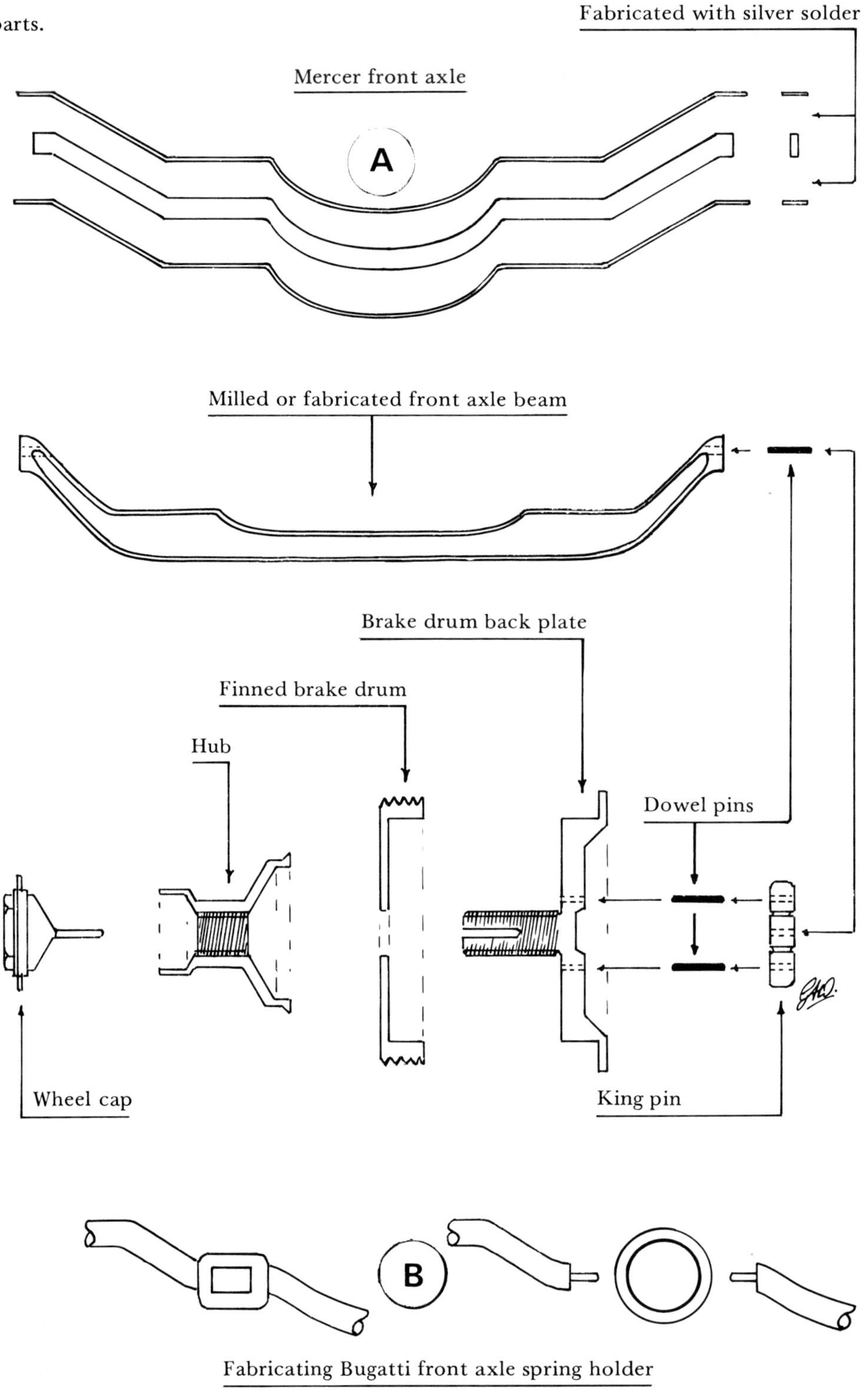

Fabricated with silver solder

Mercer front axle

A

Milled or fabricated front axle beam

Brake drum back plate

Finned brake drum

Hub

Dowel pins

King pin

Wheel cap

B

Fabricating Bugatti front axle spring holder

width and in reasonably straight lines, then I would mill it from the solid (plate 38). If, however, it is of a more complicated shape, as for example that of the Mercer Raceabout, (FIG. 18'A'), or it is of large size, then I will laminate it from three pieces of sheet, with the aid of silver solder. The only axle beam I have found that cannot be constructed by one of these methods is that of the Bugatti, as can clearly be seen from plate 45. The answer here is to turn all the pieces from bar, square off the two parts that fit over the springs, then dowel and silver solder all the parts into a single piece (FIG. 18'B').

For the rear axle, if, as with the Blower Bentley, it cannot be seen on the finished model (because the undertray extends to the very back of the car), then all we require is a bar with a step and a short thread on each end, as can be seen in plate 39. For those vehicles not fitted with undertrays, then some form of bell shape will need to be fabricated around the centre part of the axle, and a sample prop shaft led from this forward to a block representing a gear box. It should be borne in mind though, that the type of model being discussed is only required to look correct when viewed from a distance at eye

Plate 38.

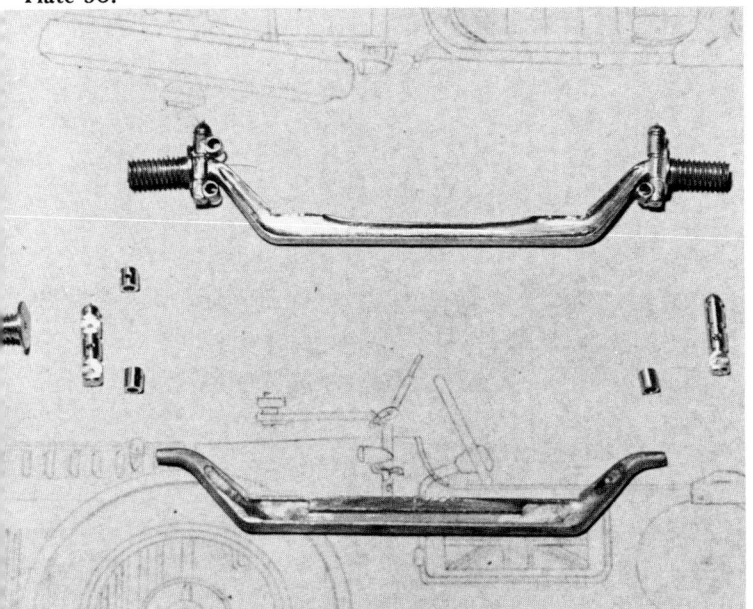

Plate 39.

Plate 40.

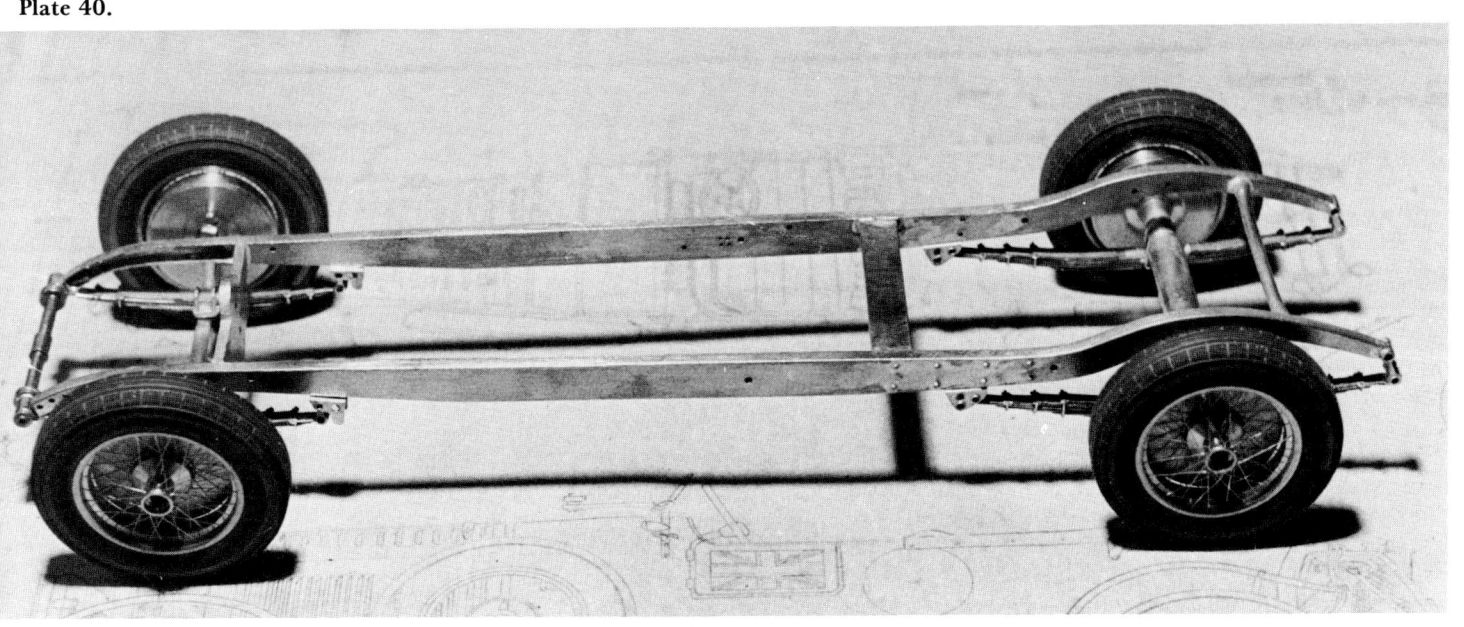

level, in other words, it is a kerb-side model, so all that is really necessary on the underside is something that will present an acceptable profile when the model is standing the right way up.

We have now reached the happy state of plate 40, when, for the first time, with all the pieces made so far assembled, we have something resembling the character of the subject being built.

From now on the model will grow with each new piece made, for what we now have is the basic platform on which everything else is built. I do not intend to discuss in detail all the fittings that will be required to complete this chassis, as this volume is meant to assist the automodeller in general, as distinct from someone wishing to construct a miniature Bentley. What I will do is pick out one or two representative items to show how we break down and build up these parts and also I will examine the logic of these operations.

The first such item is the supercharger FIG. 19, plates 41-42-44 and plates 7-8-9-10. This is not only an ideal subject to start with because of its complex shape, and also because of the materials required in its construction.

The first thoughts that probably cross your mind when you look at the prints of the actual car, are, "where on earth do I start." The fact is you will never find the answer to this, until you can learn to look through the mass of detail and concentrate your attention on one specific point. It does not matter much where or what this point is, but with experience you will soon train your eye to find the one piece to which all others are attached. It is, in most cases, the largest single lump, so it is not too difficult to pick out. When you have found it you should mentally strip off all the accessories that are attached to it and also any knobs, bolts or brackets that may actually be part of it. What you should now have in front of your mind's eye is a clean, shaped, block. The next stage is to look for squares and rounds, as this will be the first indication to you of how you will reproduce what you are looking at. If you have squares (flats of any sort) then the work will entail milling or filing, if there are rounded parts then the work will be carried out on the lathe.

Some basic blocks can be filed or machined from a single piece of material, but most will be found — as we will see with the supercharger — to be made up of both squares and rounds, which will mean splitting the block into several pieces.

So much for the theory, now to put these thoughts into practice. In FIG. 19 we have another of my third stage drawings. This is the stage, you may recall, when the actual working dimensions are sorted out and put onto paper and also the time when means of manufacture are determined. However, before any work can begin we have first to decide on the materials from which to make the various parts. The most convenient, is brass, because of its ease of working and even more important, its compatability with silver solder and soft solders. But this raises the question of how to obtain the dull silver finish of cast aluminium as in the original, and the polished aluminium finish of some of the carburettor parts. It is possible to overcome both these problems with electro-plating, the first by making use of a dull nickel plate and the second, by bright chrome plating, both of which can be applied to brass. This, of course, gives us one more important point to consider when sorting out the details illustrated in FIG. 19, for it is not really practical to

Plate 41.

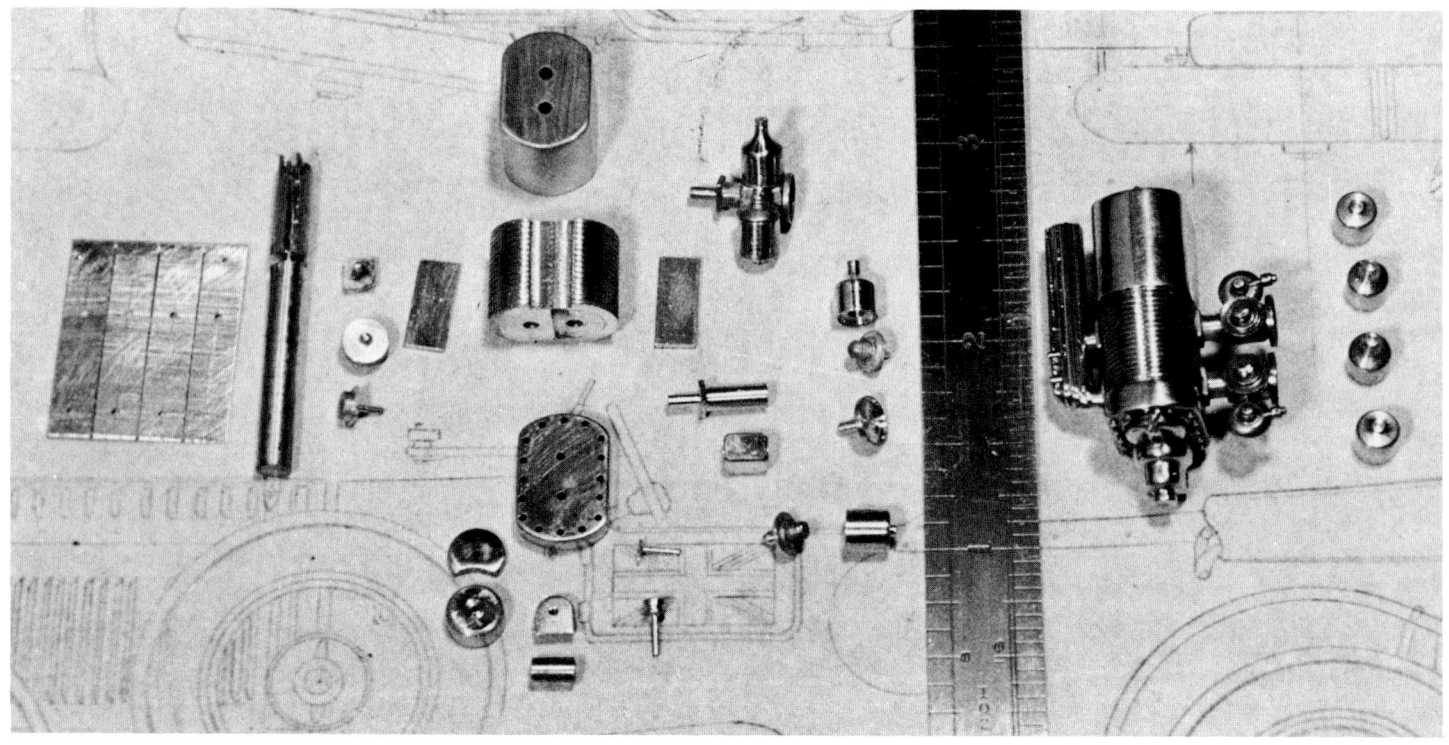

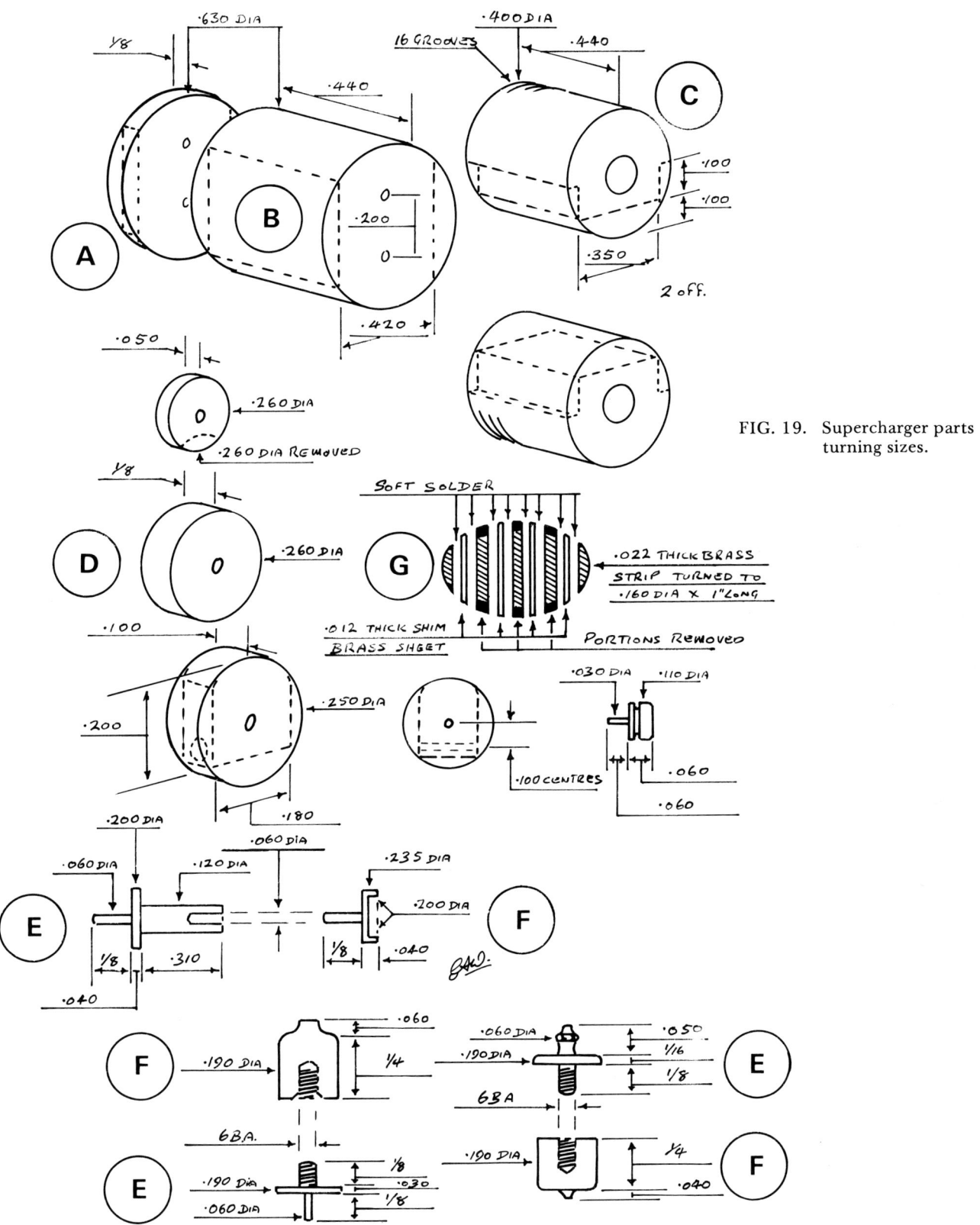

FIG. 19. Supercharger parts turning sizes.

apply both sorts of plated finish to the same piece of metal. When the finish changes from bright to dull a break has to be made and a means provided to join the two pieces together after plating.

Incidentally, the reason for not using aluminium is that it is not an easy material to solder, the melting point of the special solders required, being very near to that of the material you are soldering. Although this is not too much of a problem when soldering two pieces of aluminium together that are of the same bulk or thickness, such as two pieces of sheet, it is almost impossible to solder a very small piece onto a larger mass, without special equipment, because the small piece tends to melt before the main bulk of aluminium has reached the soldering temperature.

Returning to FIG. 19 and plate 41: On the top row of the former, you will see that I have split the main body of the supercharger into four convenient pieces. In fact both 'A' and 'B', the front and back, and the two points of 'C', the centre section, can be combined so that we have only two pieces to turn and mill or file, they being separated when all the machining has been

45

completed. Then the two parts of 'C' are dowelled together on the milled faces and dowelled and silver soldered between 'A' and 'B' to give the starting block to which all else can be fitted. The parts at 'D' when added, will complete the front, and those marked 'E' and 'F' will complete the carburettor side. The ones marked 'E' will be soldered to the main body and be dull nickel plate, while those marked 'F' will be bright chrome and assembled later.

At 'G' we have an altogether different problem. This concerns the making of the finned pipe that takes the compressed mixture from the supercharger to the engine. The pipe in question can be clearly seen on the left in plate 7. My method of tackling this type of subject, i.e. the finning on an air cooled cylinder is to build up laminations of brass sheet of different thicknesses with soft solder, then, to turn or file this block to the correct overall shape. The piece is then reheated and the laminations separated. It is now but a simple matter to remove, with a file, being careful to follow the contours and angles, sufficient metal from the outside edges of the thicker parts to represent the valleys between the fins. When all is correct, the parts are treated to a spot of flux, reassembled and heated to remelt the trace of soft solder remaining on each side of the laminations, so making once again, a single block, but this time with fins on. Of course, one or two dowel pins through the laminations will greatly assist in the assembly.

On the right of plate 41 we can see the completed supercharger with all the parts dowelled and/or bolted together. Note that everything is polished, even the main block, which as can be seen from plate 44, is to receive a dull nickel plate. For those not familiar with the limitations of electro-plating, the main thing to remember is that the plated finish is only as good as the surface before plating, in other words you cannot plate a mirror finish. The mirror finish must be worked on the surface, before the part is plated, with the aid of fine abrasive papers and metal polishes. The only electro-plating that will actually change the texture of the metal surface, is the dull nickel finish, which only looks its best, if plated onto a highly polished surface.

In FIG. 20, we have another example of breaking down an item into manageable parts, in this case the outside handbrake. The full size part can be seen on plate 2. Remember to look for squares and rounds, although in this case flats, rather than squares, would be more

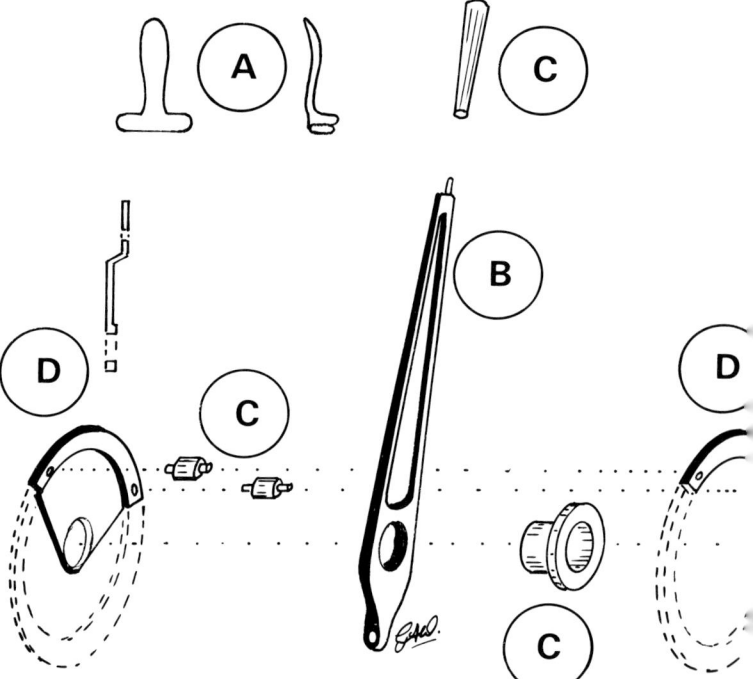

FIG. 20.   Hand brake parts.

appropriate. Rather than make use of the milling machine, these parts have been produced from two thickness of sheet metal. These are at 'A', a thin sheet cut and bent to form the trigger and at 'B', the main shaft cut and worked from a thicker strip of brass.

The recess down the centre of this part, which on the actual car is shown painted, was milled out with a dentists' burr, the small tool used to drill holes in teeth. I have, over the years, collected together a large variety of these in a number of different sizes. Although I now purchase them direct from a supplier, I did start my collection with a few secondhand ones from my local dentist. It has been my experience that almost everyone looks favourably on the model-maker, perhaps because most people at some time in their life have attempted to make something, even if it was in their childhood. So, if you do see someone using a tool or material that you think could improve your own work, do not be shy in disclosing your interest. Let them know what you do, always have one or two photographs of your work with you to show people, and you will be amazed at the response.

The parts 'C' in FIG. 20 are simple turning operations, as also are parts 'D', but seventy per cent of these are removed with snips before assembly. With a part such

Plate 42.

Plate 43.

Plate 44.

as this, where the finish is a combination of paint and chrome plate on a small compact item, it is best to assemble all the parts with silver solder, polish, plate and then mask those parts that are required to remain chromed and paint the remainder. However, I will have more to say on this point when we deal with finishing in a later chapter.

The last major lump to fit to our chassis, that will present any worthwhile problems, is the radiator shell. With the Bentley, I machined it from a single block of brass in the sequence of operations set out in FIG. 21. Although these obviously present little trouble when one has a milling machine at hand, nonetheless, they can be done equally well with a file. Regarding No. 3, one would need to drill a series of holes just inside the line so that the centre can be knocked out, then cleaned up back to the line with files. Note: I found it much simpler to cut out a clean hole and add the arch to accommodate the supercharger rather than try and cut round it, while in the solid.

In plate 46 we have another style of radiator, in this case a Bugatti. As this is a thin shell of almost equal thickness, it is easier to make it up from strip material, bent and formed to the correct shape around a previously shaped block of hard wood, than to carve this from a solid block. In the case of both these shells, they are eventually fitted with blocks of hard wood to which the wire mesh grills are attached. When we deal with the larger scale and more detailed type of miniature, I will discuss a third method of radiator shell-making using a steel former.

The last item of the chassis that we need to give some thought to, would, at first sight, appear to be

Plate 45.

Plate 46.

insignificant and one of those things that could quite well be either left off the model, or at most, represented with the minimum amount of work. I am referring, of course, to the radiator ornament or mascot. It so happens that the Blower Bentley was never fitted with one, so I have turned to several other subjects for my illustrations.

To me the mascot is a vital part of the miniature, for it is in the most prominent place on the car and backed with highly polished metal and paintwork. The con-

trast against this background of a minutely worked detail can be quite exceptional. It is also a fact that the whole of the model can usually be judged by the quality of this one item. Although the mascot is small — in plate 52, we can see it is only about the size of a match-head — it is still possible, with the aid of dentists' burrs, plate 47, to get a great deal of recognisable detail on it. The first thing to remember is to make sure you have something to hold. I invariably carve it on the end of a short bar, plate 47, which also makes it a simple matter to turn down a spigot below the carved part for fitting into the top of the radiator cap.

In plates 47-48-49, we see the Amilcar mascot, which was carved from a single piece, in this case nickel silver. In plates 50-51 and 52 we have examples built up from several pieces, but as can be seen from the first of these, the Hispano Suiza Stork, the main body of the bird was carved while still attached to a substantial handle, and the wings were cut from thin sheet, and soldered in place before the bird was eventually cut from the bar. A complication on this mascot was having to make a second silver soldered joint on such a small item, when fixing the tips of the wings to the base. However, seeing is believing. With a spot of solder deposited in the right place on the base, before the wings and the base were held in the flame together, made sure that only the minimum of heat was required to make a single item of the three main parts. The legs were attached with a spot of soft solder as a final operation.

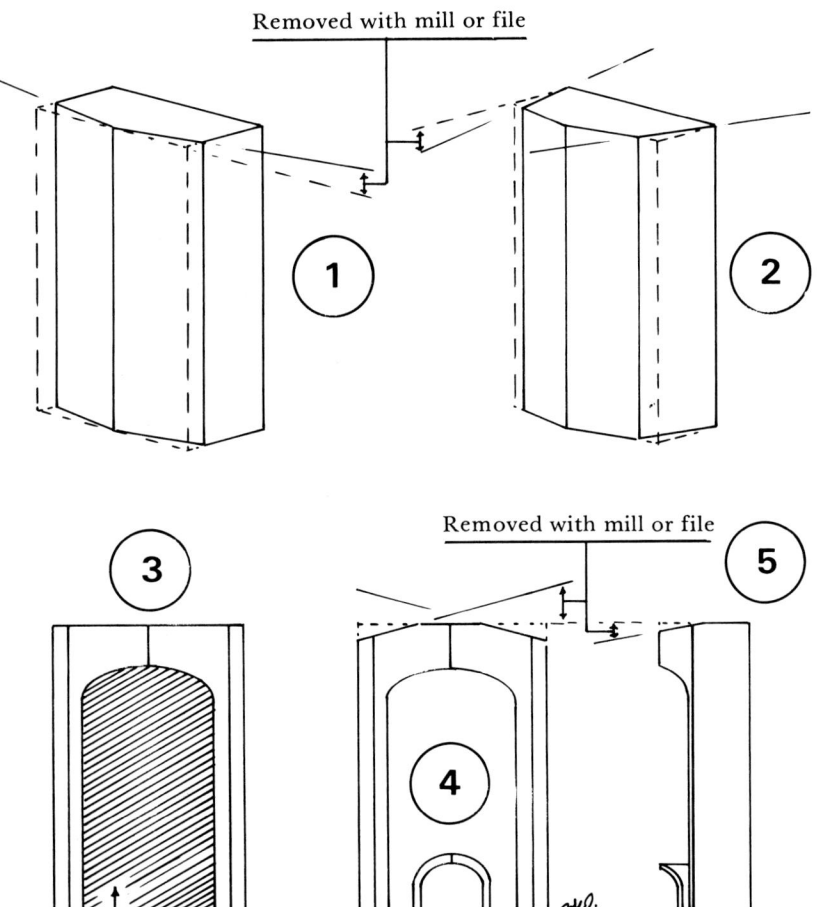

FIG. 21. Bentley radiator from solid.

Plate 47.

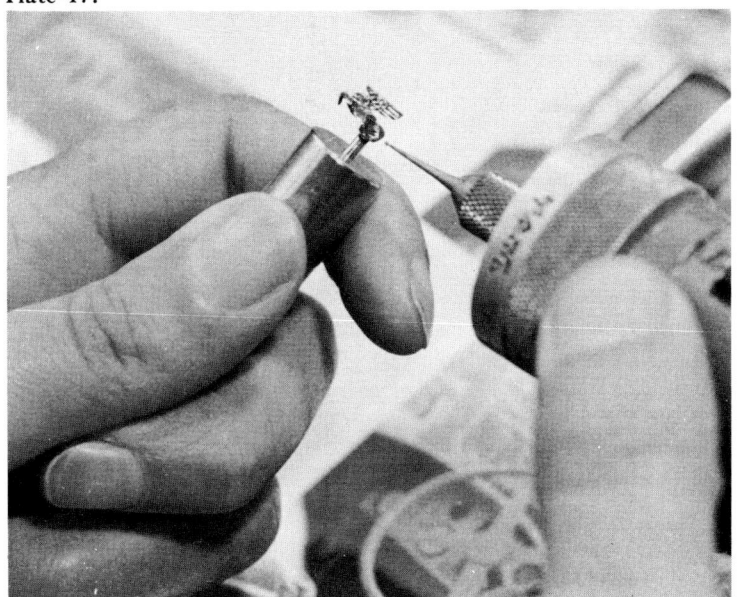

Plate 50.

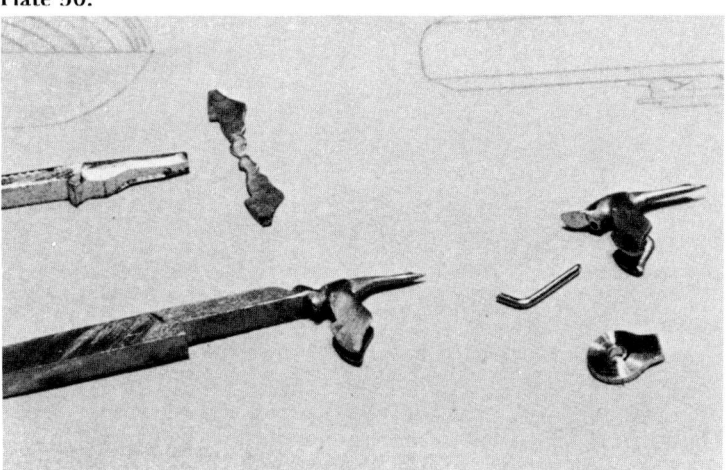

Plate 51.

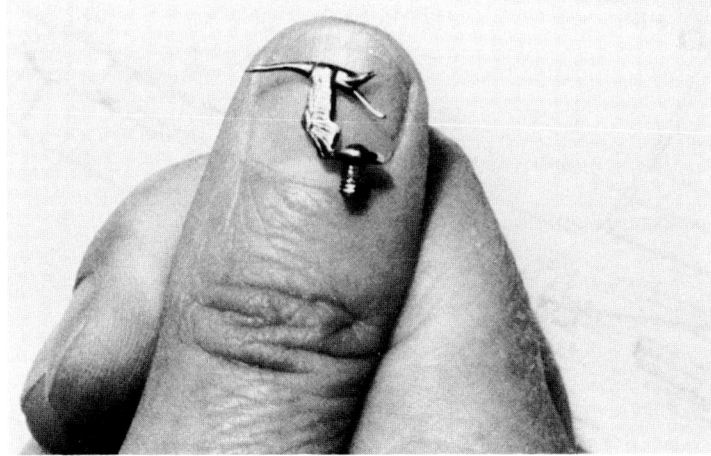

Plate 52.

Plate 48.

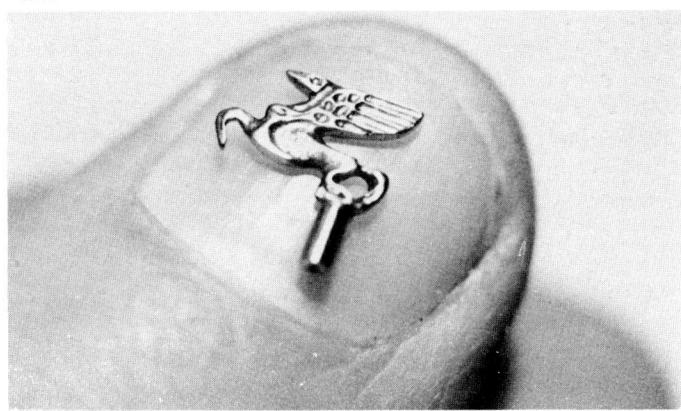

Plate 49.

The Stutz mascot, plate 52, comprises a head carved from a single piece with a short spigot, the radiator cap and two wings attached to the cap. It was the two wings that presented the problem, because they were not attached to each other as with the Stork. However, by making them on each end of a short strip of metal and bending this into a loop, it was then a simple matter to solder the cap between the two ends and trim off the loop, leaving one wing on each side of the cap. The head was then soft soldered into the cap via its spigot.

For those not equipped or skilled enough to undertake all the foregoing chassis work, you can, of course, purchase a kit and rework as much or as little as you are able. This is one of the unique attractions of auto-modelling, in that the motor car has such variety, that no matter what subject the kit is supposed to portray, it can be modified in innumerable ways to show a dozen different varieties of that particular car. Although a few of these modifications could be in the chassis, the most will undoubtedly be in the bodywork, which is the subject of our next chapter.

Chapter 4

Bodywork

My usual practice in dressing a chassis, is to build and fit the body first, then the fenders and finally seats, controls etc. However, for the benefit of my readers, particularly those who are new to this subject, I propose to deal with the fenders first. It will be much simpler with these smaller less complicated items, to go through the various stages which are essentially the same as for the more complicated body.

For our first example I have chosen the 12/50 Alvis fenders which, as we can see from plates 53-54 and 55, are of a simple swept style.

The first task is to transfer the side profile from the plans to a block of hardwood, my own choice here is pearwood, although it is somewhat difficult to find a stockist. The block should first be planed smooth and square on all sides. The width should be equal to the full width of the fender, although in the case of the Alvis I did manage to make two patterns to produce the four individual fenders. With these the main 'U' section has as part of it, on the inside, a short angled apron, this can clearly be seen in plate 55. By marking out the width of the 'U' section down the centre of the wood pattern block and making allowance for and carving an apron on each side of this, it is possible to use the one pattern for both left and right fenders, for either front or rear. An obvious advantage here, apart from saving some work, is that by making use of the same pattern block for both left and righthand fenders you can be sure that the angles and curves will be identical.

The marking out and carving of the fender shapes should be on the end grain of the wood, as this is better able to stand the working of the sheet metal over its form. In plate 55 it should be noticed that I carved the two patterns, one on each end, of the same block of wood with sufficient between to hold each clear of the vice when being worked.

So with the pattern block marked out from the plan with the aid of carbon paper, rough sawn to shape and finished off with chisels, sand paper, etc., we can get down to the material for the actual fenders. There are a number of metals that in thin sheet form could be tempted around this simple shape. The three that first spring to mind are steel (as per old tin cans), copper and aluminium. I, personally, steer clear of the first of these because of the problems of rust from soldering fluxes etc. Copper would be ideal, but the original called for a polished aluminium finish so, of course, the choice was aluminium, of a cold working type and a thickness about .022" (25SWG).

As with all sheet metals, before they can be worked into new shapes they have to have all their stresses removed. This is called 'annealing' and is done by heating the metal and letting it cool gradually. With aluminium, however, the heating is rather critical as too much will blister and then melt the thin sheet. If, after playing a flame on the metal for a short period, it is momentarily removed, a thin piece of wood drawn across the surface will indicate — if it leaves a dark brown line — that sufficient heat has been applied. When cool the material previously cut into suitable lengths can be worked very easily with a hammer, to conform to the shape of the wood pattern.

It will be observed from the plates, that I am using two different hammers. On the right, in plate 53, I am using what appears to be a hide-faced hammer on the bench. It has in fact a plastic face on one side and a rubber face on the other, and it is used to rough the metal to the shape of the pattern. After this preliminary operation the metal will become quite hard, this is due to metal fatigue, so before the final tapping to shape with the repousse hammer, plate 54, the aluminium should be again annealed.

The repousse hammer is a tool of the jewellery trade and can be obtained from trade suppliers. Note the very thin shaft which makes for a very light and delicate touch.

After working with the hammers, the fenders are trimmed to shape with snips and cleaned up with fine papers and metal polish. For fitting to the chassis frame, each was provided with a single stay or bracket rivetted to the frame, directly over the axles front and rear and the stays were made from flattened 1/16" diameter brass. The polished aluminium fenders were resined to them with an epoxy resin adhesive. Had the fenders been formed in copper, they could have been soft soldered in place.

The running boards were also made in aluminium, in the form of an envelope, with an open slot at each end. This was dowelled to the frame with tabs from the bottom end of each fender and fitted into the slots, also with a spot of resin adhesive.

Plate 53.

Plate 54.

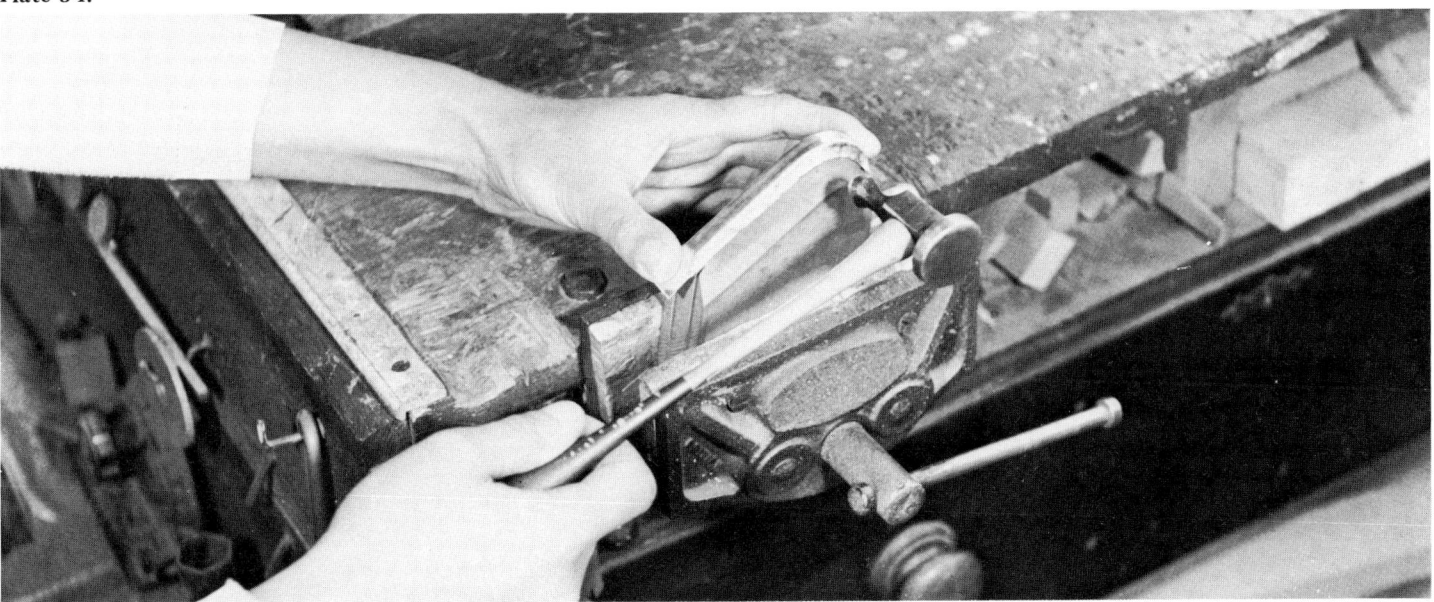

Plate 55.

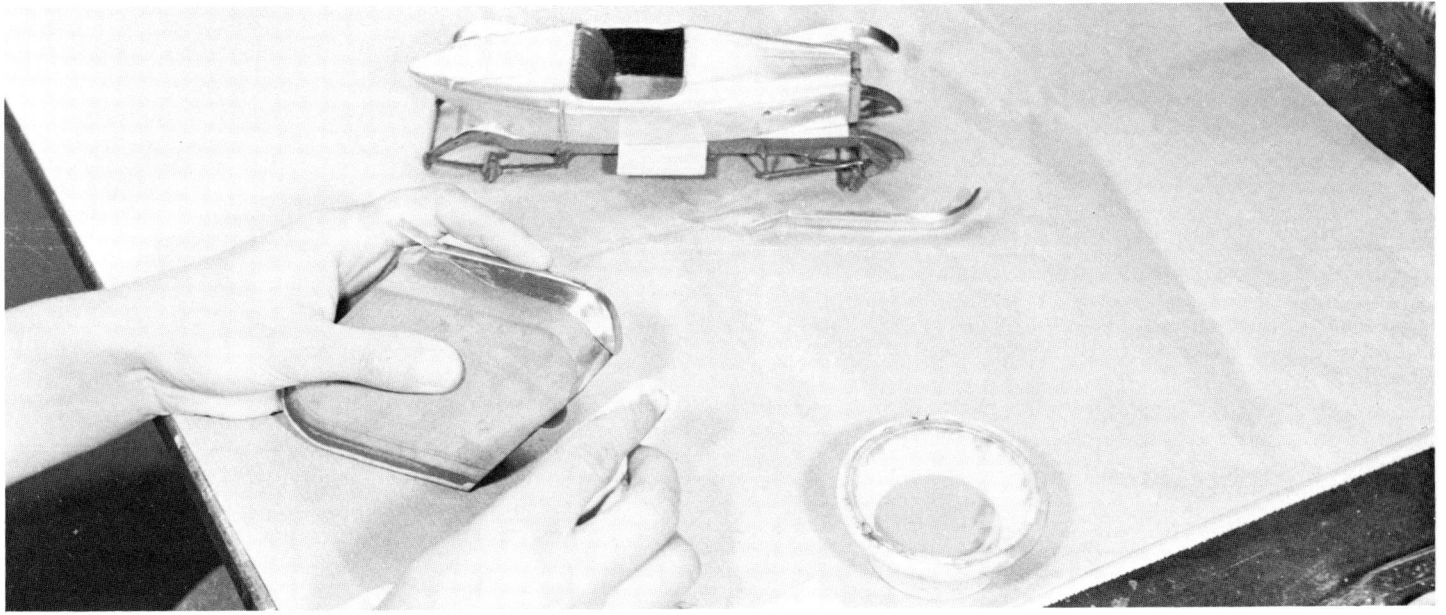

In plate 56 we see examples of what are termed cycle fenders, in this case for a type 43 Bugatti. Note that in this case a single pattern will suffice for all four fenders. It was just a case of trimming those for the front to make them slightly shorter than those for the back. In plate 57 four individual patterns are called for. However, each is marked out and carved on the end grain, just as described in the first example. To assist in keeping the shapes the same for both left and right fenders it can be a great help to drill and dowel the two front pattern blocks together, and the same for the two rear blocks. These can then have the side profile carved across the blocks in pairs. The remainder of the shaping would, however, need to be done to the four patterns individually. In plate 58 we can see the extent of the problem in a shot of the actual car, a 30/98 Vauxhall. This type of fender with compound curves, means it is necessary to anneal the aluminium three or four times to form it around the patterns without cracks or splits.

There is one other fender style we need to consider, to cover all eventualities, and this is the Pontoon fender. Although a popular style in the late 1920's and 1930's (with probably the 810 and 812 Cord's front fenders being the most classic example), the only car fitted with these and illustrated in these pages, is the 1924 Hispano Suiza dealt with in Chapter Six. However, because this is a particularly advanced model I intend to deal with it separately, so for the moment we need only concern ourselves with a look at the shape of the fenders.

To make these in metal one would be advised to choose copper or soft brass, unless the finish called for was to be polished aluminium. The reason being that each shell would be made in two halves and soldered together along a centre line. With the shallow curves that each of these halves would form, they could either be shaped over a male pattern, of the type we have been discussing up till now, or formed into a female (concave) pattern or mould. The latter method, which could be done with the same tools, would probably make it easier to square up the two faces for soldering. With the use of copper or brass, any stays or fixing for the chassis could, of course, be soldered in place.

With all these examples you may well be asking, why it is necessary to go to all the trouble of carving a fender in wood, only to use it as a pattern and then

Plate 56.

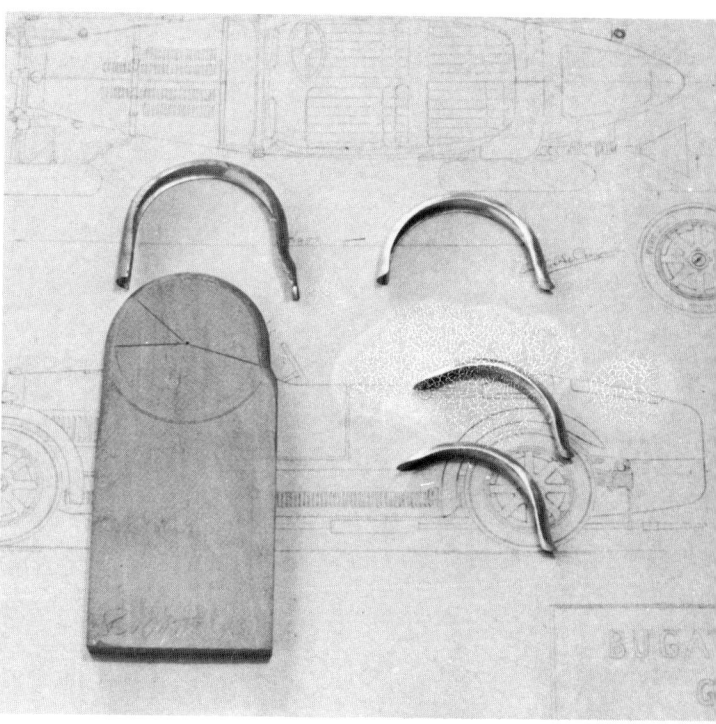

throw it away? Why not make the fenders and body in wood, particularly where the finish is only to be a painted one, and this would save all that messing about with sheet metal. The answer is that wood is very unstable and is apt to shrink and expand from day to day depending on temperature and humidity. This, as may be imagined, is disastrous for any highly polished paint finish, as the surface will be covered with hundreds of minute cracks. If the model is to be kept out of direct sunlight, away from radiators and in a constant temperature, then good quality hardwood can be made to hold a highly-polished paint finish, but very few models can be guaranteed this treatment.

One should not be apprehensive about working with sheet metal, as the finish obtainable, be it with paint or polish, far surpasses that of any other material and the finish remains under almost any conditions.

Let us turn to the car body. For this I have picked as a subject the beautiful 'S' Type Invicta. Plates 59 to 62. In the first of these we see the planed and squared pearwood block, together with two card templates, marked out from the plans. Note that the one for the

Plate 57.

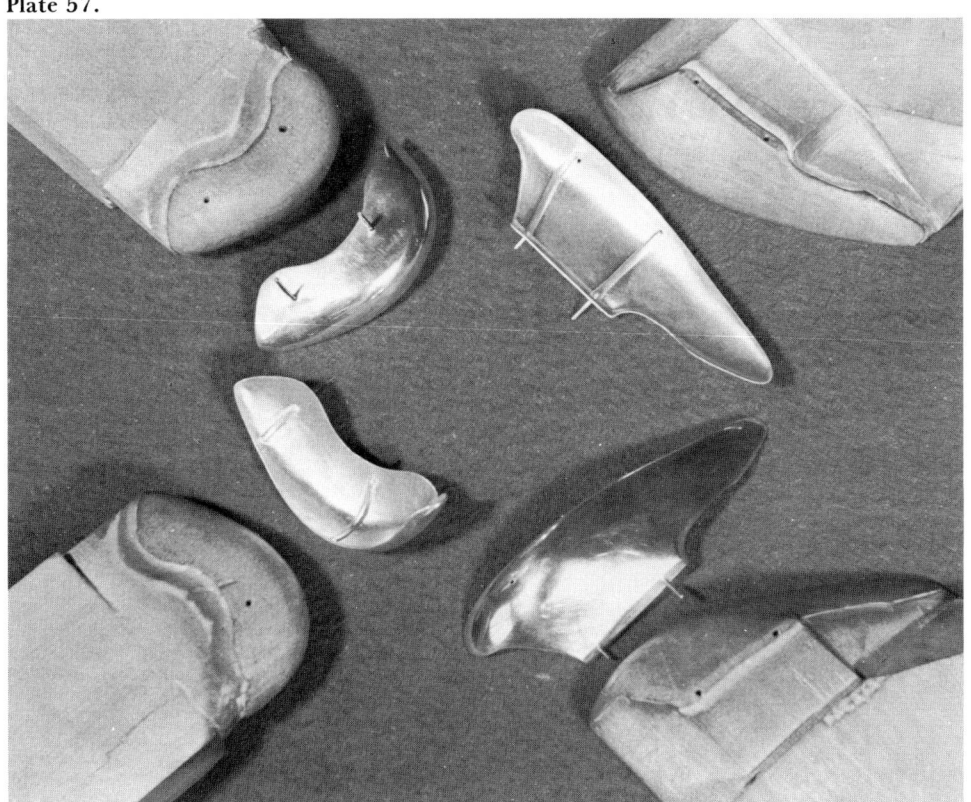

Plate 58.

YM 225

top only covers half the block. By using this to mark out and check both sides of the centre line, there is less chance of error. With the block marked out and carved to shape, I drill two holes through the centre and screw it — with two long wood screws — firmly to a second block for mounting in the vice, plate 60.

Once the body block has been carved and checked as per the plans, a sheet of stiffish card is taken and folded around it to make a pattern for cutting the sheet metal. The card will need to be cut and trimmed several times to get it just right, but the aim should be to start on the cowl, fold down each side, then around the rear quarters, ending with a butt seam down the centre of the back.

The card is now layed out on a sheet of aluminium, of the same gauge as used for the fenders, and marked around the edge with a felt tip pen. Then the shape is cut from the sheet with an allowance of about 1/16" to 1/8" added all round. After annealing, it is worked over the wood block until it conforms exactly, trimming off where necessary any waste metal particularly where the seam is to be down the back. It is most important that the two pieces that form this seam should meet precisely, as aluminium solder is not good at filling gaps.

With the metal shell made to fit perfectly over the block, it is now slipped off and made ready for the back seam to be soldered. The metal should be manipulated so that when the shell is standing on the bench, the two parts are exactly in line and form a perfect seam. With this now standing on a fire brick, a gentle flame is used to slowly heat the whole area of the back, not just the seam. When hot enough to produce a black mark from a sliver of wood, as in the test when annealing, the flux should be applied to the seam. Only apply the solder, which is in the form of thick wire, when the flux starts to run, as this is the indication that the metal is at the correct soldering temperature. The difficulty with soldering this metal is that you only need to heat it just a few more degrees and it will blister and melt away. If you have not tried this method before, the best plan is to perfect a technique on some scrap metal before you try your hand at the real thing. With the soldering done the metal work is put to one side and we turn to a little woodwork.

When I reached this stage on my first model car, I discovered that although I had produced a very good metal body shell, it was much too flimsy to use as it was, and anyway, to be correct, the inside would need

Plate 59.

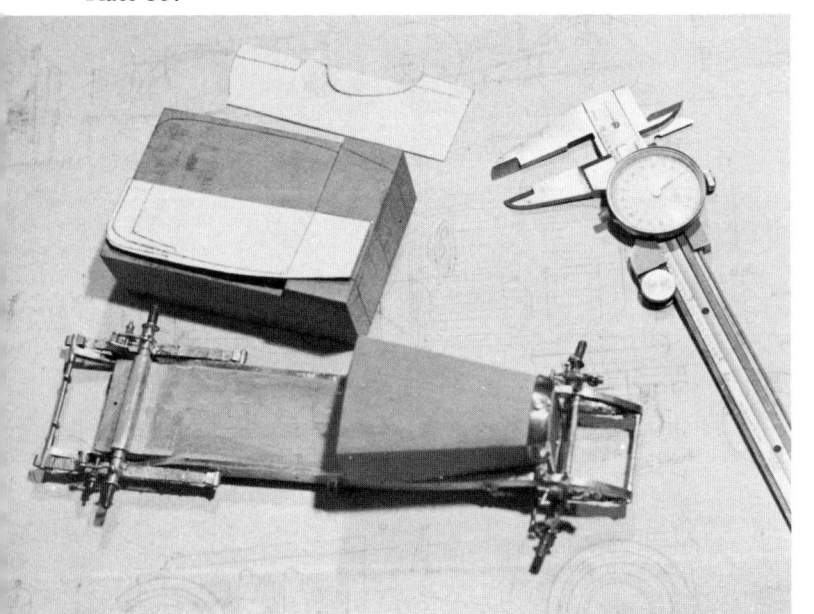

Plate 60.

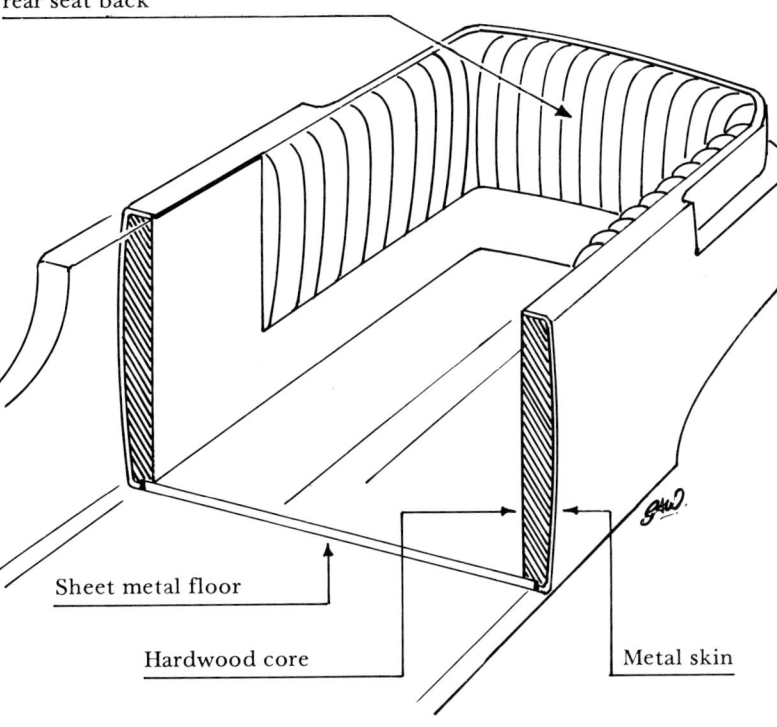

Wood block carved to represent
rear seat back

Sheet metal floor

Hardwood core

Metal skin

FIG. 22. Cross section through body.

some padding. On a car body of this period, the thickness of the sides would be made up by a wooden frame work. On a miniature at this scale, I decided the logical answer would be to carve out the centre part of the pattern block and resin it inside the metal shell, after all it would be a perfect fit. (FIG. 22).

In plate 61 we have the body pattern rough-carved to the inside shape, together with the metal body shell. Note that sufficient material has been left at the back for carving the rear seat back. It should also be noted that a strip of wood has been left across the floor at the front, at the rise of floor, under the cowl. This is most important, as when a block of wood is carved away in this manner, leaving only a thin shell, the sides

tend to twist inwards. By leaving this small triangular strip in place, we can be sure we will keep the original shape.

The simplest way to remove all the wood from the centre of the block is to first mark it out for the correct thickness of sides and back, then to drill a series of holes, about 1/8" diameter, right round the centre of the block, keeping just inside the line. The holes should be placed as close together as possible so that when complete, the slightest tap from a hammer will remove the centre section with ease. The sides and back are then cleaned up with chisels and files, taking care to remove equal amounts all round. On a thin wood shell like this, if one attempts to finish one side completely before cleaning up the remainder, you will invariably find you are having to hold the block for carving by a thinner section than the one you are actually working on. More often than not this means it will split or break off. The aim should be to work around the inside, maintaining an even thickness all the time, completing all the rough shaping before the finishing and detailing is started.

With the wood work complete, it is slipped back into the aluminium shell with a liberal coating of epoxy resin adhesive. The two parts are then held together,

Plate 61.

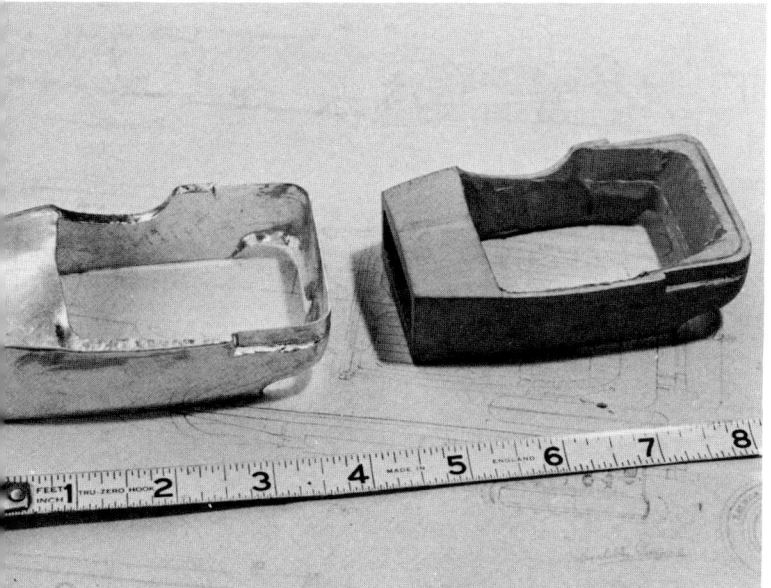

Plate 62.

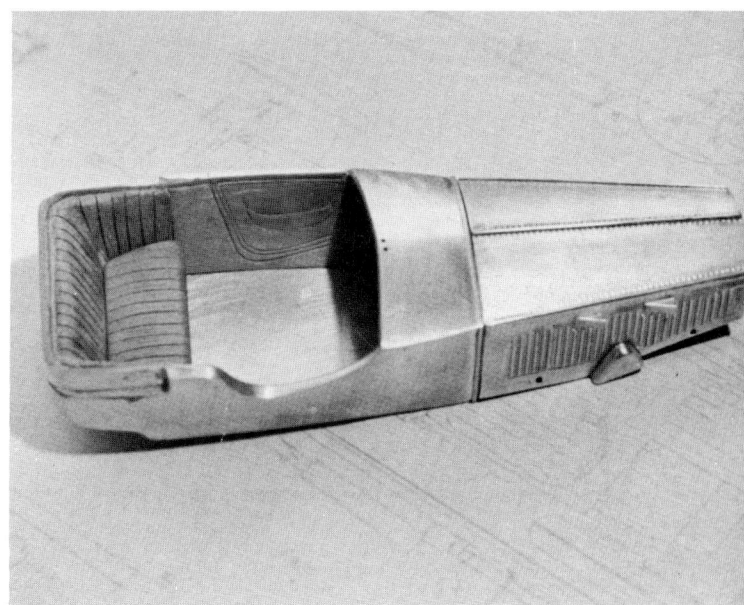

tightly, until the resin has set, after which they can be cleaned up and mounted on the chassis. Holding two complicated shapes together like this can be a problem. I get over it by the generous use of clear adhesive tape, I make use of it on everything. In this case it should be bound around all the parts that it is possible to get it around, in this way one obtains an even contact between metal and wood all over.

Another useful item for holding small parts together for glueing or soldering, are ladies small hair grips, not so much the ones in the form of a bent wire, (although even these can be of use) but the ones sold in strips of six with small springs in one end. They are obtainable almost anywhere and only cost a few pence.

Plate 62 illustrates the stage at which we have now arrived, showing the Invicta body complete and ready for fitting out. Plate 63 shows the same stage on a miniature of a 1913 Mercer, with all the sheet metal work in brass. Brass can be worked to the compound shapes called for in the fenders and bodywork just discussed, but while easier cold working metals like copper and aluminium are available, I only use this metal when the fenders and body panels are the simple flats and curves shown here.

Plate 63.

Plate 64 illustrates a complete set of parts for a Bugatti, including the undertray and hood or bonnet, all worked in sheet aluminium and fitted with hard wood blocks or cores. Mention of the hood, of course, brings our attention to the louvres, particularly with this Bugatti, for it is covered with them, as is the bottom half of the body. This is another of the details of a car that one should pay particular attention to, for if it looks scruffy then it will make the finished model look the same, no matter how much work has been put into it. The problem is two-fold, keeping the louvres in a straight line and spacing them out equally.

Many years ago I was offered a small press called a 'Prestacon' plate 65. I had no immediate use for it, but not being one to let a useful-looking tool go by at a giveaway price, I bought it and put it away in the back of my workshop, where it stayed for half-a-dozen years. Then came my interest in modelling cars and inevitably the question of how to make regular-looking louvres. The Prestacon seemed to be made for the job. In fact, in a way, it was. Evidently this tool was put on the market in the early 1930's as part of a model engineering kit consisting of sheet and angles of thin gauge aluminium. By fitting various punches, bending and cutting tools into the miniature press, I was able to transform these basic aluminium sheets into all manner of cranes, buses, ships and cars etc. In fact, the kits seem to have been very much like 'Meccano', except that you made all the parts and punched all the holes yourself. Having also obtained a complete set of tools with it, when the need arose I was soon able to modify one of these to produce a very crisp louvre. This press tool and die plate can be seen on the left of plate 66. As the base of the press is quite large it is ideal for fitting various guide rails, along which the pieces of bonnet or hood can be passed while pressing out the individual louvres.

Although this is the ideal tool for the job, and I have one, I appreciate it is not going to be much help to the reader to know how to make use of a tool they are unlikely to acquire. For this is the only one I have seen, and I have not met anyone else who has seen one before. Had I not found this press and only intended making one or two car miniatures, then I would mark out all the louvres on the back of a piece of metal I had selected for the hood, grind a piece of steel for use as a punch, place the sheet metal on a block of fine grain wood, not too hard, and then

Plate 64.

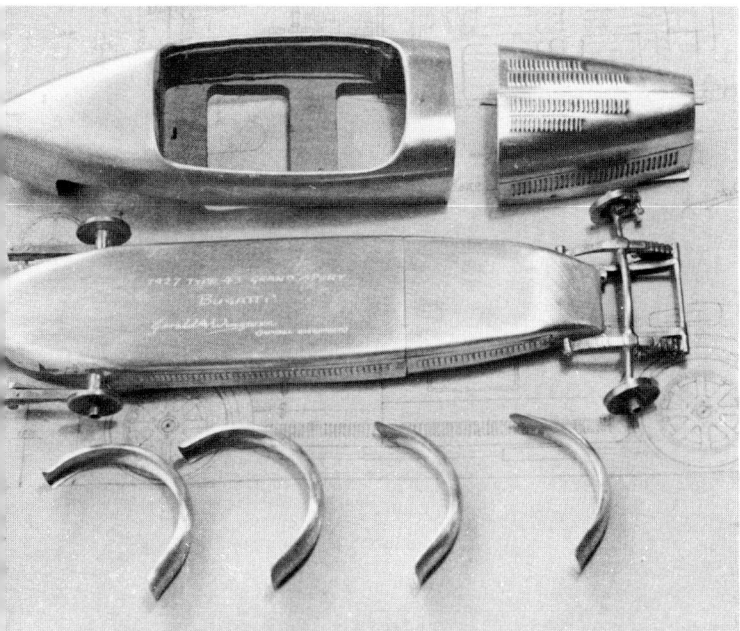

Plate 65.

Plate 66.

proceed, very carefully, to punch out the louvres free-hand.

Several years after the original publication of this book, I came up against the inevitable problem of a subject with a set of tapered louvres along the full length of the hood. This was the 1932 P3 Alfa Romeo, plate LP1, with a total of some 41 different louvre widths. With the Prestacon now showing its age, and the thought of making up 41 separate press tools, I decided my energies would be better spent designing and building a completely new machine that would meet all of my needs for now and in the future – one that would be capable of making louvres of any size, shape, width and combination of widths.

After some thought, I settled on the idea that the only way I was going to be able to cut and form a louvre of variable length with a single tool would be for that tool to take the form of a small 'D' shaped roller. For this to work I would need a table that could be moved accurately on two planes. The table would have straight-sided grooves milled across it for the press tool ('D' shaped roller) to form in to, (plate LP2). The sheet metal that was required to have louvres formed on it would then be clamped on top of the grooved plate, the press tool brought down so that the flat side of the 'D' would cut through the metal and the rounded side form the louvre by pressing it into the grooved plate. If the table is now moved back and forth under the press tool ('D' roller) then a variety of widths can be made. If, in fact, an adjustable stop is now provided at the front and back, and between these is placed a flat strip of brass attached to each side of the grooved plate, on which the stops may operate, then it would be but a simple matter to cut profiles in these brass strips to allow a number of louvres to be pressed out as tapered, stepped or just parallel. Provision, of course, would also be necessary to place each groove of the grooved plate precisely beneath the press tool in sequence, and so was conceived the louvre press, plate LP3.

Plate LP1.

Plate LP2.

Plate LP3.

With these thoughts, it was becoming apparent that the actual press was going to form only half the new set-up, with almost as much work going into providing the movable grooved table. However, I did now have an idea to work on, the first job would be to secure a new press and then make the rest. The main requirement for the press would be the accuracy of the ram and tool holder rather than great pressing power, and that it should be small, with space at a premium in my workshop. To my surprise, there is nothing at all on the market; it appears that the only tools available are small fly-presses for several hundred pounds apiece, suitable only for pressing out bushes and taper pins. This was perhaps an advantage, for it meant that I could build the two parts together rather than have to compromise my ideas to fit someone else's press.

There are several ways of getting mechanical power to the ram of a press, but the cam action of the old Prestacon seemed to be one of the neatest and easily manufactured, so I decided to use the same principal, plate LP4, though I did increase the size of the cam to 1-3/8" diameter to give a movement to the ram and tool of 3/4". This was not so necessary for this application of the press, but if you are going to design and build a new tool from scratch, you might as well make it versatile. I also made provision for the head and ram assembly to be bolted to the column at several different heights from the base, and provided the base with a master plate on which form dies may be mounted, should the need arise for a later project.

Plate LP5 shows the complete press unit with the side removed, with the handle which is in two parts, in the back position, and the ram at the top of its travel. The small rectangular cut-out at the bottom of the ram with a bolt in the top centre of it, is for locating and holding the press tools – in this case the holder with the 'D' shaped roller/cutter that actually forms the louvre.

The depth of throat of 2-3/4" was decided upon as being ample for the purpose and convenient for the width of gauge plate I happened to have in the workshop. This was 4" wide by 1/4" thick and in fact most of the press and louvre assembly are made from this width, the remainder being either of 5/16" or 1/8" thick gauge plate. I machined the base from an old cast iron inspection plate of 5/8" thickness. I never throw anything away; you never know when it

Plate LP4.

Plate LP5.

might come in handy, particularly heavy metal.

The press tool was turned from silver steel as a 'D' shaped roller with a short stub spindle on each side. The holder for this was made in two parts, pinned and screwed together and then clamped with plates and screws in a recess in the bottom of the ram. All these parts were of course hardened.

The louvre assembly, plate LP2, is comprised of a steel block mounted on four small ball races set in a tracked cage which is itself bolted to the base of the press. A handle is provided on the right, also mounted on small ball races, which moves the steel block back and forth between two adjustable stops. The maximum movement is about one inch, thus making it possible to form louvres from one inch down to a width of about 1/8". A threaded rod and two guide bars are passed through the steel block at right angles to its movement in the cage, the right hand end of the threaded rod being provided with a calibrated hand wheel. This forms a lead screw for the grooved table. Mounted across the ends of the guide bars and lead screw are two small rectangular bars which at their outer ends are provided with slots and locking screws to hold the flat brass stop bars. Threaded holes are provided between the lead screw and the guide bars at each end for fixing in place the grooved plate. This plate is made from 1/8" thick steel gauge plate

and has milled across its centre section a number of straight sided grooves 1 mm deep, 1.25 mm wide and 2 mm apart, this last measurement being the same as the spacing of the louvres on the P3. After milling, the grooved plate was hardened and then had its top surface honed with a small oil stone to give a keen edge to each of the grooves, after which it was fixed in position over the steel block. Onto this, and held in place at each end with knurled locking screws, was placed a holding plate also machined from 1/8" thick steel gauge plate, and this, when locked in place, holds the strips of thin sheet securely to the grooved plate while the louvres are being formed.

With a 6 mm lead screw having a pitch of 1 mm, it will be seen that two full turns of the hand wheel will precisely place each groove directly under the cutting edge of the press tool, and the shape of the brass stop bars together with the adjustable stops will account for any length or combination of lengths of louvre.

In operation, plate LP6, the flat sheet that is to receive the louvres is clamped on the top of the grooved plate with the holding plate and the louvre assembly wound back to the left to locate the first louvre. The left hand is then used to lower the press tool by moving the top handle from the back position over to the front, while at the same time traversing the assembly holding the grooved plate back and forth

Plate LP7.

Plate LP8.

Plate LP9.

Plate LP10.

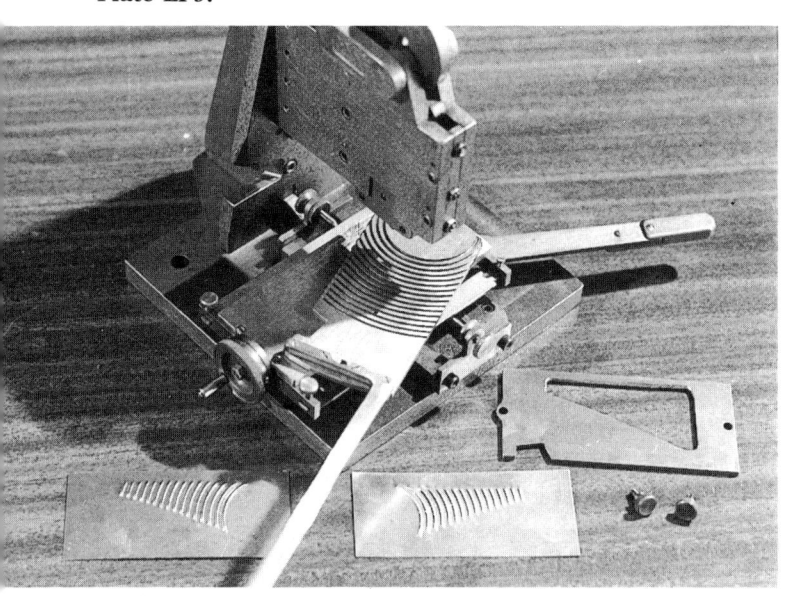

with the lever on the right, with the right hand. The effect is much like that of a can opener; as the 'D' shaped roller comes into contact with the flat sheet, the sharp edge of the 'D' set against that of one of the grooves will cut through the sheet, while the rounded side will roll out a perfect louvre shape in the groove.

To make the complete press and louvre tool occupied about 90 hours. When finished and set up, it took less than one hour to produce a complete set of P3 Alfa Romeo louvred parts. It may sound odd to spend 90 hours making a special tool that is only needed for one hour's work. The answer is to be found in the character of the subject. A car is a precision being, its whole essence is 'preciseness', anything that deviates from this will destroy the character, and it is to capture the character that distinguishes a miniature from a model. Details that are in quantity and close together must be as near perfect as it is possible to make them or they will draw the eye like a magnet, and it is sometimes the longest way around that will get you there the soonest; the wire wheel is another prime example. Apart from this of course, I have now added to my workshop a new precision press, that will itself open up new fields in producing shaped sheet metal parts from matched dies, as, in many cases, the original full size car parts were made.

The curved louvres that are a feature of the 'J' Duesenberg when fitted with its more normal internal exhaust system, plates LP7 and LP8, were a problem waiting for a practical answer for some time. Although I had previously mentioned the steel die and a block of fine grained wood as a last resort for pressing out louvres, even I felt there must be a better way of tackling this one.

The problem presented by this subject was the set of curved hood louvres, the centre point of which is the centre of the side mounted spare wheel. The original louvre press was designed to produce any size or combination of sizes of louvre, but of the straight variety. Here we have 16, each of a different radius and length.

To accommodate this the straight grooved table and clamping plate was replaced with a circular grooved table with its own profile-shaped reversible clamping plate, plates LP9 and LP10. The new table consists of two gauge-plate steel plates, with a ball race fitted-pivoting point at one end. The bottom plate, 3/16" thick, was mounted on the lathe face plate, and provided with the requisite number of grooves, the centre of the radii being the point at which the top and bottom plates are pivoted. To this was added an operating handle on the left side, and a detachable clamping plate for holding the work piece on top, both of which were machined from 1/8" thick gauge plate. The original 'D' shaped roller cutter was retained to cut the louvre grooves.

The clamping plate was provided with an aperture through which the cutter could work, which was of a shape that when the table was privoted about its axis, and the cutter fully in its groove, the contact of the cutter housing with the aperture sides at each groove setting, would determine the correct length for each louvre. The aperture was also so placed that with the clamping plate turned over, a left and right hand 'hood side' could be made.

In operating the press with this set-up, the two adjusting stops at the front and the back are fully extended to lock the table in a position that places the press tool directly over the central pivot point of the grooved plate. In this position, the table is only allowed to move to the left or right, and this only along the centre line of the radius-ed louvres. The louvre assembly is indexed along under the press tool in exactly the same way as in the straight variety. However the actual forming of the individual curved louvres is undertaken by moving the lever on the left in an arc with the left hand, while the press tool is brought down with the top lever by the right hand. As stated previously, it is the internal shape of the clamping plate that in this example determines the length of the individual louvres, and by reversing the single clamping plate, it is possible to produce both left and right handed louvred panels. In Volume 2 of *The Complete Car Modeller*, I show yet another modification to this most versatile miniature press. This shows the press being used to produce the door type louvres on the Bugatti Royale that were also a

feature of a number of most interesting subjects from the late 1930s and early '40s.

Let us now turn to some of the items that go to fit out the body. The most bulky of these are the seats. Up till now you may have noticed that I have endeavoured to make a part in metal if the original was so made and of course the tyres were made in rubber, of sorts. With the seats, I decided at the start, that to use conventional materials such as fabrics or leathers was out, for apart from the problems of sewing and making seams, the actual finish of these materials would inevitably be out of scale, and consequently ruin the effect and character that I was trying to show.

Having discarded the idea of using original materials, I took a new look at the subject, with an open mind. The only qualification was that the finish should be to the correct scale. For anyone who has sprayed paint, whether from a spray gun or can, the 'orange peel effect' on a paint finish is a familiar sight. It is caused by spraying a paint that is too thick, or if it is the correct consistency, by holding the spray gun too far from the item being sprayed, so that the droplets of paint start to dry before they reach the paint surface. Most sprayers curse when they get this finish, because they are usually trying for a high gloss. However, a little experimentation with paint consistencies, low air pressures and the distance between spray gun and surface being sprayed, will reveal any number of different finishes. If we then add to the paint a proportion of matting agent, it is possible to almost exactly match, at the right scale, the finish on the seats to be seen in plate 67.

I should perhaps point out that whenever I mention paint, I refer to cellulose paint as used for actual automobile finishes. I will, however, have more to say about its advantages over other paints later.

Having found a suitable finish I needed a material from which to make the seats. I have already mentioned the disadvantages of using wood to build car bodies, because of its tendency to produce minute cracking of the paint finish. If you have ever seen a well worn leather seat, you may have noticed that this also appears to be covered with fine cracks and creases, also to be seen in plate 67. And wood, of course, is the ideal material on which to carve all the details of pleating and folds. The type of wood, should be as hard and fine grained as possible, my own choice being the inevitable pearwood. My mention of the cracking and splitting of carved wood seats, does not indicate that you should go and find yourself a piece of split wood from which to carve your seats, on the contrary, only the best materials should be made use of at all times, but it is as well to know before you start, that should the worst happen, the effect would tend to enhance the character rather than distract from it.

Those knowledgeable in matters of timbers will be saying that if the wood has been seasoned correctly, then there will be little chance of cracking. While this is correct, except for something stood very close to a radiator for a week or two, it is a fact that these days one cannot be sure that the wood has been seasoned properly, and it can be a bit late to find out when you have spent many hours making something, only to find that it has been spoilt.

We saw in the final stages of building the Invicta body, that the rear seat back could be carved, while still part of the body. This was also the case with the back and sides of the rear seat in the 30/98 Vauxhall plate 68. The front bucket seats, however, are carved separately, but with the seat and back from the same piece of wood. When presented with a diamond, or half-diamond-tufted pattern as this is, you should mark it out as per the original, drill holes where the buttons are required, then carve all the seams and cushioning

and fit the buttons as the final operation. On the scale we are using here, 1/20, I find a 1/32" diameter round head rivet just the right size. If the heads look too rounded, as they would for the Vauxhall seats, then the tops can be flattened with a file, before they are fitted. When carving the seats, the grain should, of course, be in the direction of the pleating. As a final operation, just before painting, the seat blocks can be given a good hard scrub with a brass wire brush, in the direction of pleats and grain. This on pearwood seems to burnish it in such a way that it looks exactly like natural leather, even without any paint on it.

With plate 69 we see the more simple form of French Pleated seat cushions, in this case for a Hispano Suiza. They were made exactly as above, except, that they were fitted with a cord or beading around the edge. Although this an be carved in the wood, by virtue of the fact that the grain follows the direction of the pleat, it will be seen that the greater proportion of this beading is across the grain. A much better idea is to carve a groove where the beading has to go, then carve the pleats into this and finally resin into the groove a length of thin copper wire. One last point, before we move on. When I carve any detailing in seat cushions I always make them look as though they have been sat on, by gouging out a shallow depression in the seat bottoms and backs. Then when I carve the pleats, I make them look flatter in the centre, than around the edge of the seats. In fact some of this can be seen in the Hispano Suiza seat parts. This is one of those small things that can make a miniature look right as against looking correct. A plastic kit can be correct in every detail, but unless they are extensively 'doctored' they very seldom look right. Remember, the aim is to build a miniature with character.

I once saw a quite good model of an early Bentley spoilt by not having any details on its dashboard. Of all the cars, I cannot think of one that has more clocks, knobs and taps crammed on its dash than the Bentley and the whole effect was spoilt by this unnecessary omission. In plate 70 I have illustrated the dash fitted to an early model of mine, the Blower Bentley, which though quite moderately detailed, does give some idea of method and assist the general character of the miniature as a whole. The clocks, it should be noted, do not have numbered faces, although at a glance the right impression is given. This is a good example of how ones work improves over the years, through

1910 Type C24/30 hp Russo Baltique

1912 Model 'T' Ford Runabout

1913 Type 35J Mercer Raceabout

1932 Model 'J' Duesenberg Chassis ▶

1924 Hispano Suiza (Tulipwood)

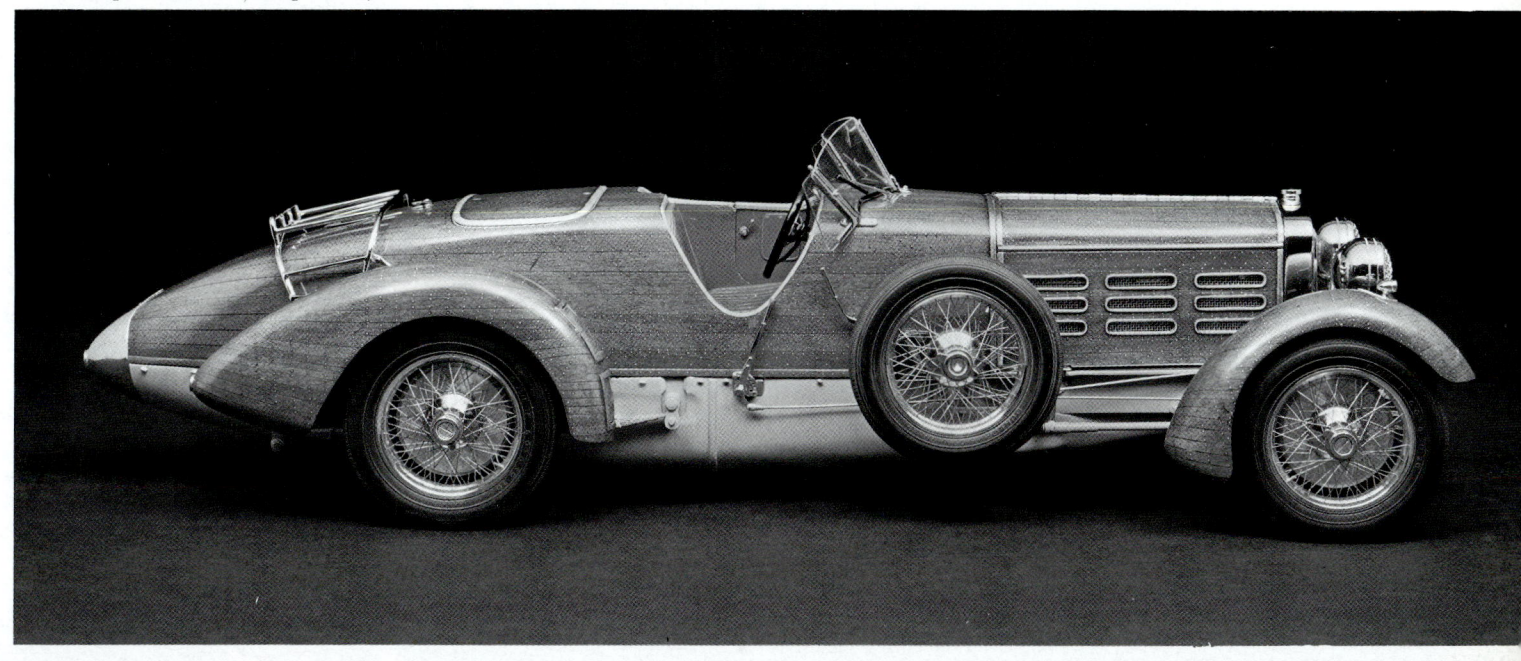

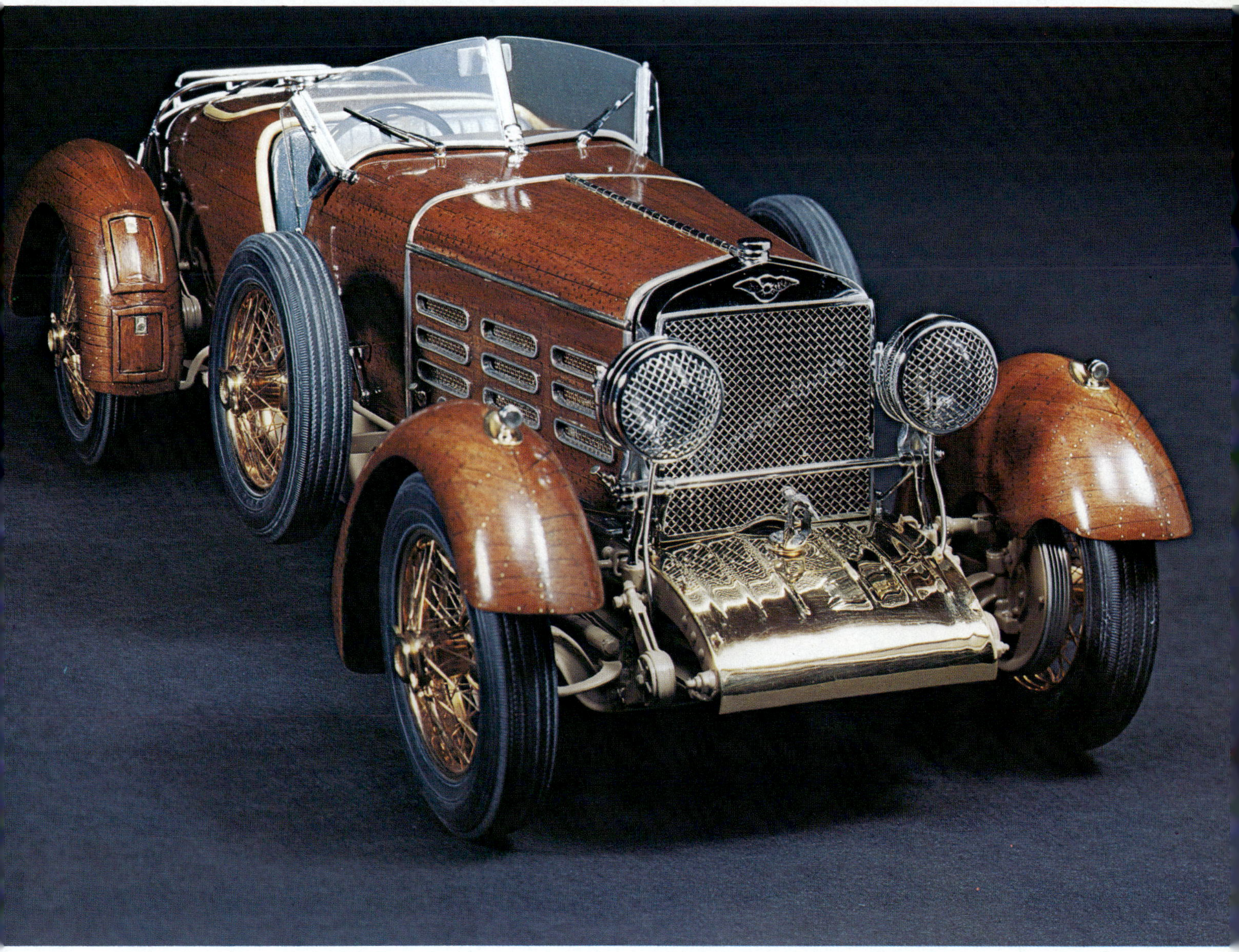

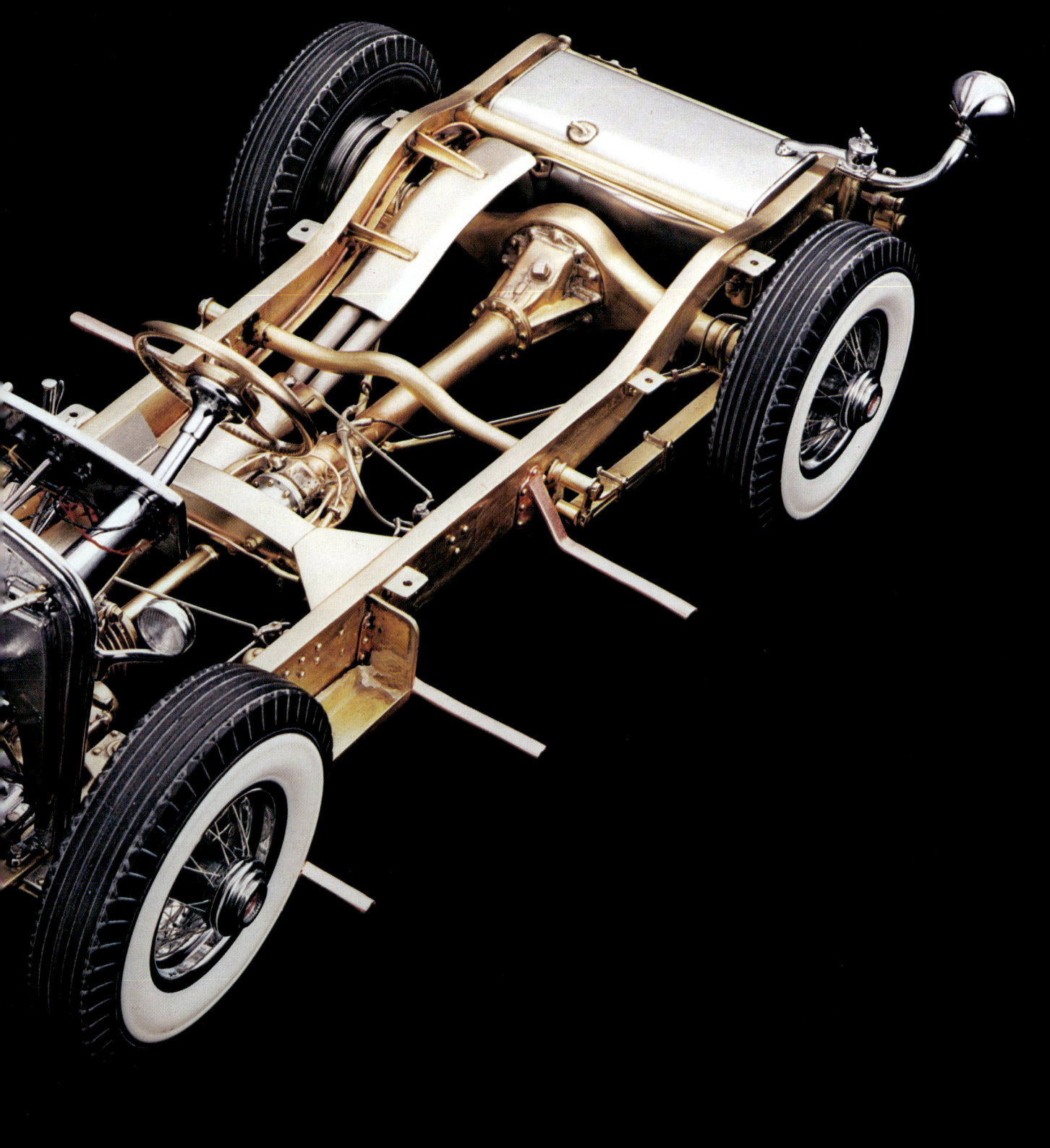

1929 4½ litre 'Blower' Bentley

1933 Derham Tourster 'SJ' Duesenberg

1963 250 GTO Ferrari

1974 M23 McLaren

Plate 67.

Plate 68.

Plate 69.

developing new techniques. At the time I built the Bentley, I was pleased as punch at having made and put together the twenty or so pieces and have it look something like the original, let alone put numbers on the clocks. I saved that problem for when it was no longer a novelty to make a recognisable dashboard. This I think is how it should be, first build your model as best you can, you can then sit back and note its shortcomings and how best you can improve this or that detail. Some of these may be just a case of improving your technique, but others, as with these clocks, may entail much thought and time, perfecting completely new techniques. I do not think it a good idea to attempt the latter until you have perfected what you can already do. To me it is quite acceptable to have clocks with spots of white or black paint to represent the numbers on a reasonably finished model. However, if we are talking about the ultimate, the last word in miniaturisation, then only a correct scale reproduction of the original, numbers and all, will do. In plate 71 we have just that, although this particular example is built to the larger scale of 1/15, the subject being a Model 'J' Duesenberg.

In plate 72, we have the original art work for two sets of clocks, the Duesenberg and Hispano Suiza. Unless you are able to remove the actual clock faces from your subject to photograph them, you have to redraw each, because it is not possible to get anything reproducable through the glass face. However, there are two distinct advantages in draughting a set of faces from scratch. The first of these concerns the detail to be included. If an actual clock face, oil gauge or speedometer etc., is reduced from, say three inches to .200" (1/15 scale) or .150" (1/20 scale) then more often than not it will not look right, for two reasons. First the numbers etc., will all but disappear, because of the small size of the original and secondly, some gauges have a lot of fine lettering on them that tends to smudge the effect when reduced. To overcome these two problems a little licence is used in preparing the art work. Firstly, the numbering and marking that represents the recognisable features of the face are made slightly bigger and thicker — more prominent. The remaining detail is made slightly smaller and less prominent. When this is reduced to the scale size it looks exactly right, for we see clearly what we know should be there.

Plate 70.

The second advantage in drawing new faces for the dash clocks, is that it can be done to the most convenient size. You must have guessed by now that the process of reproducing a fully-detailed clock face in a diameter of anything less than 1/2" must be a photographic one, as it would hardly be possible to do it any other way. Through trial and error I found that with my 35mm camera, I was able to produce a clock face on the negative, of the correct scale size if I made the art work ten times the final size and photographed it with the camera placed exactly two feet from the art work. It was then only a case of taking the film in for developing and contact printing, and I had a perfect scale set of clock faces every time.

Actually drawing the clock faces is not as difficult as it might seem, although one does need to use a good black ink on the white faces. The numbers are, of course, of the instant variety as are the larger letters.

Plate 71.

Plate 72.

The biggest problem was producing the black faces, as I have yet to find a white ink that is really white when used on black card. Then one day I was browsing through an art shop and came across something called Scratch Card. This is a thick paper card with a layer of white plaster on it, covered with a matt black finish, the idea being, you draw on it with a sharp pointed tool, scratching through the black surface, to reveal the white underneath. The finer the point on the tool, the finer the detail obtainable on the scratch card.

In plate 72 both varieties, black on white and white on black are illustrated, produced by the above methods, note even the mileage can be included. When these were reduced to the scale size, all the detail could still be picked out, albeit with a magnifying glass.

As to the actual fittings on the dash, these are never very complicated, being in the main, simple turning operations. The only questions arise with regard to materials. In my early miniatures I went to the trouble of having the clock surrounds chrome-plated, but it is not really necessary. Nowadays if the original is chrome, then polished aluminium or nickel is used on the miniature. If the original is black, then I turn the miniatures from black perspex (acrylic sheet). The

dashboard itself, is usually cut from a thickish aluminium sheet and fitted to the model, complete with all the clocks in the final stages, to a previously worked back-plate resined into the model. This would be cut out and drilled to take the clocks at the same time as the dash, so that if the clocks are turned with a small pin on the back, when all is assembled, these pins will assist in locating and holding the assembly in place.

To cover all the remaining body fittings in detail would take far too many pages and would by and large be a repetition of much that has gone before, so I propose to finish with the construction details of the 1/20 scale miniatures at this point and move on to finishing and presentation. However, I think my reader will find items that are missing here, such as the screen and folding top etc., will be dealt with in the final two chapters, which cover the more advanced and slightly larger miniatures.

Plate 73.

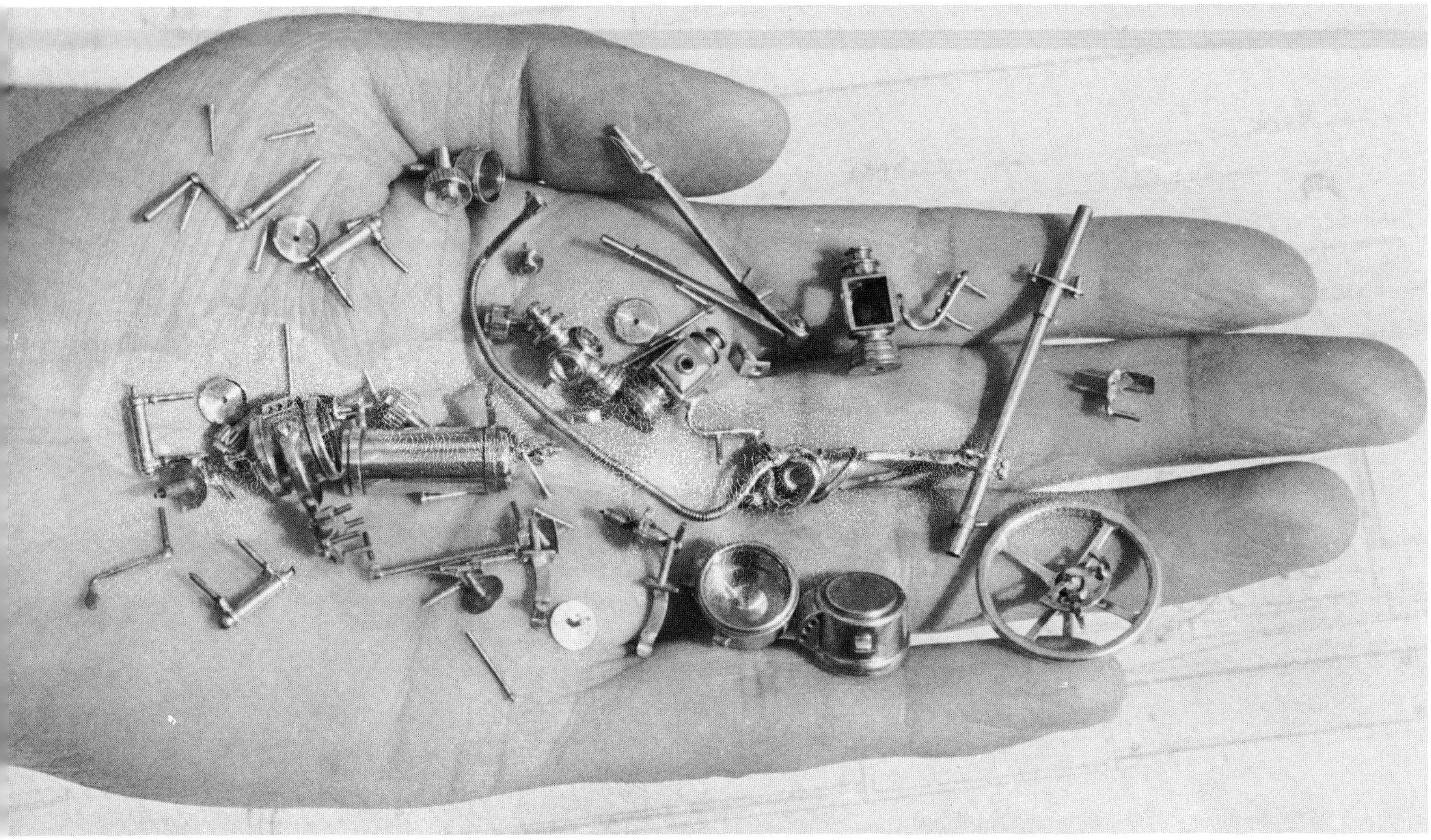

Plate 74.

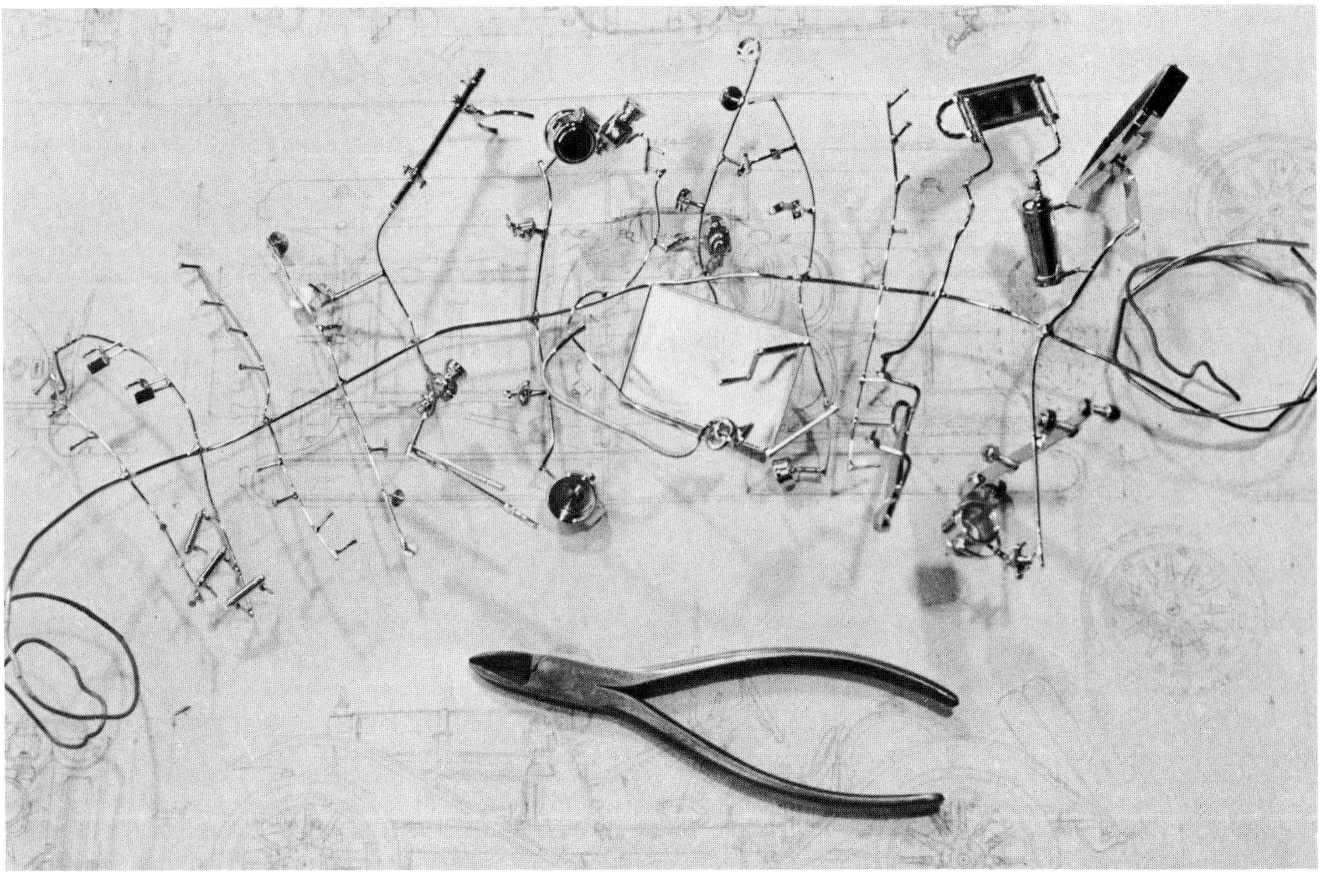

Chapter 5

Paintwork & Material Finishes

There are two ways of building and finishing a model. One is to construct, paint and permanently assemble each piece as it becomes available, and the other is to build, but only temporarily assemble everything, then strip it down and do all the painting and finishing in one go.

There are two disadvantages with the first method, in that invariably work tends to improve as one progresses through a model, and this can show particularly if it is an early item in the modeller's career, built over several months. If the painting etc., is left to the last, then the final impression of the finished work will be that of the experienced modeller. The second disadvantage lies in the fact that when building models from scratch, one has to make each piece exactly fit the previous one, which can mean a great deal of handling for the early pieces, leading to knocks and scratches for the painted items.

My own recommendation, as mentioned in a previous chapter, is to build and only temporarily assemble the model. Only when every part is made and fitted is any finishing work undertaken. I should perhaps make the point here, that in fitting all these pieces together in their bare state as-it-were, due allowance must be made on the close-fitting items, for the thickness of paint or plating that is to be applied to them. It is much less trouble to assemble everything without disturbing the finish, rather than find you have to scrape some paint off here, or plating off there, before you can get the model back together again.

So, with our model stripped down to its component parts, we can proceed with the finishing operations. The first of these is to see that everything is scrupulously clean. All the parts built up with silver solders should, after each soldering, be pickled by placing the item in a bath of weak sulphuric acid, which will remove all trace of the soldering flux. I always keep a small plastic container of acid and a large one of water next to my soldering hearth so that I can pop the pieces in while they are still warm. This assists the acid and the scale is removed in about five minutes, otherwise a good ten to fifteen minutes are necessary for pickling. Please be warned, particularly those young in years and those new to these techniques that 'ACID' of any sort, weak or otherwise, is a dangerous substance. It should be kept in well-marked containers and well out of reach of small hands. My practice of putting warm items in the pickling bath to save time is not to be recommended, as there is an added danger of fumes eminating from the heated acid.

After pickling, a good scrub with a brass wire brush will burnish the items and complete the cleaning process. A good brass wire brush is another of those essential, but hard to find tools. Small ones can be found in most hardware stores for cleaning suede leather. However, by far the best, are the much larger ones used in the jewellery trade and obtainable from trade suppliers. They are about a foot long, half of which is handle, and are distinguished by the number of rows of wires. Thus a one or two row brush will be a narrow one and a five or six row will indicate a wide brush, one of each will be most useful.

With all the metal work clean, we divide the parts into three. First, the items that have been made in a material which is of itself the correct colour, these may just need a polish to make them ready for assembly. Secondly, the parts for painting and lastly, those items requiring a plated finish. Of these last two, let us have a look at the treatment of the plated parts first.

In plate 73 we see a typical handful of car parts requiring a plated finish. In this case, the finish called for, was a gold plating, as the parts are for a 1913 Mercer Raceabout. Each of these is very carefully polished, for as I stated in an earlier chapter, the plated finish will only be as good as the finish worked on the part before plating. If there are scratches on the item before plating, they will still be there after.

Before plating, the items need to be put on some form of frame as they cannot be plated loose. In plate 74 we see the Mercer Parts wired together to form one length. The essential here, is to be certain that each item makes a positive electrical contact with a central wire and that the main wire has enough spare length at each end to mount it on the frame used in the plating bath. As can be seen from this plate, my method is to make a sort of tree with the model parts soldered onto short lengths of copper wire and these are then soldered to a main length of thicker (about 19SWG) copper wire. As a guide, the length of the wire is about thirty inches, with all the parts fitted into the central twelve inches of this. As a source of copper wire I watch out for short lengths of heavy duty electrical cable and unravel this for my supply.

With regard to the actual electro-plating, I feel this is such a specialised subject needing as it does, so much expensive equipment, that it is really outside the scope of this volume. In fact, it is the only part of my own miniatures that I do not undertake myself. Find yourself a small plating company, seek out the boss, show him your work and in my experience he will be only too pleased to plate your parts for you for a pound or two. Do not take him a handful of little pieces though. Present him with all the parts firmly soldered to lengths of wire, as in plate 74, so that all he has to do is twist each end around his frame and pop the lot into the plating bath and you will have no trouble.

Of the types of plating useful to the auto-modeller, there are in the main just three, dull nickel, chromium and gold. In addition there is also bright nickel, which is similar to chromium but on the yellow side, and silver, which is again similar to chrome but on the white side. Personally, I would not recommend either of these for the very small car parts as they are susceptible to tarnish and will need to be polished from time to time, to maintain the required finish. Unless it is possible to remove the item from the model, repolishing is not practicable.

Of the first three electrolytic finishes I have already mentioned the main use for the dull nickel, is in connection with the Bentley supercharger. The chromium plating is, of course, used wherever called for, from the original subject. I make use of gold plating on such items that on the original are polished brass, thus ensuring a permanent bright finish. When asking for parts to be gold-plated, request that they are first given a nickel plate and then a flash gold, which is just sufficient to turn the metal yellow.

When discussing plating with the people who are going to do it for you, always ask for light coatings, as thick build-ups of nickel and chromium will make the very thin parts as brittle as glass. A piece of soft copper wire with only .001" of these metals plated onto it will break in two, if one attempts to bend it. One other point I learnt from experience, that is worth passing on, is the fact that nickel will not plate on nickel. A nickel deposit will form on a nickel item, but it will flake off at the first opportunity. To overcome this, the part should first be copper-plated. The copper will then stick to the nickel and

the nickel plating will bond permanently to the copper. So, if you have some parts that have been fabricated from brass and nickel silver or german silver as it is sometimes called, and it is to end up with a plated finish, ask that it be dipped in the copper bath first, just to make sure. The only metal that cannot be successfully plated is stainless steel, so this metal should be avoided when building parts for eventual plating.

Now we come to the parts of the model for painting. As with those for plating, it is essential that each is thoroughly cleaned, first by pickling in acid and then by application of a fine abrasive paper where this is possible, as this not only gets down to the bare metal, but also makes for a key for the paint finish. The ideal medium for cleaning metal, no matter how complicated the shape, is fine sand-blasting, but again we are getting into the realms of expensive equipment.

Having cleaned everything, I then proceed to group the various parts according to their eventual colour, should there be more than one used on the model. The problem now, is how to hold the parts for painting. A piece of round dowelling, about twelve inches long, tapered at each end will accommodate two wheels. A length of hardwood or ply, about one inch by half an inch by fifteen inches, with an eight-inch piece of balsa wood or cork glued to one end, will hold many of the smaller parts, that are fitted with dowel pins. Those parts that have a flattish back, not requiring paint, can be held in place on another length of hardwood, with double-sided adhesive tape. The more complicated parts requiring paint on the one side only, can be held in plate with a plasticine-type material called 'Blu-Tack', a sort of double-sided sticky tape in putty form. The larger items, such as the chassis on the body, can usually have a hole drilled in them, if there is not a conveniently hidden one already there, to accommodate a small nut and bolt, so that the part can be bolted to a suitable handle, either a length of wood or a stiff wire frame. Anything that will hold a part firmly enough to get the paint on it, can be used, as any handling during the painting should be avoided.

As previously mentioned while discussing seats, the only paint finish I use and would recommend is cellulose, and I apply it with a spray gun. The advantage of this paint over all others is that each subsequent coat, when it is applied, actually bites into the previous one. If you put a spot of cellulose thinners onto a hard cellulose finish it will dissolve it. If you do the same with terpentine on an oil based paint surface, it will have no effect.

The advantage of this, is that when you have applied your several coats of final colour to your model, you have in fact a single coat of paint, and not a series of layers, as you would have with other paints. This is essential when we come to work the final polish on the model, as we do this with a fine abrasive liquid polish, that actually cuts into the paint. If you try and do this with oil-based paints, there is always a tendency, particularly on projections and corners, to rub through one or more of the layers and end up with a series of rings.

Metal presents a particularly difficult surface to 'stick' paint on and some metals are worse than others, so it is important that a definite procedure is followed. Although it is possible to get a permanent finish by starting with a cellulose primer, followed with the pigmented top coat, it has been my experience that the slightest knock will chip pieces of paint off, right down to the bare metal.

The correct method, to be followed as soon as possible after cleaning the parts, is to apply a coat of self-etch primer. This is a special paint used in the motor trade and consists of a mix of one part paint, one part thinners and one part of a special acid hardener. This, as its name implies, etches itself into the surface of the metal and once dry cannot be removed other than by mechanical means. This is not a paint that is readily available, although if you can locate a supplier of finishes to motor repairers then you should find no difficulty in obtaining a sample, it is well worth the effort if you wish to do the job properly.

With my own self-etch primer, the makers state that the overcoat, the next paint to be applied, should be put on within one hour, and that it should not be left overnight. In fact, if it is left much more than one hour, the cellulose primer, which is the next coat to go on, will not stick to it. So when you do find a supplier for your self-etch, follow the manufacturers instructions.

After the self-etch, we put on a coat of cellulose primer, and when this is dry we add a second thin coat. If the piece has some plain surfaces large enough for polishing at a later stage, then when the second coat is dry it can be rubbed down with very fine abrasive paper and given a third and possibly fourth coat, which can also be rubbed down. Any deep marks that happen to show themselves through the primer, can be filled with cellulose putty. This is like a very thick cellulose primer and is applied to the small hole or scratch with a knife or piece of wood. When dry, it can also be rubbed down with a very fine abrasive paper.

Only the minimum of paint should be applied to the finely detailed parts of the model, as there is always the tendency to fill in, or round off the corners, if too much is put on. Bear in mind that at least two coats of colour will be needed on these small parts, which with two of primer and one of self-etch makes five in all. Even though they are all thin coats, sprayed on, any more cannot improve the detailing.

Of the finish top coats on the parts such as the body, I usually put on about four, very lightly rubbing down each, and ending with one very thinned down. Before polishing, the finish should be allowed to harden for several days, for although cellulose paints dry very quickly, it still takes several days to really settle down. For the polishing, a very fine liquid metal polish is ideal. Use a soft rag, changing its position as soon as a deposit of colouring has built up. The aim should be to replace the glassy shine on the natural gloss of the paint, with the deep burnished shine which brings out the colour, and is only obtainable with actual polishing.

For finishes such as that called for on the Blower Bentley, which has a fabric body, the treatment is the same as I described for the seats. Spray from a distance with a low air pressure and paint on the thick side. A close look at the photographs of this, both actual car and model, will reveal an interesting comparison between the finish on the hood, or bonnet, and that on the body, particularly the cowl.

In discussing the painting, I have had to assume that all my readers are equipped with the most up to date spray equipment. I have had to tackle it this way in order to get down on paper methods that may be understandable. However, if you have no equipment at all, do not despair, neither did I when I started. In this case the self-etch can be applied with a soft brush, the type used for water-colour painting. For the cellulose primer and coloured cellulose gloss top coat, the touch-up spray can is the answer,

Plate 75.

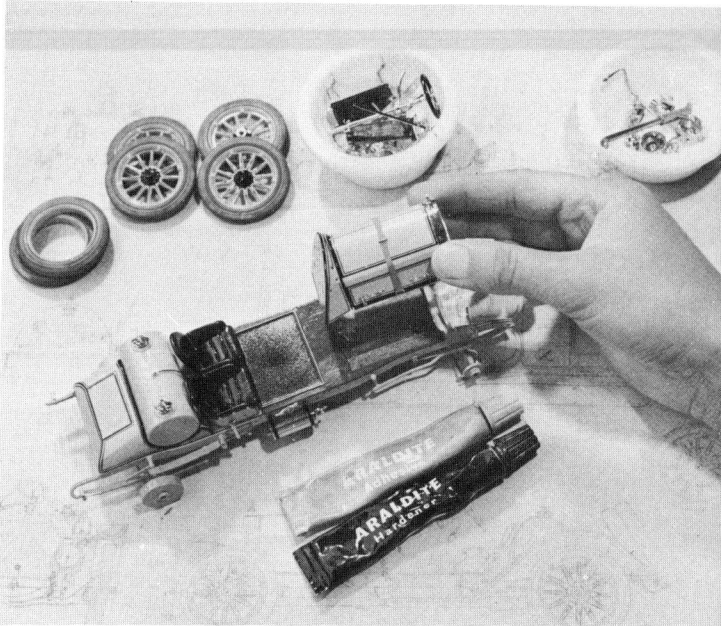

for both of these finishes are obtainable in this form. With regard to the special finish for seats and fabric bodies, if the spray can is held a foot to eighteen inches from the part being sprayed, then the paint will be almost dry by the time it reaches the part, in which case it will have a very speckled, semi-matt finish, which is all that is required.

In plate 75 we can see the final stage of the model, that of fitting all the parts back together. However, it also illustrates one other point regarding paint work, that we have not touched upon, and that is lining. This, as you will probably recognise, shows the Mercer Raceabout, if you look at the illustration of the finished model, you will notice that not only the body — such as it is — is picked out with double lining, but also the fenders.

There are three possible ways of lining your car, your steadiness of hand and general skill will determine which of these will be most suitable for you. The first is to use a very fine brush, with a very steady hand, using one finger as a guide along the edge of the part being lined and do the job free-hand, using black cellulose, of course.

The second method is to cut masking tape into thin strips and mask the areas to be lined. When all are in place, then the cellulose can again be brushed or sprayed on. The masking tape is removed when the paint has dried, leaving the lines on your model. It is important to use a plastic masking tape for this work, not the rough crepe-paper-backed sort. It is also important to run your nail along the edge of the tape that is going to receive the paint, to avoid any chance of it creeping under it. Also make sure that the masking tape is not stretched when it is taken over a projection, as given the slightest chance, it will lift and attract paint into the cavity.

It is with the use of masking tape, that the big advantage of cellulose over other finishes, (that of dissolving one coat into another), really comes into its own. When masking very fine lines, such as we have here, if you use ordinary oil-base paints that dry one layer on another, you will find that the bond between the paint and the tape is as strong as that between the two layers of paint, so that when you remove the masking tape you also take with it most of the lining detail. With the cellulose it is possible to form a single coat that cannot be removed, provided the surface of the paint is clean before the lining is put on.

With both of these methods, you not only have to get the lines in the right place, but also regulate their thickness. The third method of lining models takes care of one of these problems, the regular thickness of the lines, and leaves you with just putting them in the correct place.

Some of the companies producing the sheets of instant lettering, also produce sheets of instant lines, curves and corners in a variety of thicknesses. It is in fact a selection of these, that I used on the model illustrated, except for the very small details which I added free-hand. They are very simple to apply and are permanent if sprayed at the finish with a clear lacquer, one of the new clear plastic Melamine lacquers is ideal as it will not disturb the 'instant' lines and bonds well to a cellulose finish. They must be sprayed though, it is no good trying to do this particular job with a brush. For those without spray equipment, the 'instant' people do also supply spray cans of a lacquer to permanently fix their products, which if you cannot use Melamine will do the job. Take care though, if you try polishing the finish after using this lacquer, as it will not bond well with cellulose, leaving rings if you polish through it.

I think that just about covers the finishes so all that remains is to reassemble the parts. For this I use two types of adhesive. For large areas where there are no bolts, I make use of one of the epoxy resin glues with a hardener and for the very small parts, or where it is metal to metal and there is a dowel pin or pins to locate the parts, I use one of the new cyanoacrylate adhesives. This is the latest in the ever-increasing range of glues on the market and is the one that carries a warning to children not to get it on their fingers, as if they do and put their fingers together, it needs surgery to get them apart. It is a very expensive adhesive to buy, although it probably is not too bad in the long run, as only the slightest drop will hold quite a lot together. Unlike the epoxy resin adhesives, there is no mixing with hardeners, so there is no waste.

There should be no problems in the final assembly of the model if due allowance has been made for the added thickness of finishes as I stated earlier. So let us now look at what we can do with the finished miniature. My own view, is that they look much better standing on a prepared base, rather than just placed on the sideboard or shelf in a glass cabinet. If this is accepted it is a simple matter to incorporate with the base a dust cover of some sort, for the biggest enemy of finely detailed miniatures, apart from small children, is dust.

In FIG. 23 I have shown a cross section through a typical base of the sort I make for my own works. The wood should incorporate a nice grain but not too bright. If you work the lengths out beforehand and cut your wood so that you have just two lengths, each of one side and one end piece. Then the planing, grooving and chamfering of corners can be done to these two pieces. It is much easier to work two pieces of wood and get them looking the same, than working four.

When fully shaped, the two can be cut into four, and the corners mitred to form a tray or frame. A piece of plywood is then cut to fit neatly into the centre of this. The thickness is not important, except that it should only half fill the step 'A', FIG. 23, allowed for it. When all is ready, a wood glue is applied to the mitres and the edge of the ply, and all is fitted together, small panel pins being used through the ply, into the frame to help hold all the pieces together. When this has set it is cleaned up with abrasive paper and given a coating of French polish, button polish, or just wax, whichever takes your fancy, and then put to one side.

A second piece of substantially thicker ply is now cut to fit the recess in the frame, making sure to leave a gap of about one sixteenth of an inch all round. The ply should be thick enough to stand proud of the frame by at least a quarter of an inch, so that it will take the dust cover.

A piece of fabric — I personally favour velvet — of a suitable colour is selected and cut to fit this plywood base, making sure enough allowance is made to take it around the sides and about half an inch underneath all round. This is secured in place with either a spray (can) adhesive or lengths of double-sided adhesive tape fixed to the underside. The fabric-covered base is then secured in place in the polished wood frame with two small wood screws on the underside.

The actual dust cover can be made from glass or clear perspex (acrylic) sheet. My own preference is for the perspex, as it cannot be shattered and the five pieces needed to form the cover can be glued together, thus eliminating the need for a frame. Framed cases are all right for very large models, where you can stand back and see the model before noticing the frame. With small objects, such as we are discussing, a wood or even a very thin metal frame, will distract the eye from the model every time.

Plate 76 illustrates this point very well, imagine a frame around this case, the model would appear to be caged in. This dust cover is built from quarter-inch thick clear perspex sheet, mitred all round and the parts glued together with the special acrylic adhesive supplied for the material. Acrylic sheet can be worked with most wood-working tools, it can even be planed on the edge if the plane is sharp and set for a fine cut. It is important though, that all the joints make a good close fit, as the adhesive is not a gap filler. Should gaps be present, they will show as air pockets on the finished job, which do not look very good.

The final touch to a craftsman's work should be his signature. Although this can be engraved on the underside of the individual models, it does lend a nice touch to set a small polished nickel silver plate in the velvet, with the builder's signature scrawled across it. The motorised dentist burr is the ideal tool for this sort of thing. To mount the plate on the velvet, silver solder two 1/32" rivets, heads down on the back of the plate, drill through the velvet into the plywood base and with a spot of resin adhesive on the pins, press them into the holes. This will make the plate sit in the velvet, rather than sit on as would be the case if you just put a spot of glue on the back and laid it in place.

If you engrave your name on the plate before you solder the pins on the back, you will find on repolishing the plate, that the name stands out much more because of the heat darkening the engraved lettering.

Although I have not given precise instructions on how to make and assemble every part of a particular model, I would hope I have given you some food for thought on possible ways of overcoming the many problems that present themselves, when one starts on a new subject. In fact, I have always found it of much more value, in the long term, to learn how to think your way through problems, rather than be told how to build one specific model, hence the format of this book.

For those wanting to know what you can do when you have got this far, I say read on. For the second half is devoted to a more advanced miniature on a slightly larger scale. I have kept this work to a separate part of the book because I do not believe it is a good idea to try too much at once. The best plan is to start with plastic kits, then add to these, a piece at a time, the parts we have been discussing, until you finally arrive at a one hundred per cent scratch built model. An intermediate stage in car modelling may be achieved through the construction of predominantly metal kits (usually white metal) and to assist the reader, I have listed a representative range of these on page 122. Only when you have built several of these would I recommend you move on to the sort of detailing about to be discussed. Learn to walk before you run and you may win a race.

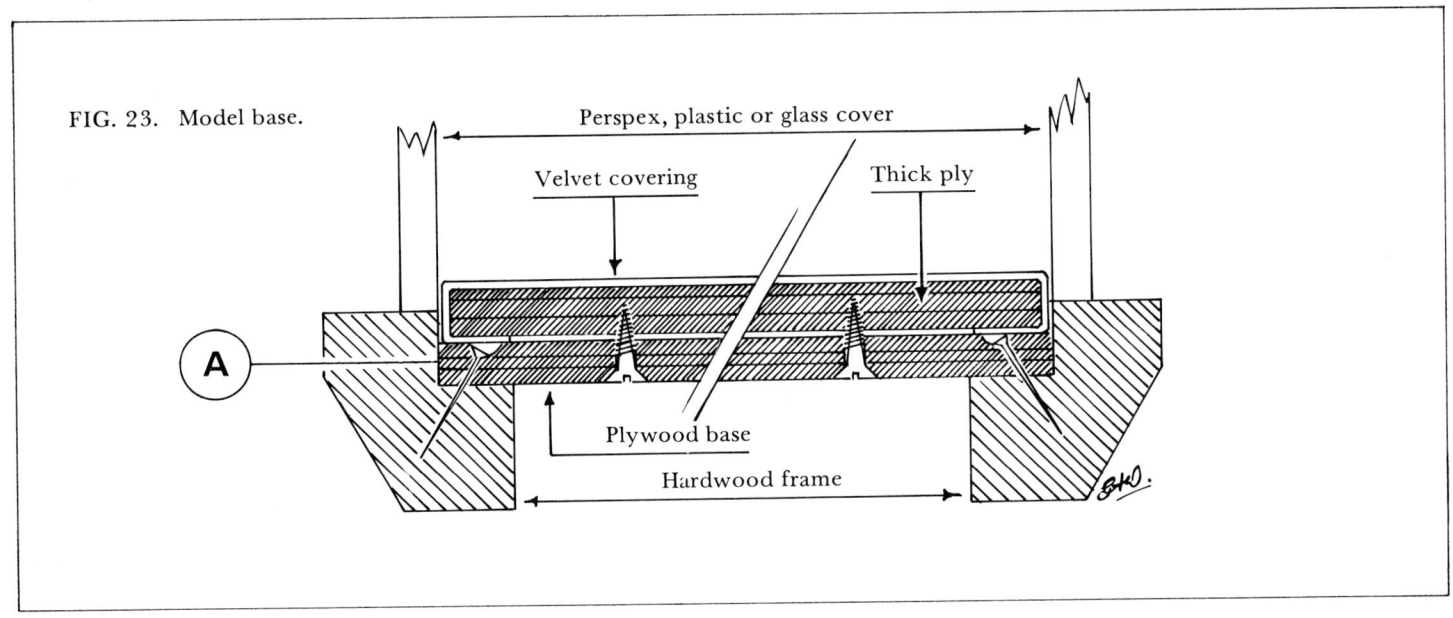

FIG. 23. Model base.

Perspex, plastic or glass cover

Velvet covering

Thick ply

A

Plywood base

Hardwood frame

Plate 76.

Chapter 6

Part 2

Special Bodywork

As a start on the more advanced type of automodel, what better subject could we have than the fabulous 1924 tulipwood Hispano Suiza. It probably presents the most difficult body of any car to reproduce in miniature. Now, although only very few of my readers may ever get around to having a go at an actual model of this car, there were several classics of this period fitted either in part or in whole with planked bodywork.

The main reason for starting with it is not that you may want to build one, but more for the fact that when you see a subject such as this for the first time, your first thoughts are, as mine were, that it is impossible. However, being a professional model engineer, who has to earn his living from building such things, I soon learnt that one must not allow oneself the 'no way' option, or one simply does not eat.

In discussing this subject, all I want to show, is that even with the most daunting subject, if you can learn to look at it with your mind's eye and strip the detail away, down to the bare bones, then a simple solution can be found for all the problems, if tackled one at a time. Always remember that the only time you see your model, as you see the full size car, is when you have finished it. At all other times you will only be seeing parts of it and at the earliest, only the one piece you are actually working on. So do not be put off by first impressions, say to yourself "If it has been done once it can be done again".

First thoughts on the car inevitably turn to the tulip-wood planked, brass-pinned, body and fenders. Here we need to ask ourselves several questions, so let us go through them one at a time. Number one, can we use tulipwood on the model? I would suggest no, for the same reason I do not recommend using actual leather for miniature seats. The scale grain of the wood would spoil the effect. So can we find a wood with a scale grain, of a similar colour, or can it be coloured, to match that of the tulipwood? This we can do with pearwood, although it does need a slight touch of a reddish stain to bring it up to the right colour.

Having taken a positive decision, we now proceed to the next stage, which is to decide how to work the pearwood. Do we cut it up into planks and work them as on the actual car, or, having had a good look around the car and noticed that the woodwork is in

convenient blocks, are we tempted to use the wood in blocks and just mark the planks on them?

I have seen a model of this particular car carved from the solid, and although it was a very well made miniature, it did suffer from the inevitable shortcomings of the method, in that you must have end grain showing somewhere. My own view, is that one should accept that planks were used to build the original, so they should also be used on the model. My reason for this concerns another detail to be considered, that of the thousands of brass rivets. Again we need to ask, can we put them in and would they be missed if they were left off the model? To me the second question is the most important. For the final aim of the miniature is to capture the character of the original. A glance through the plates showing my Hispano Suiza model will show clearly, that the pattern on the planking, is an integral part of the overall character of the car. Then, how to show this characteristic, is there any way of doing this, other than by fitting each one in individually? It is possible to employ a fine paint brush and a pot of gold paint, but even then there is still the problem of having to spot the rivets one at a time and the end result would bear no comparison with the original.

So we are left with fitting all the brass rivets in place individually, which would appear to be quite a job. To me it would seem silly to go to all this trouble on anything less than individually laid planks. The problem is like that of the wire wheel, having found the only way to make it, it is going to tax your patience and time considerably but it is only logical to make sure you have all the spokes in the right place.

So we now have accepted the planking and the brass pinning let us now look a little deeper to see what the foundation for this work can be. The materials that come to mind are metal, wood and resin/fibreglass. Metal is the best of these because of its strength and permanence. However, we do have to provide each of the thousands of rivets with a hole, which means the use of tiny drills, and I know to my cost that these are expensive and to be treated with the greatest respect. I passed over the use of metal this time. Wood should be O.K. if it is well seasoned and hollowed out to leave a shell, to avoid the tendency of splitting. However, resin/fibreglass, offers more advantages than both metal and wood, in that it can be made into a tough, though not hard, permanent shell.

Plate 77.

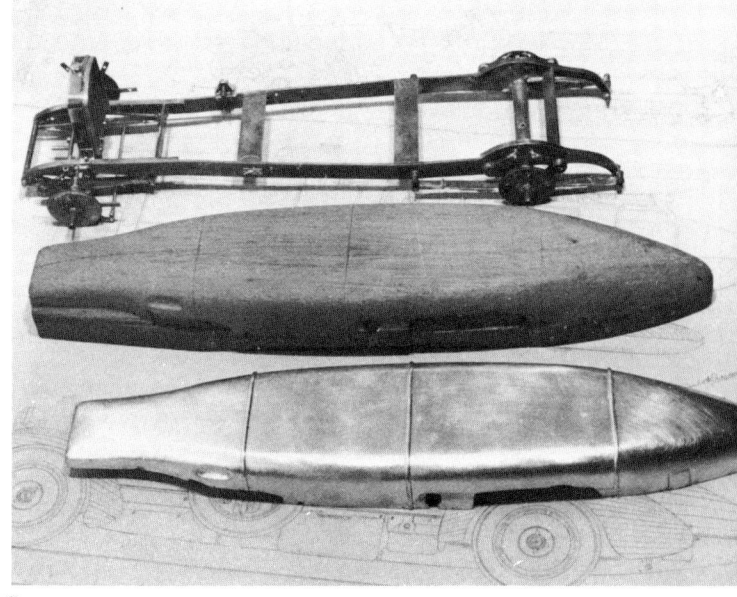

Plate 78.

Having roughed out our answers to the problems presented by this body, we are now ready to start some practical work. If it is something new, or the combination of materials are new, as these were to me when I built this model, then it is a worthwhile proposition to make up a small test piece to see if your ideas work. So I mixed some polyester resin and with a sample of glass fibre, made up a small curved section in a make-shift mould. On this I resined, with epoxy adhesive, some strips of pearwood, trimming the edges to accommodate the curves, the pieces of planking being held firmly in place with Sellotape. When set, the woodwork was first cleaned and flatted with adhesive papers, then marked out and drilled for pinning. For the pins I decided that rather than try using pins of the correct length at the start, I would use them in the form of a length of wire. So with the holes drilled, a short length of brass wire, about two inches long, had one end first dipped into some ready-mixed epoxy adhesive and then inserted into a hole. When it bottomed, the holes were about a sixteenth of an inch deep and the wire was snipped off flush with the wood. This was repeated with several lengths of wire, until each hole contained a pin. When this adhesive was firmly set, the surface was again sanded with fine graded papers, so that it was completely smooth.

Several wood stains were now procured and mixed to give a selection of about four shades very near to the one I required. These were then applied to the test piece in stripes across the planks, so that no variation in wood of the individual planks could give a false colour. When dry it was given several coats of shellac varnish in the manner of French polishing, worked up to a perfect shine and then the piece was put to one side in normal daylight, for two weeks, to settle down. Only then was it examined to see if all was well and to select the appropriate stain for the authentic colouring.

From this simple test piece, which only took an hour or so to complete, I was able to try out and perfect all the techniques and materials, even the finishes and colouring, before ever starting the actual model. It is one thing to have ideas, but if you want to build anything really worthwhile it must be done with confidence, and this can only be accomplished if you have tested and perfected these ideas before you actually start the miniature. It is not necessary to build a dozen models before you build a good one,

Plate 79.

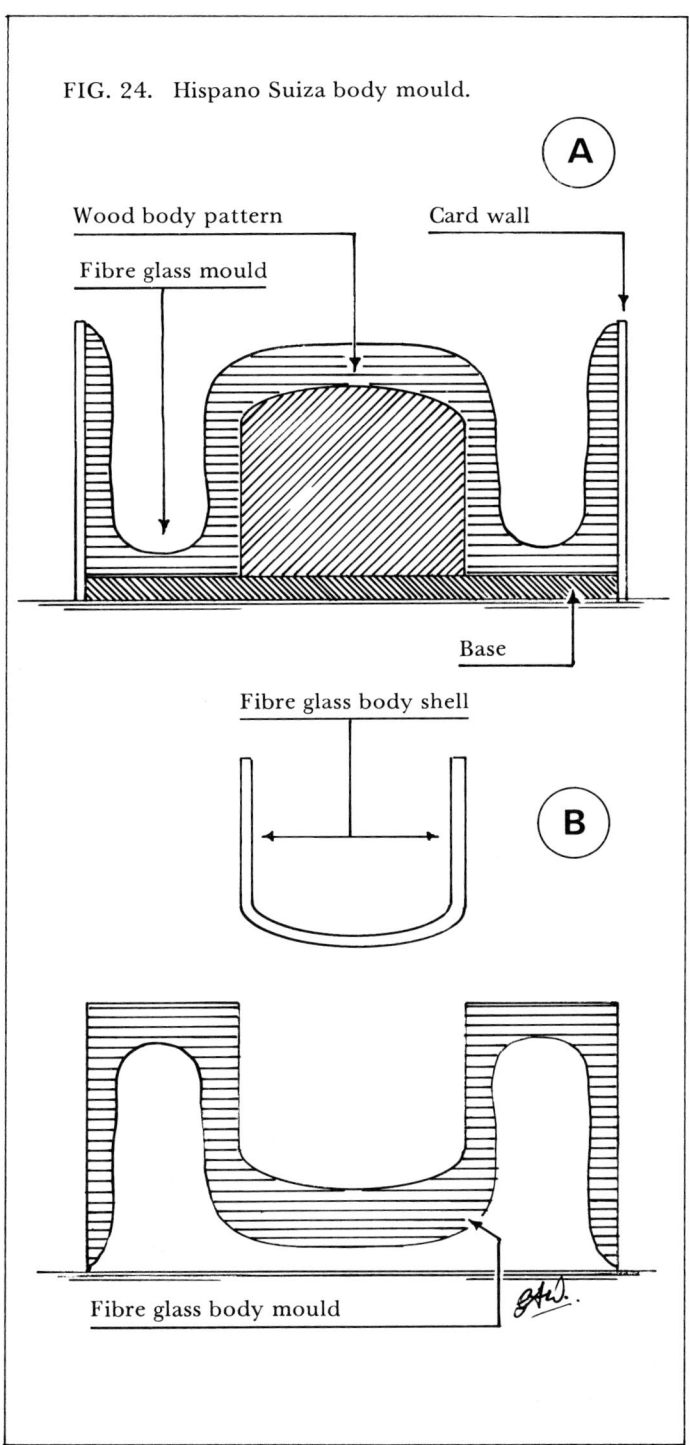

FIG. 24. Hispano Suiza body mould.

A

Wood body pattern

Card wall

Fibre glass mould

Base

Fibre glass body shell

B

Fibre glass body mould

a dozen test pieces and one or two models, is far less frustrating and less costly in materials, time and money.

With all the new techniques settled, plus those discussed in detail in earlier chapters, we should now be ready to take on the real thing, so let us have a look through the plates illustrating just how the actual model went together.

We begin with the completed chassis stage, plate 77, made exactly as described in part one except that it is to the larger scale of 1/15. Conveniently, on this first example, we have as with the earlier Bugatti, an undertray from the radiator right back to the tail. This, together with the hardwood former, can be seen in plate 78. The undertray was formed in cold working aluminium with the three bands of beading cut from the sheet and resined in place after the undertray had been cleaned up.

Plate 79 illustrates the early stages of working the main body pattern, from the initially squared hardwood block. Do not be put off by the fact that I use an expensive machine tool for this work, it can just as easily be done with normal every-day wood working hand tools albeit with a little extra time. The wood in this case is mahogany, as the larger scale does require larger blocks and mahogany is much easier to locate than pearwood. In most cases the larger blocks are built up from several thicknesses, as one usually gets ones wood in thicknesses of between one and two inches. As the width of the Hispano Suiza body is just over three inches, it meant two layers. It can be very useful when this happens, to glue a piece of light coloured wood veneer, or paper, between the two pieces and use it as a permanent centre line for marking out the various shapes and details at later stages. This can be clearly seen on the pattern block in this plate. There is one vital point to be remembered at all times when carving patterns that are to be used for mould making: there must be no undercuts. If you look at FIG. 24(A) you will see what I mean. If there was any detail on this pattern that made the bottom less wide than the top (an undercut), then the pattern could not be removed from the mould. If by virtue of the shape of the pattern, undercuts are unavoidable, then the mould has to be made in several parts, as we will see when we come to the fenders.

Unlike previous wood body patterns this one will not be used in its naked state, but will require a finish of some sort, applied to its surface. This can be either a wood type finish, such as shellac or French polish, or it can be treated as if it were metal and given a cellulose finish. The important point is to fill the wood grain and work it up to a high polish. When this has been done it is fixed to a base board, the surface of which also has a smooth polished finish. A piece of plastic-coated chipboard is ideal for this. The size of the base board should be such, that the edge, which should also be clean and smooth, is at least two inches from the side of the pattern.

Four walls are now prepared and fitted to the base, they can be made from thick card or plywood. Whatever material is used, it should have a smooth sealed surface on the side facing the pattern and should be of a height at least two inches higher than the top of the pattern. We now have our body pattern set up to produce a female fibreglass mould in which the actual car body can be made. All that is required to complete it is an application of release agent.

Now there are literally dozens of books on the market and in public libraries on all aspects of fibreglass, its use, resins, release agents, pigments and polishes, etc., so I feel my reader would do well to seek out one of these and to acquaint himself with the techniques and materials associated with this comparatively new material. I feel this is more satisfactory than trying to describe everything in a few paragraphs. Most of the fibreglass suppliers have leaflets on the use of materials, that are also very useful for the beginner.

Having directed your attention to a source of knowledge on this subject, I will assume the reader understands the terms used in dealing with this part of the operation. However, before we do proceed, just a word or two on release agents. When you do read-up on the subject of glass-fibre laminates, you may find, as I did, that it is all quite straightforward until it comes to the choice of release agents, of which there appear to many varieties, and these can be used either singly or in combination. When I first had a go I got into terrible trouble with things sticking in moulds, or, if they came out they had horrible finishes. I now use only one release agent, known as P.V.A. (Polyvinyl Alcohol), which I spray on. This forms a skin between the mould and the resin that can be washed off the finished parts with water. So when you do venture into this field for the first time try, this release agent first, it may save you much frustration and wasted materials.

Having prepared our pattern FIG. 24(A) we now apply a gel-coat, which when almost set, is followed by a thoroughly mixed resin/hardener mix and a layer of one ounce of chopped strand mat (chopped fibreglass). When this has set it is followed with a second layer of resin and mat. Great care should be taken with the gel-coat to see that it gets into every corner and that there are no air bubbles, as this is to be the working surface of the finished mould. If the average thickness is about a quarter of an inch this can now be left to properly cure for several days, after which the card or ply sides can be removed and the fibreglass/resin mould carefully eased off the wood pattern and base. With the mould washed in warm soapy water to remove the traces of old release agent, it can now be dried and sprayed with its own coat of P.V.A. ready for use.

We make the body shell, FIG. 24(B) in exactly the same way as we made the mould, except that only one layer of resin/mat follows the gel-coat, as we only really need a thickness of about one-eighth of an inch. Plate 80 shows the stage we have now arrived at, one mould, one wood pattern, and one body shell, with surplus removed.

Forgetting for the moment the fenders on the chassis. Plate 81 illustrates the next job, that of tidying up the inside of the body shell. A feature of making things in fibreglass is that you need a mould to get a good finish and that the other surface, the one on which you have actually been working is usually quite rough. It can be smoothed out with a resin filler, a thick mixture of Polyester resin and talcum powder with, of course, hardener. However, it will be seen from this plate, that I preferred the use of sheet metal panels. Most of these panels were cut from thin sheet aluminium, although the ones surrounding the side door and the opening for the dicky seat, were cut from sheet brass so that door locks, hinges and frames could be soldered to them before they were all resined into the body shell.

As this miniature was to be fitted with engine detail, an opening hood (or bonnet) was called for. These I always make in sheet metal as I fit them with fully working hinges (to be dealt with in detail later).

Plate 80.

Plate 81.

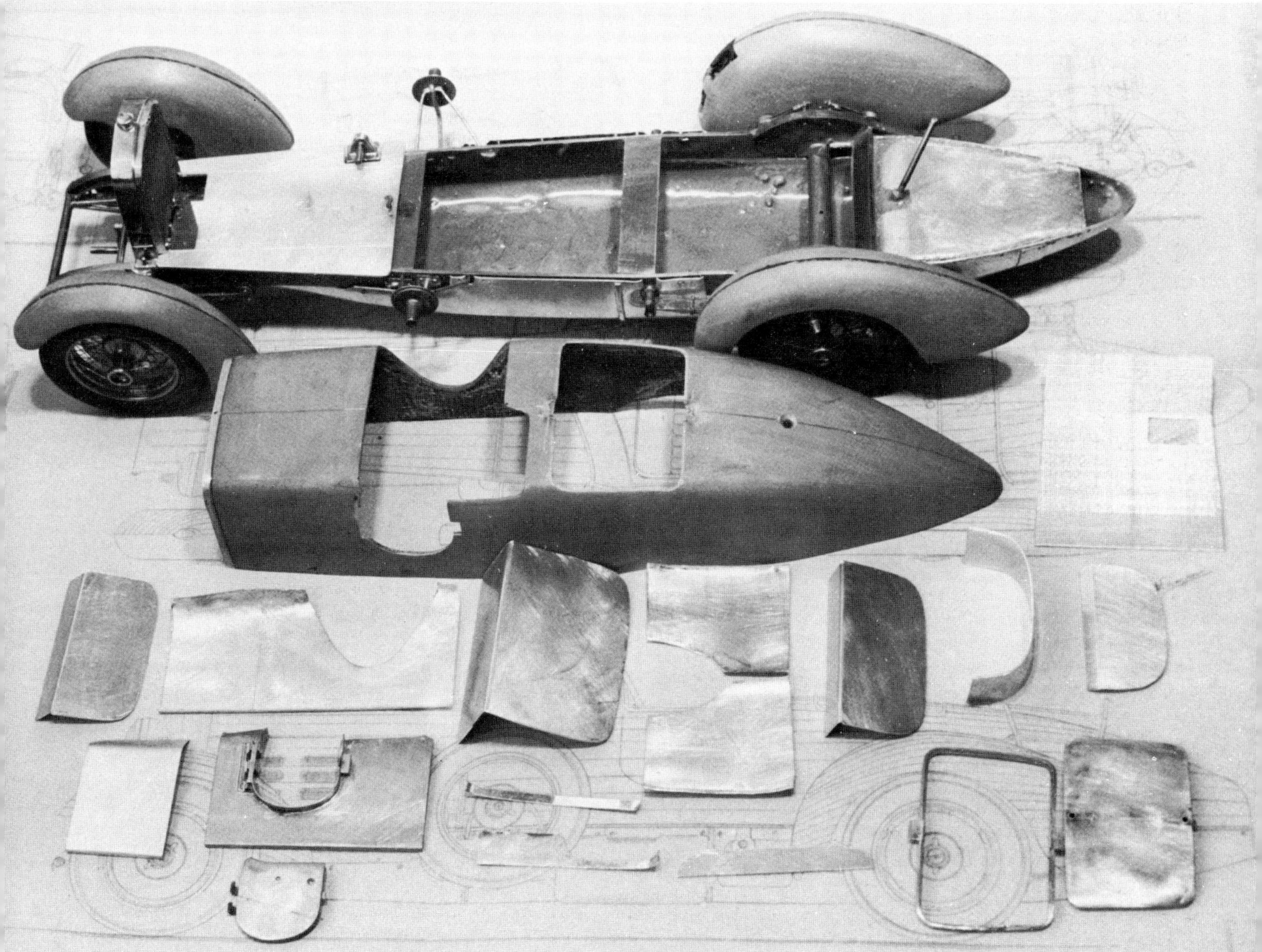

Plate 82.

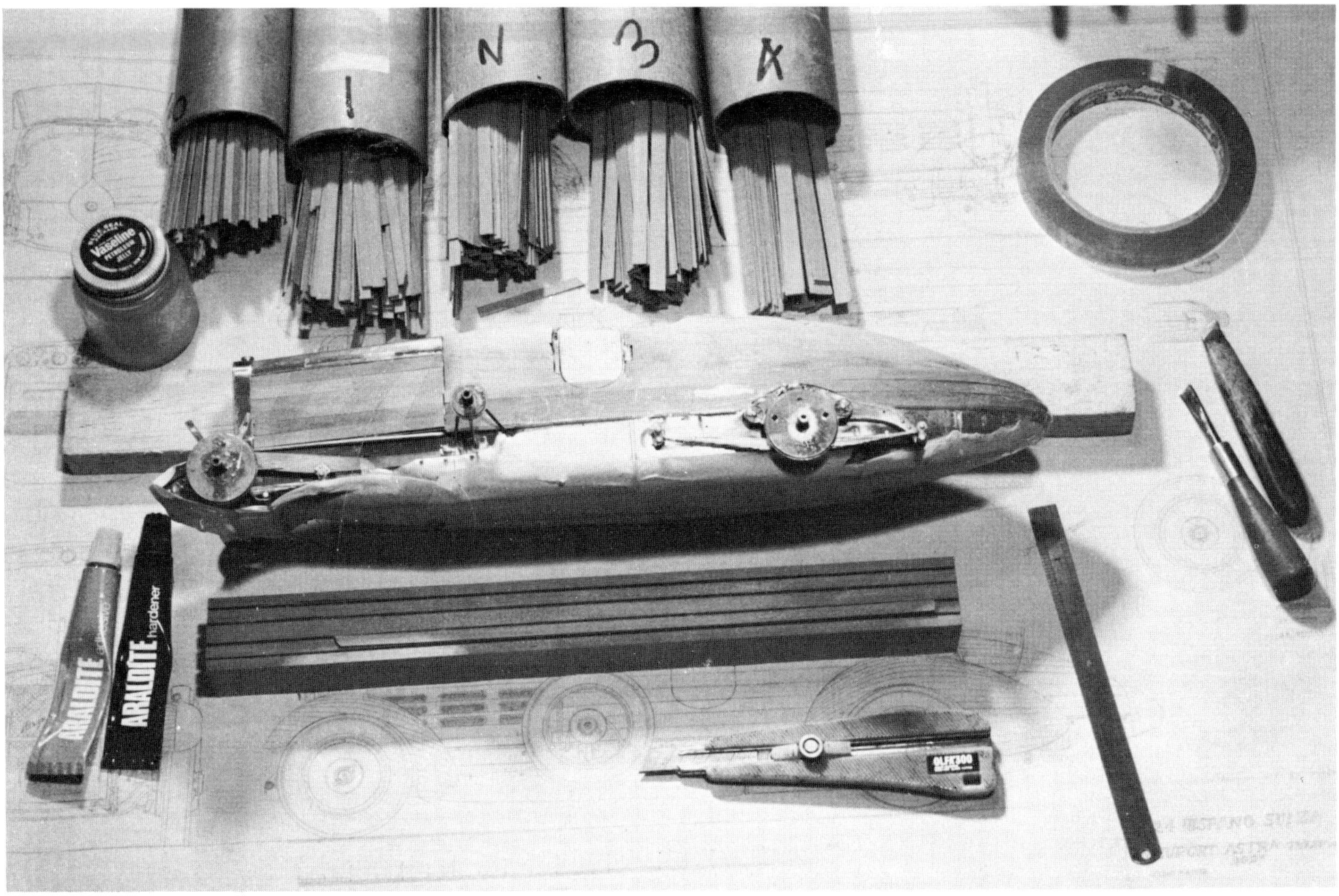

Plate 83.

As the hood was also to be planked, I decided on a very thin gauge metal for this part only .012" thick, as if it had been much thicker than this, the whole car would have looked out of proportion with the hood open.

Our next two plates 82 and 83 show the start of the planking. As I said earlier, the wood used was pear-wood. For those not equipped with a mechanical means of cutting wood into very thin strips, I would suggest the use of wood veneers. These, at the present time, are readily available at hobby shops. If in difficulty though, a few minutes with a trade directory, at your local reference library will give you several suppliers.

The actual planking is started at the bottom of the body, working both sides together. My own method, as can be seen in plate 83, is to cut and trim half a dozen planks at a time and mount them all together with sellotape, before finally glueing them to the body with an epoxy resin adhesive. By working in this way, it is possible to check that both sides exactly match, which is vital if they are to meet down the centre of the body.

This, of course, is very much like planking a ship's hull, in that none of the planks, when fitted, have parallel sides. All are trimmed to take account of the curves of the body. For anyone wishing to expand their knowledge of this subject, I would suggest my book 'The Techniques of Ship Modelling', in which I go into considerable detail on planking and the tools for making and working them.

With all the planks in place, the body and hood were cleaned up with abrasive papers, great care being taken not to sand through the very thin wood skin, which at this stage was only about .020" thick. Having settled for an even thickness all over, and a nice smooth surface, it was prepared with a grain filler, and a moderate finish built up with a shellac polish. When this was dry, it was very lightly sanded to remove the shine, ready to mark out for the brass pins. The reason for applying polish at this stage is two-fold. Firstly, it seals the grain, which prevents it soaking up surplus adhesive when the pins are resined in place, which could make for nasty looking rings around each pin head. (Remember the wood has yet to be stained.) Secondly the polished surface can be used as a guide when cleaning off after all the pins are in place. It is very easy to work an abrasive paper

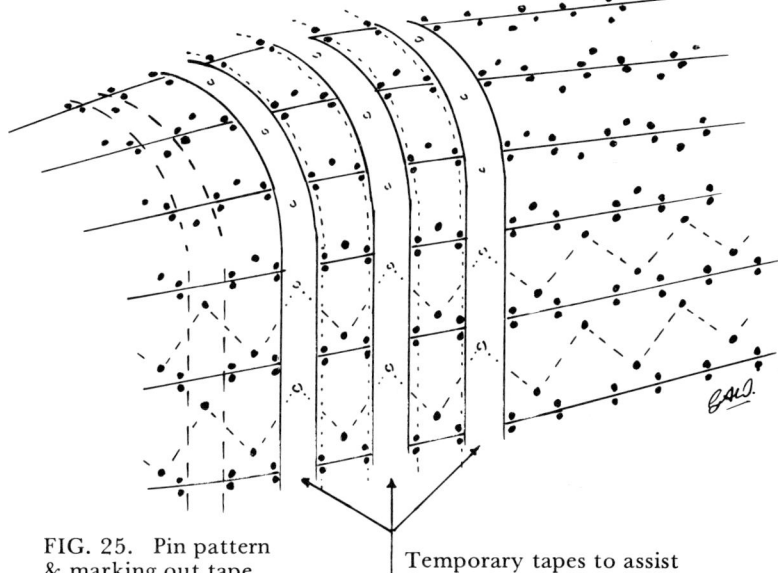

FIG. 25. Pin pattern & marking out tape for Hispano Suiza body.

Temporary tapes to assist marking out pin holes

through wood veneers, which would spell disaster on a subject such as this.

When I first set eyes on this car it was the pinning of the planks that struck me as the prominent feature and their importance lay in the regular patterns they made. In FIG. 25 we can see that the pins in fact made two distinct patterns, one horizontal and one vertical. The problem was how to mark this out on a miniature, the overall length of which was less than fifteen inches. I estimated that together with the four fenders, there would be almost thirteen thousand holes required, each correctly placed in relation to those around it.

With all problems of regular spacing there are two ways out. You either measure each individual point, or find something of the correct width and use it as a regular spacer between all the points. It might, at first, seem to be a lucky coincidence for me to have found a sticky tape of exactly the right width for this particular job. However, there are now on the market a very wide range of narrow tapes, of widths down to one sixty-fourth of an inch, which are used by the graphic artist and designers and in advertising work. These tapes are made by the same companies that produce the instant lettering and are usually obtainable from the same suppliers. The tapes are also provided with a very handy dispenser as can be seen in plate 84.

The obvious advantages of marking out the pin positions using this method can be seen in this plate.

Using the correct width of tape, the tape itself can be used to provide the correct spacing without resorting to measuring tools. But far more important than this is the fact that the spacing of the pins can be equalled out over the entire area before actually starting any of the holes, thus avoiding the possibility of getting even one in the wrong place. When using a natural wood finish on a model, it is all but impossible to conceal a hole or even a slight dent in the wrong place, as it tends to fill with stain and polish when the finish is applied and so show itself as a black dot. Unfortunately, the fillers that can be used under a painted surface are of no use in this instance. The only way round the problem, if it does occur, is to drill a small hole in the dent, if there is not one there already, and knock in a peg of the same wood. When this is sanded smooth with the surface, it can be almost undetectable.

With all the tapes in place, a small dimple was made, with a pointed tool, like a small bradawl, where each hole was to be placed. The tapes were then removed

and a fine drill, only .012" diameter was used to make the pin holes. A supplier for engineering tools is about the only place I can think of where you would be likely to obtain such fine drills, and even then, he would probably have to order them for you. On the other hand, if you were using a hollowed wood block as a base for the body, you could quite easily make your own drills from a very short piece of piano wire. To sharpen this for use as a drill, you only need to thin down one end on a fine oil stone to the shape of a screwdriver bit, then stone the end of this to a sharpened point, as per a normal drill.

Although these drills can be used in a pin vice, working them with the finger and thumb to make the holes, it is not a very practical way of doing this particular job, considering the number required. A better way is to mount the drill, either in a motorised flexible shaft, as I use, to be seen in the foreground of plate 84, or in one of the inexpensive low voltage hand drills, now obtainable in most model shops.

Plate 84.

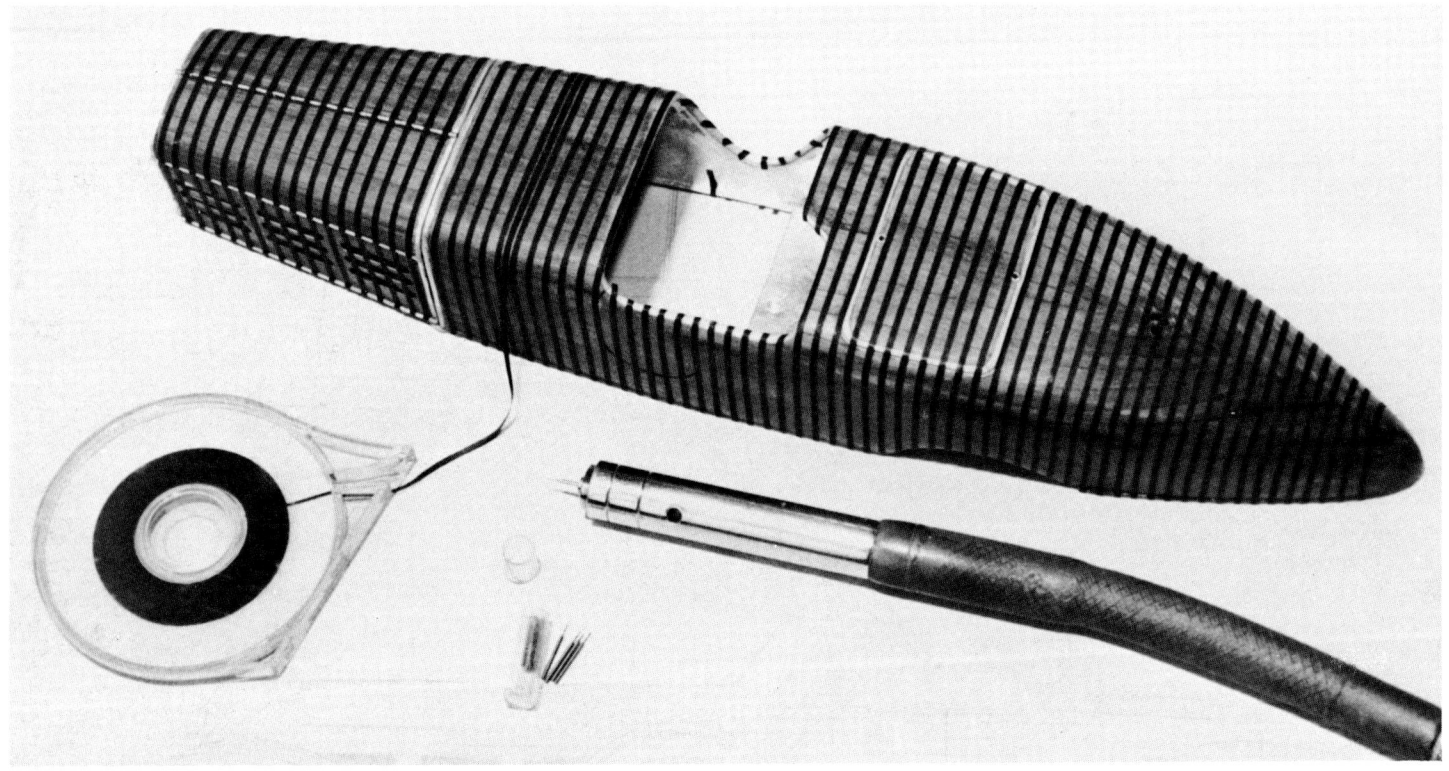

With all the holes drilled, several weeks have gone by and we still need another week or two to fill each with its pin, which, as I described with the test piece, can be clearly seen in plate 85, is in the form of a length of brass wire, .012" diameter. If difficulty is encountered in getting brass wire this fine from your metal supplier, then a suede shoe brush, of the brass wire type, together with some snips, will provide all your pins. With the pins in place and the adhesive set, the parts are cleaned up with files then abrasive papers. These are worked until we are just down to the surface of the wood again, through the polish. The next step is to stain, then the final polish is applied until a deep rich shine is built up and the job is finished. In actual fact there is nothing very difficult in this work at all, the only real skill is in keeping your patience intact long enough to complete the work, the techniques are all rather basic, cutting thin strips of wood, marking out and drilling holes, pinning and polishing.

I have left the fenders until now as the technique used to mould them is slightly different from that used previously. You may recall that I mentioned earlier the problem of undercuts on patterns when they are to be used to produce a mould. The pontoon fenders of the Hispano Suiza are a good example, as it is obvious that they cannot be made in a one-piece mould, as used for the body, without having to destroy the mould to get them out. The answer is the same as that used to make the tyre moulds. First make your pattern, set it in some modelling clay or in some way mask one side completely, so that you can make a mould of the other side. When this is ready, the masking is removed and a mould is made of this side, using the first half mould as a base. When this has set it is opened, the pattern removed, fixing bolt holes drilled and your mould is ready for use.

The two halves are set out and made in exactly the same way as was the body mould, with release agent,

Plate 85.

gel-coat and chopped strand mat. It will be noticed in plate 86 though that the base surface of the moulds is not flat, one side having two square mounds, while the other has corresponding square hollows. These are locating pegs, which are necessary when two or more parts are to be fitted together exactly. They are very simply made by putting small pieces of modelling clay on the base, and squaring them with a sharp knife to form tapered pegs ready for the first mould. When this has been made the clay will be removed from the mould, so that the resin for the other half can form pegs in those, that will fit exactly. Another point to note in the fender pattern on the left, is that for the right hand rear fender, 'cores' are used. These are two removable metal blocks that locate between the two half-moulds and produce, in the moulded fender, two cut-outs for the folding steps which are a feature of the fender on the right side. FIG. 26 is a cross section through this mould and illustrates these details more clearly.

The main difference between these moulds and those dealt with earlier is the fact that we do not want a solid article this time, but rather a shell, as we did with the body. To get this we make an open side to

Plate 86.

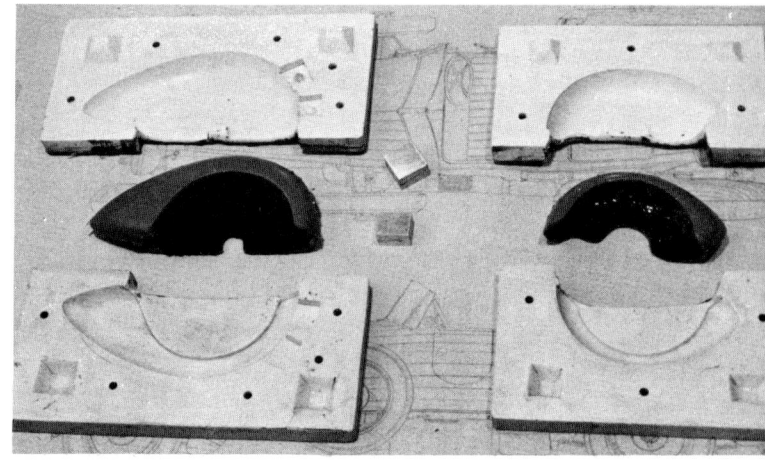

Plate 87.

FIG. 26. Hispano Suiza rear fender mould.

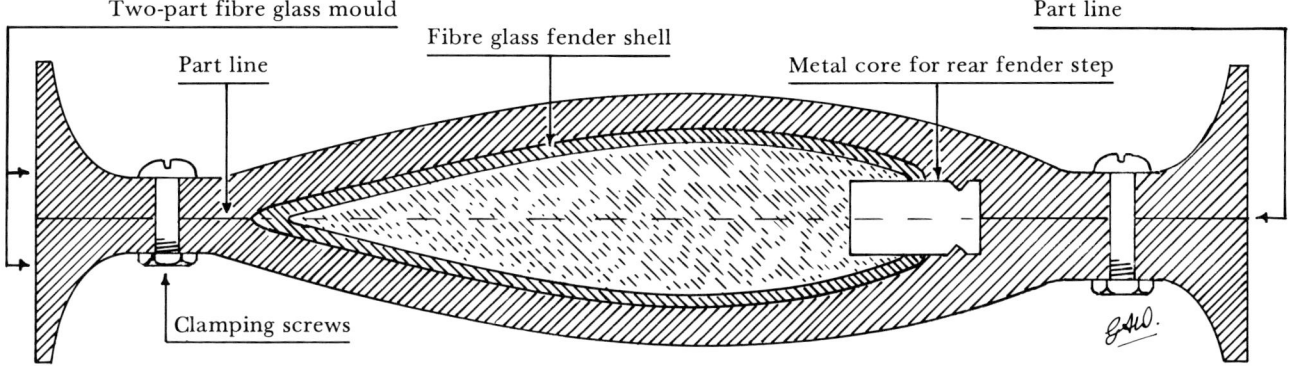

Two-part fibre glass mould

Part line

Fibre glass fender shell

Metal core for rear fender step

Part line

Clamping screws

the mould, in the case of the fender moulds, this was done at the bottom, or where the wheel protrudes below the fender. To use this type of mould everything, including the cores, is first given its coating of release agent, then with the two parts of the mould still open and with the two metal cores in place in one side, the gel-coat is laid into every part. When this is done the resin should be taken up the sides of the moulds to where the part line will be, this is the line that is to be made when the two parts of the mould are fitted together. Care should be exercised to ensure that the gel-coat is not taken over the edge, as the mould halves are not put together until the resin is almost set, so any hardened resin on the mould faces would prevent them fitting together accurately. With the gel-coat all but set, some laminating resin and glass fibre, chopped strand mat, is made ready and then applied to the gel-coat, again making a point to work up to the part line, but not over it. With the saturated fibreglass in place and while still wet, the two halves of the mould are brought together and the clamping bolts are screwed home. A narrow strip of glass fibre

is then saturated with resin and, working through the opening in the mould, is firmed along the part line to join the two halves together. When thoroughly hardened, the mould can be opened and the fender shell removed, this, together with the mould parts, is then washed in warm soapy water to remove all trace of the release agent, as if any should be left on the parts it can cause problems later.

Plate 87, shows the next stage with regard to the fenders, that of planking with thin strips of pearwood veneer. This is applied in exactly the same way as described for the body, several pieces being cut and trimmed to make up identical panels for each side, and then being resined in place on the shell. However, instead of starting at the bottom, as we did with the body, we now start at the top, with two pieces trimmed and taped together to give a straight line down the centre and gentle curves on each side ending with a point at each end. It is vital, if everything is to look right at the end, that this panel be located precisely, as the centre line will act as a guide for the meeting points of all the plank ends. When complete,

Plate 88.

93

you should have a perfectly straight line right round the centre part of each fender. When fully planked, they are pinned and finished off in the same way as the body. Plate 88 shows the various stages from the shell straight from the mould, then planked and drilled, pinned and finally cleaned and polished.

In FIG. 27 I show the catches fitted to the two opening doors on my miniature of the Hispano Suiza.

FIG. 27. Door & dicky seat lid catch for Hispano Suiza.

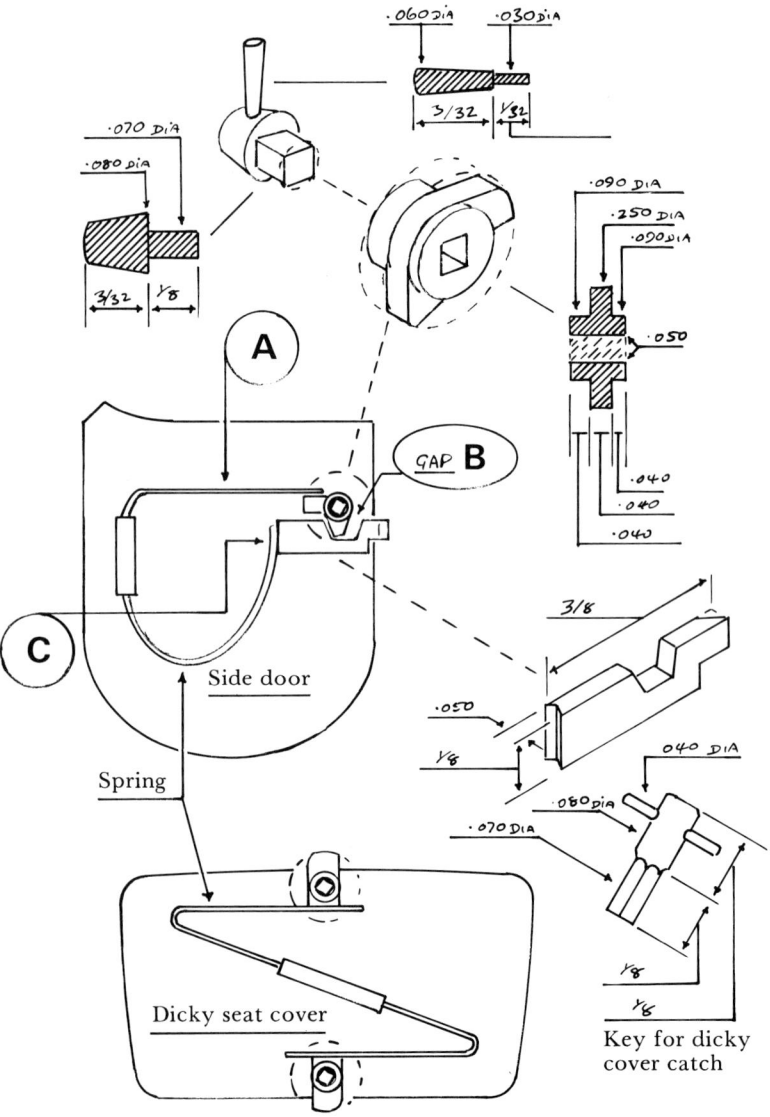

These are in fact sketches from my pad made when working out the problem. I am generally against working parts on models if they are being built for someone other than oneself, in view of the troubles involved in putting things right, if ever there is a breakdown. However, if there is an excuse, like wanting to see interior detail or the engine, then I think it can be a very attractive feature to make the hood and entry doors openable. Having decided this, however, I think we should also accept that they should be fitted with some sort of working door catch, with external features matching those of the original in scale of size and movement. This is not difficult, although it does, on occasion, involve considerable ingenuinity. I intend in this second part, therefore, to give one or two examples as we proceed. The first thing to aim for is strength and simplicity, with as few parts as possible. In the actual working of the door catch, the important detail to aim for is to make it independent of the handle, so that when the door is closed only the catch moves. To achieve this both catch and handle-cam need separate return springs. As any length of wire has two ends, we can provide both springs from the single length, as shown by 'A' FIG. 27. If we provide a gap in the catch at 'B', it will become apparent that the catch can now be moved back on its own spring, as when closing, without disturbing the cam. Yet on a slight movement of the handle-cam, the catch can also be withdrawn into the door to allow it to open.

As can be seen from the drawings, the parts for this door catch are very simple, the handle and cam being turned then filed to shape, while the catch was just filed up from a small piece of flat metal, brass or nickel silver. The door is soldered up as an open box, with the opening on the side facing into the car body. In this is soldered the small strip of brass tube to hold the spring wire and two retaining strips, between which the catch can operate. To complete the door, a panel is cut from thin sheet to cover and clip into the opening on the inside and to this is added any detail, such as pockets or fancy trim, that may form a feature of the original. It does sometimes happen, as with this example, that the working handle for the door is on the inside, which means the handle has to be fitted and retained after the inside door panel has been fitted in place. To overcome this, I made up a simple square punch from a small piece of hard steel and passed it through the centre hole of the cam.

Plate 89.

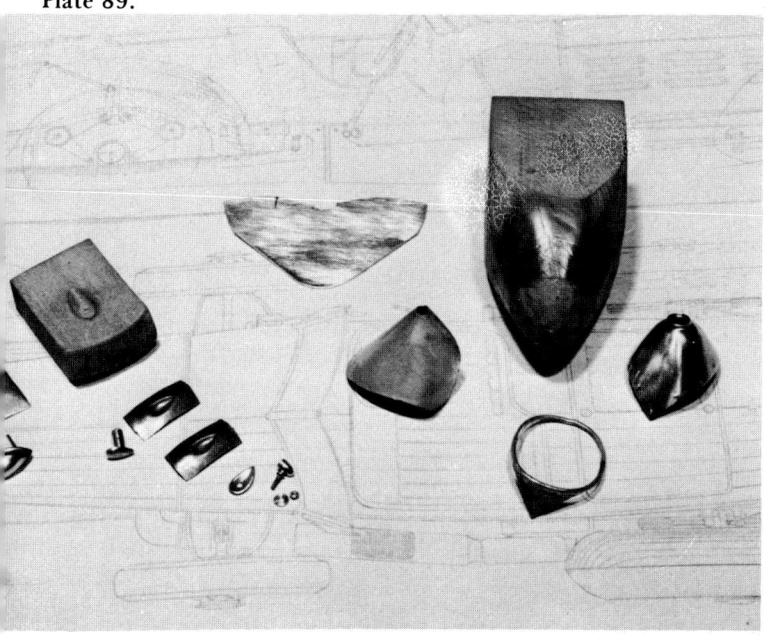

I then squared the end of the handle with a file to exactly fit this squared hole which made it possible to fit and test all the parts in the door, before finally covering them with the inside panel.

If the operating handle is on the outside, it is a simple matter to locate it in the right place. It can either be retained with a small screwed nut on the inside, or a

Plate 90.

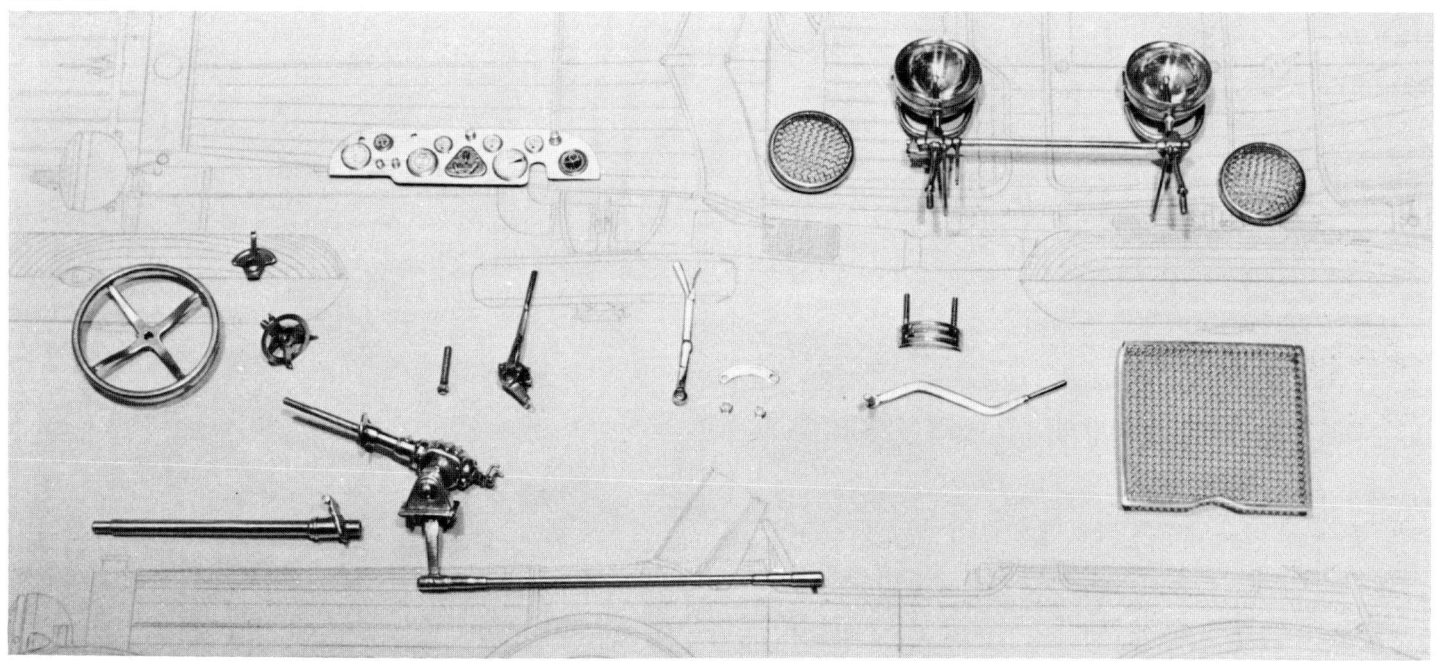

Plate 91.

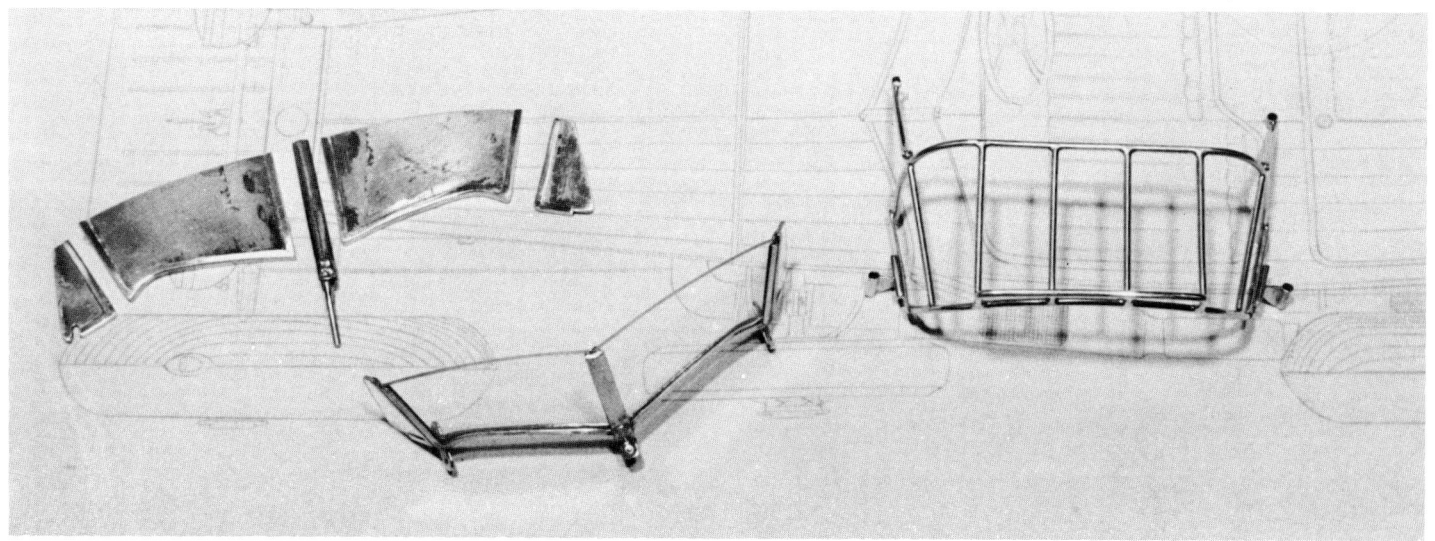

95

spot of solder between handle and cam, both of which can be done before the panel is fitted.

The last three plates to be discussed in this chapter, plates, 89, 90 and 91 cover some of the body fittings for the Hispano Suiza. The first of these illustrates some of the small parts worked from thin copper sheet. A block of hardwood, carved to the required shape and a simple punch, filed from brass rod, are all that was required for those on the left. On the right is another block of hardwood shaped to represent the pointed tail of the car on which the polished metal tail cone was formed. This could, of course, have been worked around the actual tail end of the model, however, one slip could have meant remaking a good part of it. Better to be safe than sorry.

Plate 90 illustrates some of the turned items most of which were more or less covered in part one, although two are worth a mention. Steering wheels can be turned from the solid bar as a single piece with the wheel spokes pierced with drills, and a jig saw, or they can have the rim turned from large diameter brass tube and the spokes cut from sheet and then soldered together. The latter method was the one used here. Another way of making this vital part, for those without a lathe, is to cut the spokes from sheet metal and form the rim from a circle of thick wire.

The fine wire mesh used for the radiator and head-lamp stone guards, is a commercially made item, obtained via addresses listed in the trade directories. I have had a go at making this myself, but have found it impossible to get the regular weave by hand, that is obtainable from the commercially produced article. There are many mesh and wire sizes available from the suppliers, although one usually has to purchase a great deal more than the amount required for any one model. Some useful small pieces of fine brass mesh can sometimes be found in various types of oil filter, in fact, I think most of it is used in the manufacture of various filters. Have a word with your local garage mechanic, he will probably give you an old one that can be opened up to get at the mesh. All you then need to do is give it a good clean and you are on your way.

Of the two items illustrated in plate 91 it is the screen that warrants the most interest, as these can present some difficult problems, as they need to be very fine yet strong. The main requirement is for a supply of 'U' section brass. If not obtainable ready made, try model railway suppliers, it can be made from thin sheet brass with the aid of the special cutting tool in FIG. 17 discussed earlier. The sheet is cut into strips, which in turn are given two grooves, so that they can be folded to form the 'U' section. Then with each piece in turn held upright in a flame, a spot of silver solder is deposited at the top and allowed to percolate down, through the folded corners, to the bottom. These are now cleaned in acid, washed and dried and are then ready for working into the screen frames. My method of making screens is first to make up a set of sheet metal patterns to correspond to the panes of glass — in this case four — made up of two large ones and two small quarter lights. The metal used for these patterns should be of the same thickness as the glass to be used, so that when the 'U' section channel is worked around each piece to form the frame, the correct width of the channel can be maintained. With the contortions necessary to make this frame it is apt to either spread wide or collapse into the centre. It is quite simple to work the channel around the more gentle curves of the bottom portion of the frame, however, the sharp angles of the corners will need to be mitred with a very small, three square file. These are then reheated and secured with a spot of hard solder. On the left of plate 91 can be seen a set of screen patterns with the worked 'U' section frames in place. In the centre is a complete screen with glass. The glass in this case is, of course, not the normal household window variety, but very thin, only .030" thick, perspex (acrylic) sheet. Because the screen is so vulnerable to knocks and this particular one is of the open top variety, it can add considerably to its overall strength, to bond the glass into the frame. The resin adhesives are of little use for this, as most of them are very thick when mixed and will tend to squeeze out around the glass when it is pressed into the frame, making for a very messy job. The best plan is to take the frames, one at a time, slide the glass halfway in, then place a very small spot of cyano-acrylate adhesive on the two edges of the glass so that it will take it in with it when the glass is pressed home. As this adhesive has a highly liquid consistency it will find its way right round the frame and the bond is all but permanent.

Plate 92.

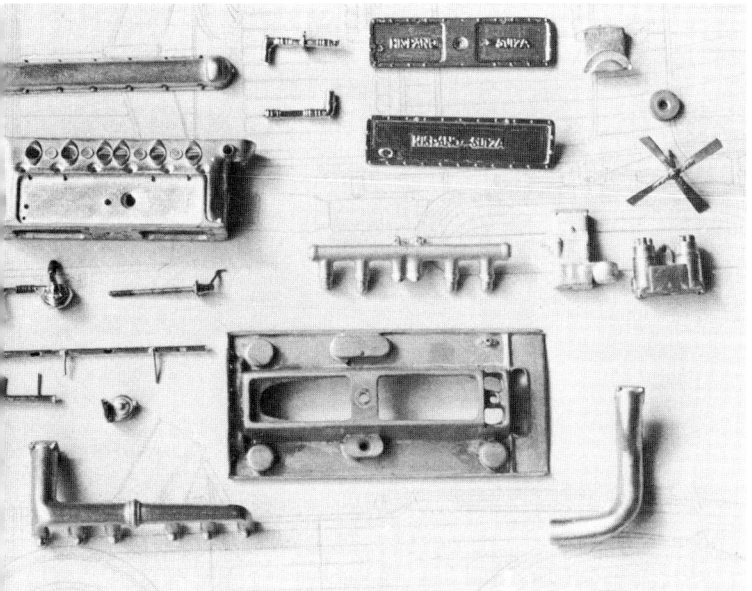

Plate 93.

Chapter 7

The Engine

I have started a new chapter, even though we are still discussing the Hispano Suiza, because we are about to enter new ground, that of building fully detailed engines. Although this was touched on in a small way with the Bentley Blower in Part One, the main engine components take our skills a step further.

From the plates that cover this chapter, you will see there are several engines to be dealt with, each will, I hope, illustrate a particular point, so that by the time we have finished — as was my aim with Part One — you should have enough ideas to be able to make a start on your own, with a subject of your own choice. I will also mention in passing, any particular details of interest, that have not already been discussed, pertaining to the miniature whose engine has been selected.

You will see from plates 92-93-94 of the Hispano Suiza engine, that because the undertray extends forward right up to the radiator and the bottom of the top half of the crank case extends out almost to the frame sides, that no part of the underside of this engine is visible, which is a good enough reason for not making it. I feel that time is much better spent in perfecting the techniques to produce perfect detailing of the parts that can be seen, and help to make up the character of the subject. Having said this, one cannot criticise the perfectionist builder, or collector, who wishes even unseen details to exist on a miniature, notwithstanding the extra labour and/or cost.

FIG. 28 gives a breakdown of the parts necessary to produce the crank case, or base, on which the remainder is built. If you remember the rule, to break the part down to squares and rounds and remove all projections, you will find no difficulty in undertaking this sort of work. All the parts incidentally are made up in metal, a good milling machine being necessary to produce the more complicated of these engine blocks, although as they are small and compact, and in most cases painted, they could be carved in pearwood, provided it is perfectly dry. The smaller parts and fittings could then be filed or turned in metal and resined in place.

Back to FIG. 28. The starting point is 'A', a simple rectangular piece of metal. After machining away the waste, the detailing is produced and soldered in place. 'B', which is all that is shown of the flywheel casing, starts as a stepped disc which is then sawn in half and added to 'A'. 'C' is a flattened length of wire and the

Plate 94.

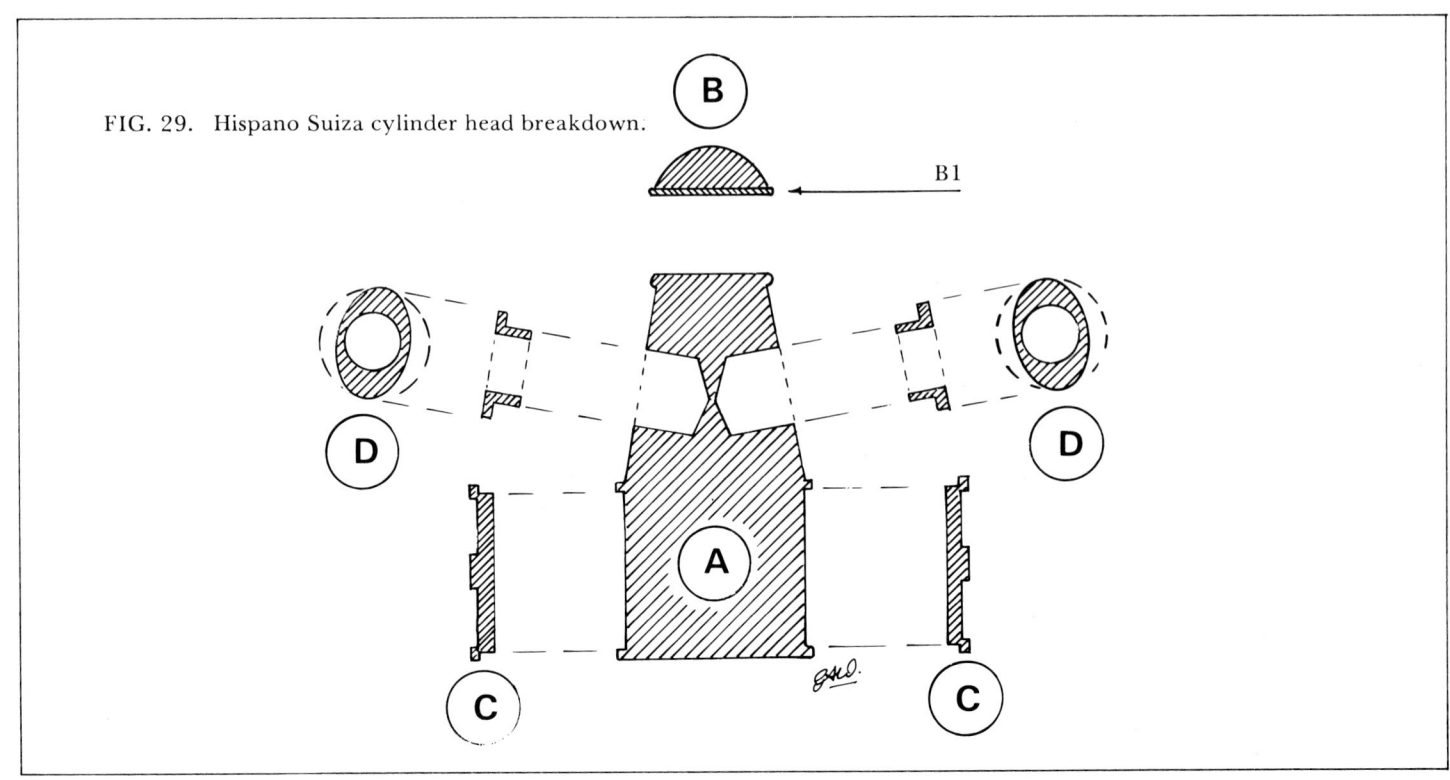

FIG. 28. Hispano Suiza crank case breakdown.

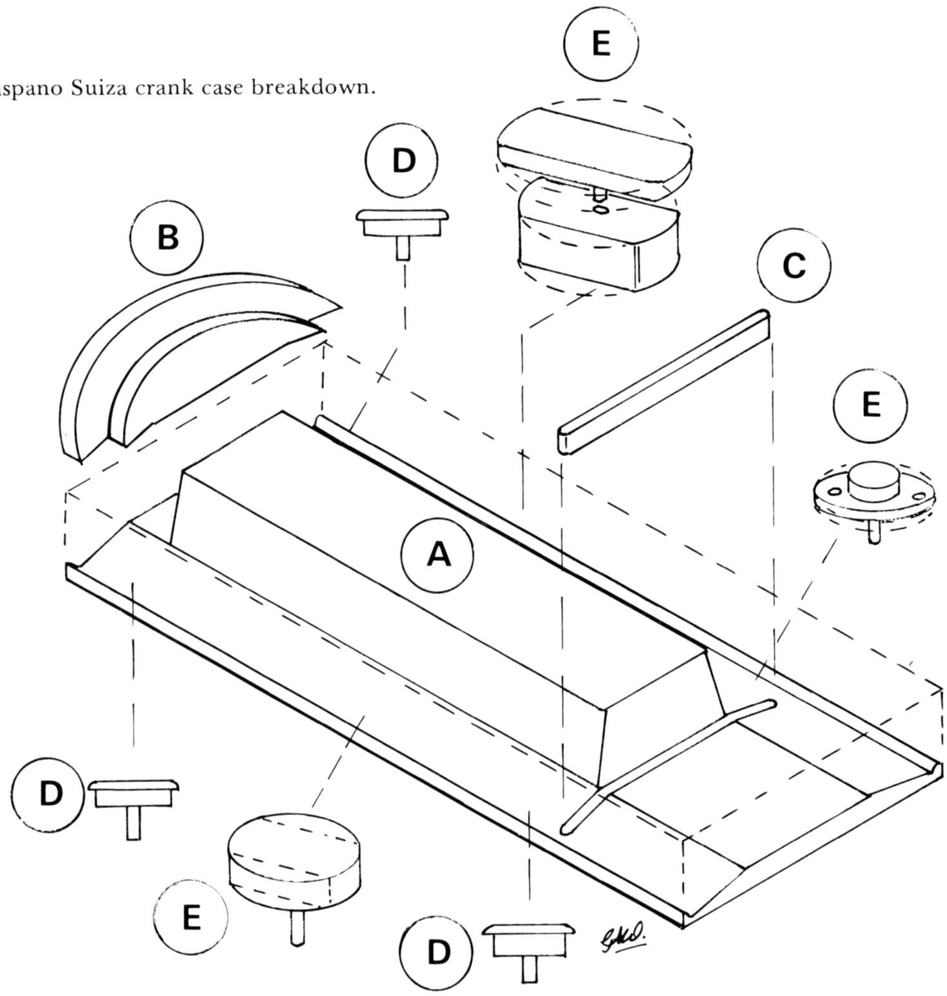

FIG. 29. Hispano Suiza cylinder head breakdown.

B1

parts for 'D' straight forward turned items, provided with dowel pins to hold them in place for soldering to 'A'. The parts marked 'E', are also turned on the lathe but before fitting are squared off on two sides with a file.

FIG. 29 shows the main components of the cylinder block. Again a simple block 'A', which could be in either wood or metal, having all projecting detail added after its basic shaping has been done. The cam shaft cover, 'B', was made as a separate item so that its flange 'B1' could be made from brass sheet and added to the actual cover after it had been shaped. It may be noticed, particularly in plate 94, that the bolts securing the cover to the cylinder head are each provided with a slight nick in the side of the cover to accommodate the bolt head. This nick is much easier to provide if the cover is separate from the flange.

The two inspection panels, 'C', were made as separate items for two reasons. Firstly, they required plating which was not necessary on the rest of the block, and secondly, the name Hispano Suiza was required in raised letters across the centre of each. Not being a natural optimist, I always anticipate disaster, so that when presented with a problem, namely producing raised lettering, then I insure that should the first try end in the scrap bin, I will not be giving myself too much work to replace it.

There are four ways of producing raised lettering, the method I used being the most direct and perhaps the most difficult to correct, should you make a mistake. A piece of thick sheet brass is cut and trimmed to the shape and size of the panel. This is blacked over with a felt tip pen and left to dry, then marked out as to the border and lettering required. The panel is then mounted on a milling machine and the waste metal removed to a depth of about .025" leaving a raised border around the edge and a raised rectangle in the centre, sufficient to accommodate all the lettering. To bring out the individual letters work around each one with a selection of fine dentists' burrs, removing all waste metal down to the depth of the milled area. Luckily I got it right the first time. However, had I messed it up I would have tried a second method that has worked in the past. With this we start with a perfectly flat brass plate. In the area that is to receive the lettering is deposited a thickish layer of soft solder which is flattened with files and fine paper, then blackened and finally marked out as was the first

example. The waste material around and between the lettering is now picked out with small sharp knives and/or finely ground pointed tools. The advantage over the first method is that because the solder of the lettering is not as hard as the brass background, it is much easier to make this flat and the lettering sharp and even. An example of lettering using this technique may be seen in plate 97, the word 'Ferrari' on the rocker covers, and in plate 103, the word 'Ford' on the gear box cover. The third way of doing this is to cut each letter out of thin sheet and solder it in place on the panel, this might be worth considering on a large scale, but it is not really practical on this scale. An example of the fourth method of producing raised lettering may also be seen on the Ford, in plate 106, but I will leave the comments on this until we reach the Ford.

The final point worthy of comment, with regard to the cylinder head, concerns the inlet and exhaust parts 'D' FIG. 29. As can be seen at the top left of plate 92 these present another example of a raised detail. In this case a dozen identical shapes were required, so it was much simpler to file a length of brass bar to the oval shape called for and then drill and part them off on the lathe, finally soldering them into place rather than to try removing the waste material from around the shapes with dentist burrs. It will be seen, that although many of the problems in model making are repeated over and over again, they do not all warrant the same answer. It should be noted also, the advantages of finding as many ways as possible of doing the same job. Even though you may have developed the perfect method of reproducing something, this should be no excuse for not keeping your eyes open for other ways, techniques and materials.

The final two prints plates 95 and 96 illustrate the finished Hispano Suiza, mounted on a base of velvet and polished wood. Note that it is bolted to the base, which need not be with quarter-inch bolts. All I have done is drill and tap two holes in each of the axles where they meet with the springs. Then I threaded four lengths of one-sixteenth diameter nickel silver bar, silver soldering a quarter inch diameter countersunk head, on the other end of each. The base was now marked out, drilled, and countersunk on the underside to take the bolts. With four on a model of this size, even though it is almost entirely built in metal and quite heavy, the bolts do not need to be

Plate 95.

Plate 96.

unduly tightened. This can be useful if the miniature is to be moved about to shows or exhibitions.

The next engine we can have a look at is that of a 1963, 250 GTO Ferrari, plate 97. This, in fact, shows the actual car. Plate 98 illustrates my 1/15 scale model of it, the width of the hood (bonnet) opening being only two and a quarter inches. With engines of this sort even less detailing is called for, in fact almost nothing was shown, or could be seen below the level of the exhaust pipes. Being a 'V' twelve engine the two banks of cylinders very usefully concealed the extensive webbing of the crank case, that is a feature of these engines. Again everything was made in metal, but there is plenty that could have been carved in wood, and then added to with metal fittings. There is usually very little bright work, all the finishes called for, being obtainable from a spray can.

For those who have stayed the course this far, a glance at these prints of the Ferrari engine should suffice to reassure you that it is far less complicated than it looks, being in the main composed of simple turned parts added to the main block.

In plate 99 we have the bright work for this car wired for plating. Of interest here are the trims for the screen and rear window. These are made up from 'T' section brass on an aluminium former, shaped and beaten to follow the contours that the glass is to follow. The glass, or in our case perspex (acrylic sheet), is given its convex shaping on a wooden former. First it is heated in an oven, or for very small pieces over a light bulb, until it softens and starts to sag. The perspex is then draped over the pattern block and if it is in the right condition, will conform to its shape. As acrylic sheet marks very easily, I make a habit of always cutting and shaping several pieces for each aperture, putting to one side the best one and using one of the others to hold the bright work trim in shape while being plated, as can be seen in the photograph. As I stated earlier, if a part is bent after plating, there is a good chance that it will crack, so it is important to make sure that these very fragile frames maintain their shape during plating.

Another part of interest on the Ferrari and shown in plates 98 and 99 is the headlamps. With modern sports car bodies, the glass for these lamps is required to blend in with the general body shape, which can be quite complicated. I found the best way to tackle this is first to complete the body, then bore into the front

fenders a hole of a size large enough to take the complete lamps, making sure that it is square with the body and parallel with the ground. A tube is then formed in a thin gauge metal (.008" brass) that will just fit this aperture. This is put just far enough into the opening and then marked around its outer surface to the shape of the opening. The surplus metal is now trimmed from the end of the tube and a thin gauge piece of metal bent to fit, and then soldered, over the opening. The outside edge of this is trimmed with snips to leave a small rim out from the edge of the tube. The centre is pierced with a drill and then filed to leave a similar small projection on the inside, which will be used to retain the glass. Rather than start with a piece of thin sheet perspex for the glass, I found a much better job could be made by using perspex rod. A piece of this is first turned to fit the headlamp tube, then one end is angled off with files, then papers and finally polish to fit and conform to the shape of the fender.

To complete the lamps, the perspex rod is parted off on a lathe so that it is about one-sixteenth of an inch shorter than the tube, and the squared end is made concave to form the lens of the lamp. What we now have is a short length of clear perspex rod, with one end angled and polished to form the convex lamp's outer glass, with the other end polished and dished to form the actual headlamp lens. With this fitted in the metal tube, it only remains to have the bulb and

Plate 97.

Plate 98.

FIG. 30. Ferrari door catch.

Catch return spring

Button holder
screwed into
door shell

Plate 99.

Plate 100.

Plate 101.

reflector turned and polished in aluminium and pressed in after the perspex to complete the unit, which can then be fitted into the car body as a single piece.

The press-button door catch of the Ferrari was another problem that needed considerable thought. FIG. 30 illustrates the principle settled upon on how it worked on the miniature. Note that because there was no actual handle to fall limp, it was possible to get away with just one return spring. In fact, because of the angle of the button, it always stayed in place whenever the door was closed.

The last item on the Ferrari I will deal with is the wire wheels, and in particular the triple spoking. Plates 100 and 101 show two views of one of the wheels, and plate 102 illustrates miniatures from the front and rear, which were both spoked in the same manner. The spoking diagram for this car can be seen in FIG. 31 and particular note should be made of the arrangement of spoke holes around both rim and hub and their relation with one another. This, in fact, is the most complicated wheel I have seen to date, having three rows of spokes, each of which crosses through the other two. It is a good idea, when confronted with a wheel of this complexity, to take more than the customary two photographs. Four or five and some sketches and notes, will all be found most useful in trying to unravel it. Note also that although the rows between the front rim and rear hub, 'A', and the back rim and back hub, 'B', can both be accommodated with single starts, the row between the back rim and front hub calls for a double start C1 and C2. Although this is probably the most complicated wheel anyone is likely to come up against, again I have endeavoured to show that these things are nowhere near as difficult as they might at first sight appear to be. The key in this particular case being to first work it all out on paper.

Let us now leave the Ferrari and have a look at several other models that I have built to the larger scale of 1/15 to see what further useful hints can be extracted. Plate 103 illustrates the interesting sort of model an engine can make on its own. In this case the subject is a 1915 Model 'T' Ford engine and it has been completed in the normal way, but instead of fitting it into a car as in plate 104, I have made, and had chromium plated, a small cradle and tray and bolted it to this, mounting both on a black perspex base. This was made up in the first place as a travelling sample, so I also added to it a Ford 'T' wheel and tyre and an

Plate 102.

Plate 103.

example of the only instrument one got with a model 'T', a speedo, with fully numbered face.

The patterns for the Model 'T' fenders, Plate 105 are still another example of a little thought beforehand, saving a lot of time later. In the centre is the master pattern, which is of the correct profile and is used in conjunction with the two outer pieces, to make up the full set, these supplementary pieces being held in place with dowels.

Plate 106 brings us back to the problems of raised lettering and in this case, raised treadwork. The Ford running board, and incidentally the word 'Ford' on the radiator shell, was worked in thin copper sheet, working on the back with a pointed, but blunt scriber-like tool. The copper, about .006" thick, is first cut to size, annealed and then fixed to a thick card with double-sided tape. The surface is then gone over with a black marker pen and when dry is marked out as to detail, which will, of course, be in reverse. When all is in order, the tool is worked with a moderate pressure, to pick out the required pattern and lettering. To avoid the chance of damage when cleaning up the

FIG. 31.
Ferrari wheel spoking diagram.

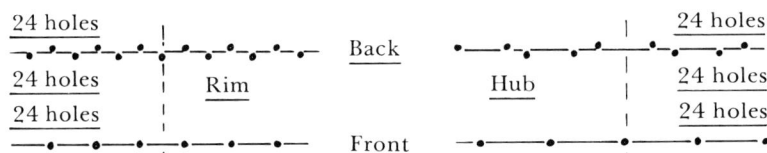

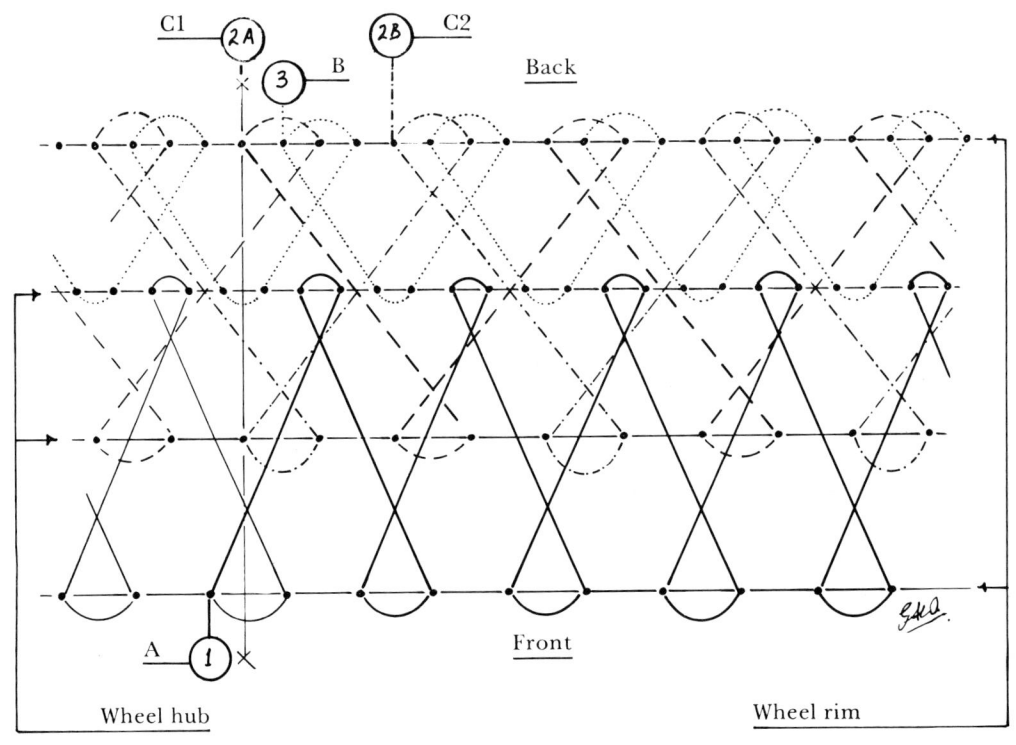

Plate 104.

Plate 105.

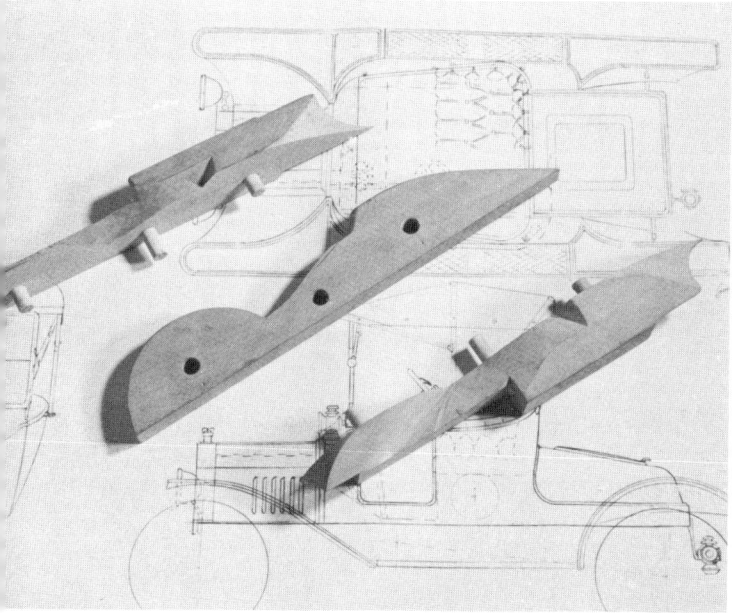

Plate 106.

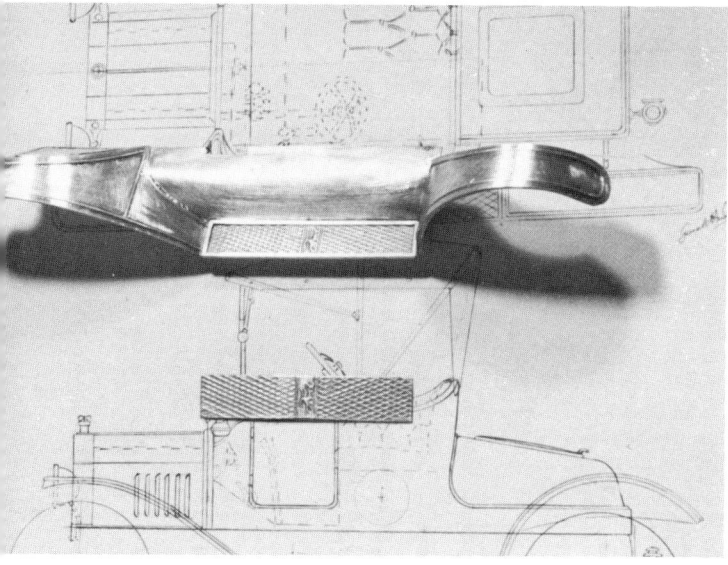

right side, some epoxy resin is mixed and spread liberally on the back, making sure to fill all the detail, then a piece of aluminium is trimmed to shape and pressed on the copper, squeezing out any surplus resin. When set, the part can be removed from the card, stripping off the double-sided tape, and cleaned up in the normal way.

One feature that I have not mentioned at all, but is evident on almost all the cars discussed so far, is the folding top, or roof. On the smaller scale miniatures I feel the best plan is to show the top down, as the scale of the materials available, in my experience, do not lend themselves to working tops. The problem is, to find a very close woven fabric, that also makes use of a very fine thread. There is also another problem, that of working the material by way of seams and general sticking etc.

For miniatures built in 1/15 scale, the fabric I find most adaptable is satin, for not only does it meet the weave and scale requirements but it can be cut without fraying and the parts put together, without

FIG. 32. Model 'T' Ford door catch.

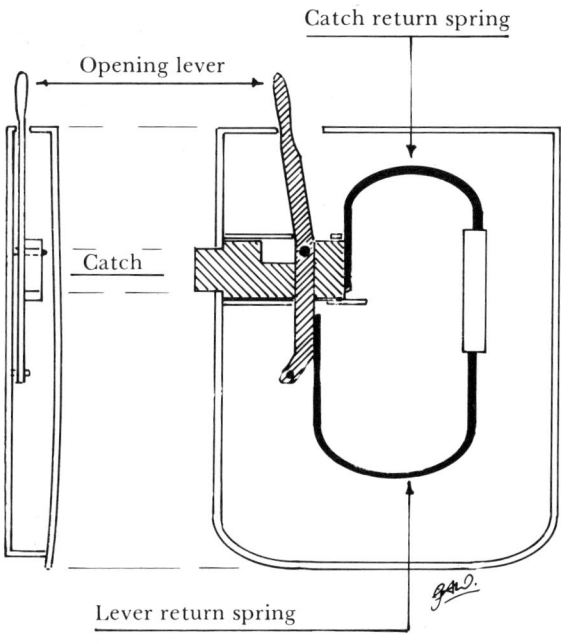

Plate 107.

sticking. Satin has a dull side and a shiny side and it is the former that we utilise for the scale finish of the top. Incidentally, although it is not correct, even the shiny side does not look out of place on the inside. The 'bows' or frames for the top are first worked out of flat brass, these should, if we followed the practice of the original, be made from wood, (ash), but I personally prefer metal from the point of view of strength. When these have been made, as per your plans, a start can be made on the fabric side. As can be seen from plate 108 I use a hot soldering iron for cutting, working around the edge of a previously cut template. The 'bit' of the iron should be filed to a sharp knife edge. In use it will be found to not only cut the material, but being hot, will also melt and seal the fibres on both sides of the cut, so preventing any fraying. With a little practice, seams and stitching can also be simulated on the satin with the hot iron.

The first pieces to be cut and fitted are the two webbing straps, as these are needed to anchor one end, and position the bows. The cutting is best done on the side that is to be seen, the dull side, as the welded ends of the threads form into a continuous line that for some reason looks correct, and for the cutting, the soldering iron is used with a steel rule or straight edge. Two squared loops are formed in a thin wire and resined in previously drilled holes, behind the seat back, these are used as the anchor points, the webbing being turned through these, with about one eighth of an inch stuck back on itself with a flexible adhesive such as Bostik No. 1. To attach the webbing to the bows, three further pieces are cut from the satin that will each just wrap around one of the bows. Squared sections are cut out of these to accommodate the webbing after which they are glued in place on the underside of each bow sandwiching the webbing in between. The seam should be along the top of each bow, so that it will be hidden by the top material.

Two more straps, this time at the front, are needed to hold the bows rigid, but these are leather — the only time I use leather to represent leather. For these and, incidentally, for hood or bonnet straps, only the finest glove leather is suitable, others being either too thick or too grainy to look right. Further squared wire loops are called for on the front bow and also on the screen frame of the model 'T' Ford in plate 107 and on the cowl of the Russo in plate 109. It is this last plate that illustrates the stage we are now at,

the two pieces in the foreground, being the cut fabric for the top on the left and for the back on the right. The window in this piece is cut from .005" acetate sheet, being held in place with another piece of satin, cut to form a frame. The whole is bonded together by painting with acetone which has the effect of melting the fabric and the acetate into one. Again this is a technique that is best approached experimentally on a test piece first. Get yourself a half yard of black satin and try these different techniques with it. Only when you know how to reproduce the exact result you are after, is the time to use it on the miniature.

To complete the folding top, or roof, we need now to fit the two satin panels. I fit the top one first, starting at the front, using the clear flexible adhesive Bostik No. 1. A thin film of this is applied to the tops of the three bows and the material is pressed in place. No glue must seep through the satin, as it will show on the finished top. The fabric is now taken over the rounded corners and down the sides slightly, so closing the 'V' darts on each side. As the fabric is quite thick and stiffish, it will not want to go exactly where you put it, particularly when it comes to working it around the radial corners of the front bows. However, a little touch here and there with the hot iron, will soon show it who is boss. It is, in fact, a most pleasant material to work with. With the top sides and front blended home it is the turn of the rear edge, which is worked downwards over the rear bow,

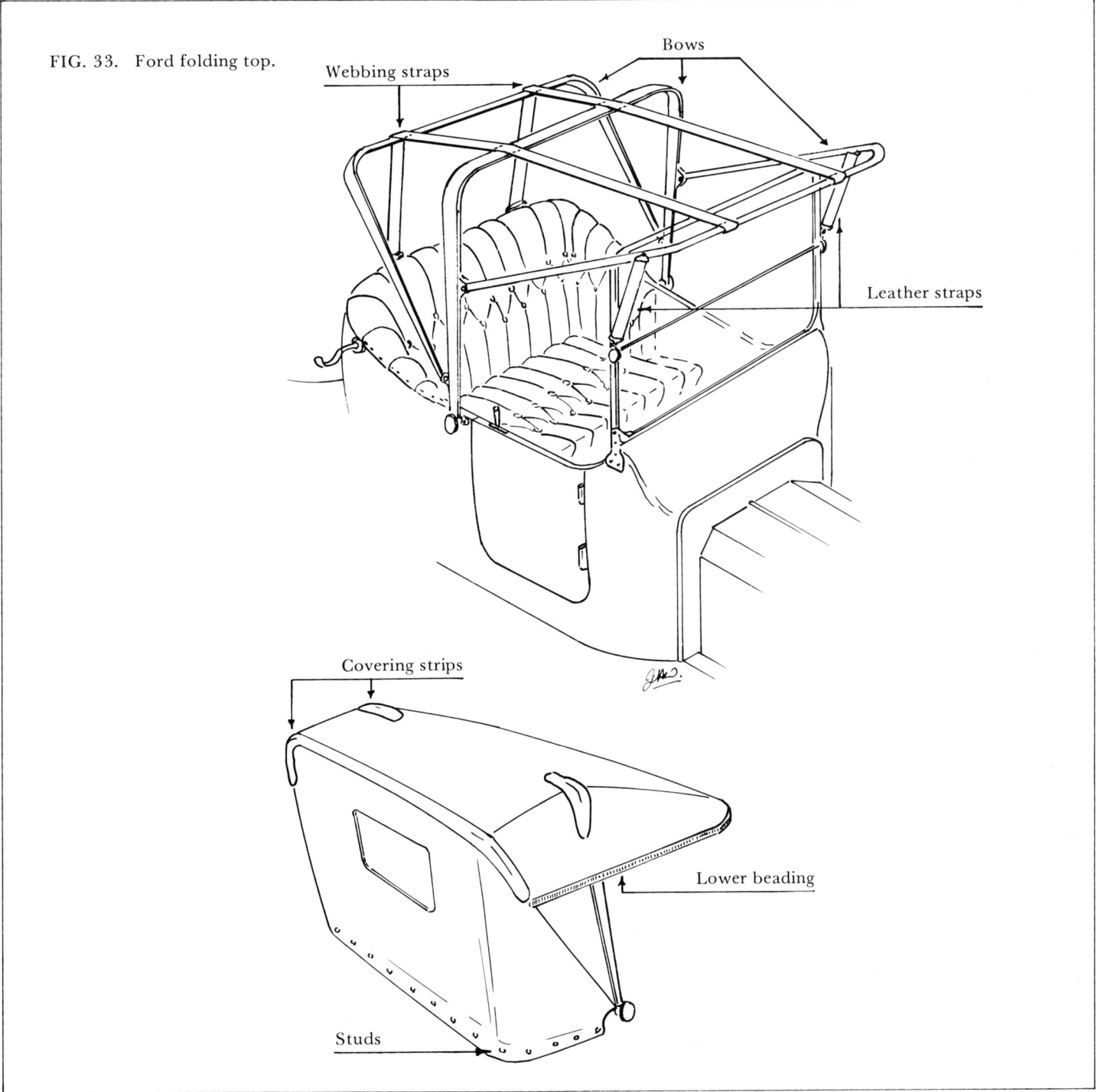

FIG. 33. Ford folding top.

Webbing straps

Bows

Leather straps

Covering strips

Lower beading

Studs

Plate 108.

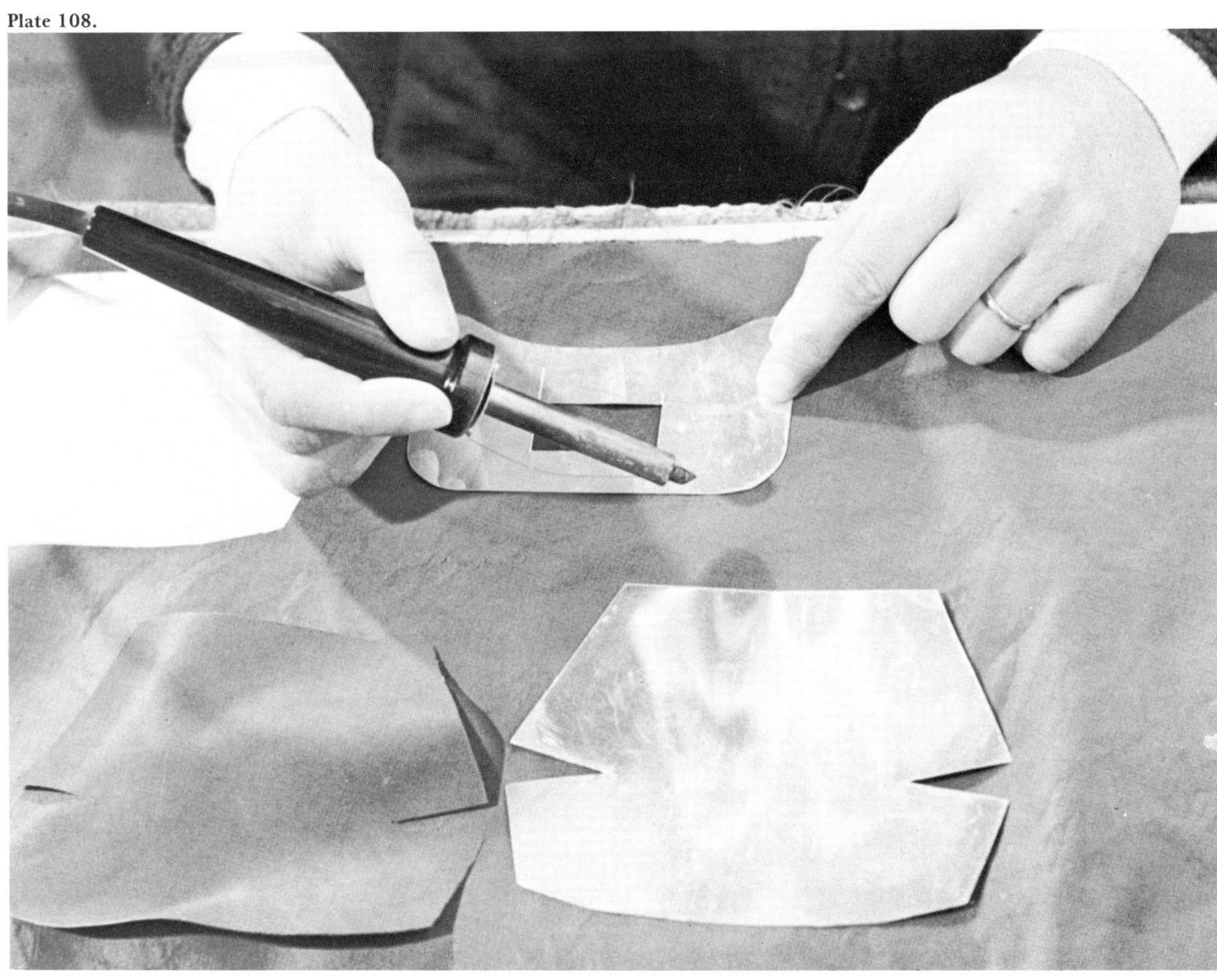

welding it to the fabric wrapped around it and trimming off the surplus with the iron.

It is now the turn of the rear piece to be fitted. This is first attached along the lower edge to the body, usually with a row of studs, which on the model are represented by the ever useful 1/32 round head rivets. Mark out the body, drill the row of holes, then find each through the fabric with a pointed tool and insert the rivet tipped with a spot of adhesive. With this done the top edge is gone around with the iron, to weld it to that of the fabric already there, again trimming off the surplus as you go. Care is needed here to see that the line of the join, and general blending in with the iron, is as narrow as possible, as the strip that will cover it will not be more than about one-sixteenth of an inch wide. A strip of satin is now cut and fitted over this rear seam, taking it around the corners. Two further shorter strips are also called for to cover the seam on the corners of the centre bow and one last strip or beading is required to follow the lower

edge of the top from one side of the rear bow, around the front bow, to the other side of the rear one. All these covering strips are held in place with Bostik, the soldering iron being used to trim, or blend in any surplus material below the lower beading.

The above comments deal in the main with the type of folding top illustrated by the miniatures of both model 'T' Ford and the Russo, but the material can be used for the larger types as well, although some difficulty might be experienced if the top for a four seat touring body was required to fold and stow correctly, on account of the bulk of material. These smaller tops, do raise and fold realistically, and look right in either position. One point of warning, as with the real thing, repeated folding will crease the fabric on the model particularly, and will soon make it look untidy in the up position, so if it is wanted up, I suggest it be left in that position to keep its shape and look its best.

Plate 109.

Plate 110.

Plate 111.

Chapter 8

The Building of a 'J' Duesenberg

This final chapter is really a resumé of what has already been discussed, except that here we will be seeing, with the help of nearly thirty prints, how all the different stages look on a single project, rather than, as we have been doing, picking out an interesting item here and there from several models to illustrate a particular point.

I think it is also a useful exercise, with this particular model, as it is about as far as one can go with the type of miniature I have been dealing with. All the subjects dealt with in the previous chapters, have to some extent been incomplete. In the first part they lacked engine detail and in this part, so far, even though the engines have been added, in most cases they have not been fully detailed because the underside has been obscured by an undertray. With this model we not only have a fully detailed engine and running gear, but also a full 'U' section frame.

The subject of the miniature is a 1933 model 'J' Duesenberg fitted with a Derham Tourster body and plate 110 illustrates the actual car. This particular car has a very special attraction for me, as I think it represents one of the most beautiful automobile body styles fitted onto the most outstanding chassis. To me it is perfection.

For those of my readers not familiar with the name, the model 'J' Duesenberg was built in the United States of America between 1929 and 1936 and less than five hundred chassis were completed. For the beginner, adapting some of these techniques to the excellent metal Hubley kit, may be a useful foot in the water, before going it alone from scratch. However, each of these chassis was fitted with a different hand-crafted custom body. This one chassis has had a wider variety of body styles fitted to it, built by a larger number of the world's foremost custom body shops, than any other automobile chassis before or since. In consequence, it probably has the largest number of the most beautiful, most exciting and most elegant bodies of any automobile ever; all designed and built when the art of the custom coach builder was at its zenith. It is also a testimony to its engineering, that it is said there are more Duesenbergs still running, in proportion to the total number made, than any other make of car. It is also the most sought after of all the classics and at the time of writing, holds the record for the highest price ever paid for an automobile in the classic car salerooms. Its place in my life is marked by the fact that it is one of the first cars to stimulate my interest to create miniatures of them and also for making me realise that an automobile need not be just a conveyance from 'A' to 'B' but it can also be a work of art.

So the subject of this last project is no ordinary car, to me it is the finest thing man ever put on four wheels, and with such thoughts in mind, my aim was to show this in the finished model. Although I had made contact with the owner of the car many years ago and he very generously sent me many photographs of his pride and joy, it was not until two years ago that I found myself five thousand miles from home, in the Mid West of the United States of America, standing beside this dream of a car, seeing and feeling it in the flesh. There is no substitute for actually being in the presence of the subject you wish to reproduce in miniature, only then can you really get the feeling of it, and it is only when you have that, that you have got a chance of showing something of its character in your model.

Needless to say, being in the presence of such a beautiful beast as this, I was soon at work with camera and pencil, and on arrival home, the workshop was given over to the task of interpreting all the photographs and dimensions I had collected, into a workable set of scale drawings. With these completed, as described at the start of this volume, and checked against the car, the building work began. As is my practice, the wheels were the first items to take shape and it so happened that the time for spoking them coincided with mid-winter, short days and poor lighting. If there is one thing you cannot do without when spoking wire wheels, it is good lighting, so I spent some time in the next few days browsing through the local electrical shops looking for a suitable lamp. All of them suffered from the same defects, in that they cast shadows where you did not want them and they gave off heat. An idea sprang to mind though, when I came across some small circular fluorescent tubes. I purchased one of these, about twelve inches in diameter, together with its starter unit, and a small plastic seed pan from a local seedsman. The result of this unlikely combination may be seen in plate 112, the ideal, cool, shadowless lighting for all small intricate assembly work, on dark winter evenings.

As can be seen from the first of these photographs, this car was fitted with white wall tyres. This, at first

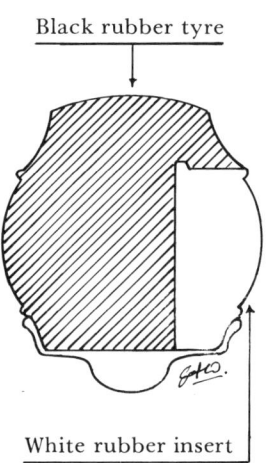

FIG. 34. Section of white wall rubber tyre.

Black rubber tyre

White rubber insert

sight, presented a particularly tricky problem, because one of the properties of silicone rubber, which we use to make the miniatures, is that it is impossible to stick anything else to it, i.e. paint, etc. As my first thoughts had been to purchase a small quantity of the paint sold for white wall tyres, to apply to the model ones, it was also the first idea to be thrown out. It turned out to be another of the problems that could not satisfactorily be got around. Only the direct approach of moulding a white rubber insert and fitting it into a moulded recess in each tyre, would give the clean crisp effect, that is the feeling one gets from a car fitted with these tyres. FIG. 34 gives a cross section though one of these tyres, to show how the insert is actually held in place, by having on its outside diameter a small step, which fits into a corresponding undercut in the tyre proper, and on the inside diameter, by the rim of the wheel. By doing it in this way, no adhesive is necessary.

Again the techniques used are exactly as previously described, first a machined pattern, then a rubber mould, followed by a rubber pattern and finally the resin moulds that are used to make the actual tyres.

Plate 112.

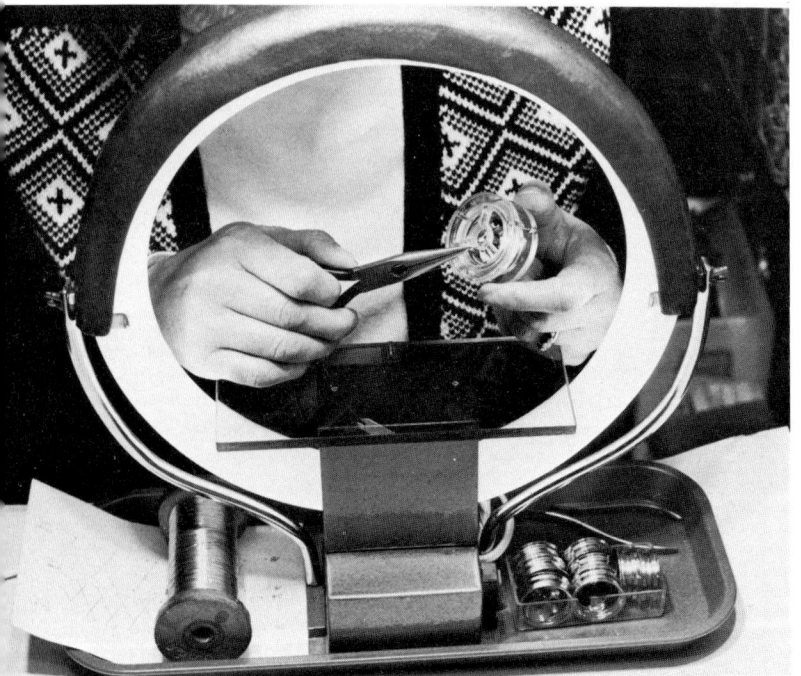

To ensure a really tight fit of the rubber parts, the pattern for the insert should be turned about .008" larger than the recess in which it is to fit, the depth of both should, however, match precisely, as the finished tyre must look as though it is moulded in one piece.

With wheels and tyres complete, plate 113, I now turned to the chassis frame, plate 114. This was made as described for the Bentley, except that instead of just making the frame ends into 'U' sections, two strips of thin gauge brass were silver soldered, one on top and one on the underside along their whole length. The side pieces being cut from one-sixteenth thick brass, instead of the one-eighth material used for the Bentley. Also, unlike the previous miniature, all the cross members on this chassis are correct as to scale, size, shape and positioning, this data, of course, having been collected from the original full size car.

There was nothing new with regard to axles and brakes, except perhaps a little more detail, and the springs of this Duesenberg chassis were booted. They were each fitted with a leather cover to keep any grit or road dirt from getting between the leaves of the springs. One can use leather as in the full size job, but the stitching together of the two edges on the underside of each, would present some problems as regards the scale of the stitches and there is always the difficulty of getting a leather thin enough, not to overpower the springs. The other solution is to simulate the boots by painting each of the springs with a thick polyester resin filler. When this has hardened, it can be sanded to the correct shape and thickness and the stitching carved where it is required, the finished job being sprayed as per seats and fabric bodies. For flexible springs, the leaves can be made in spring steel and the boot moulded into place in rubber.

The radiator for the Duesenberg was quite a large lump, so being ever conscious of the cost of brass and of hard work, I thought twice about trying to carve this one from a solid block. Instead, I decided to have

Plate 113.

Plate 114.

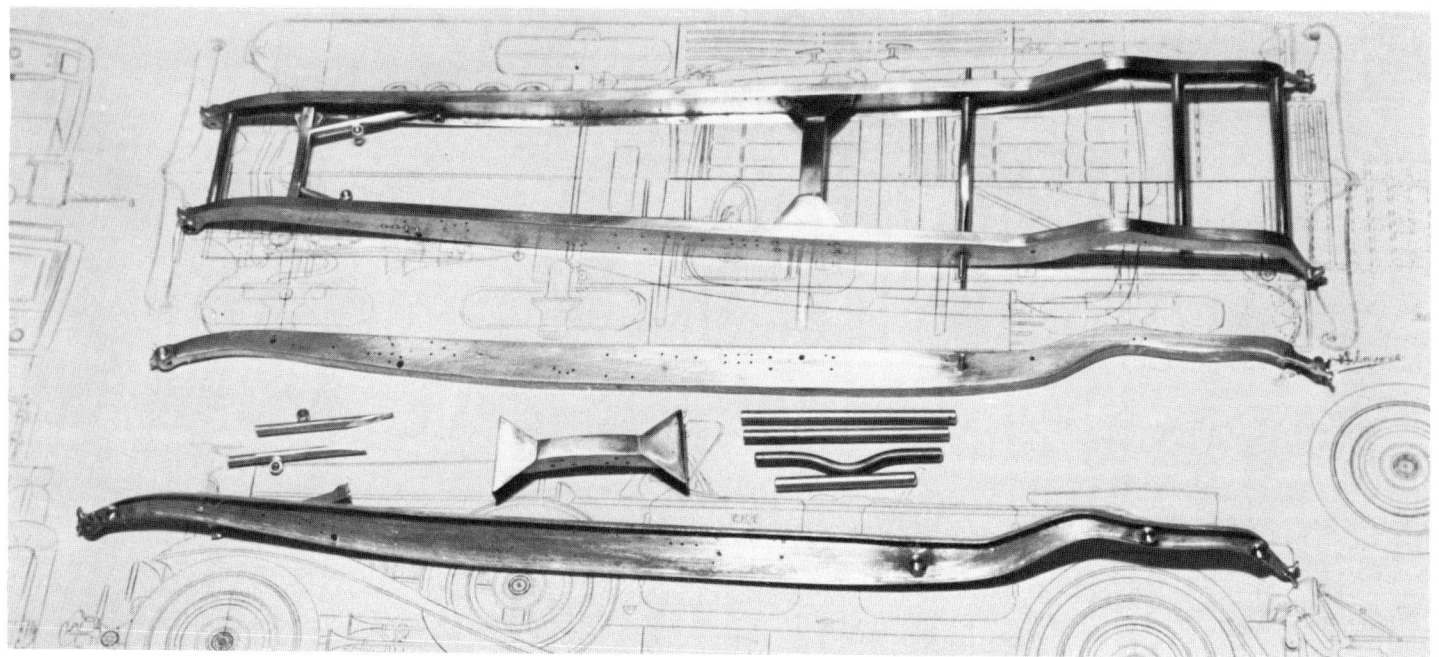

Plate 115.

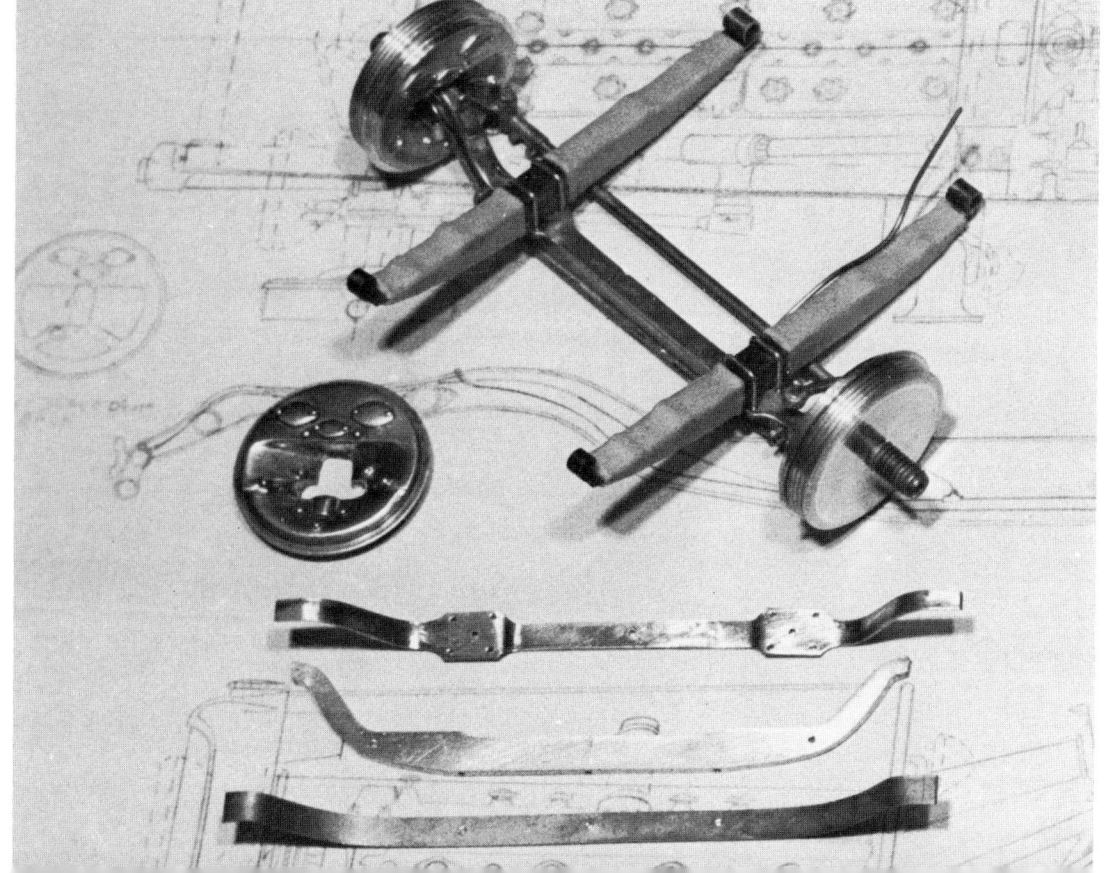

Plate 116.

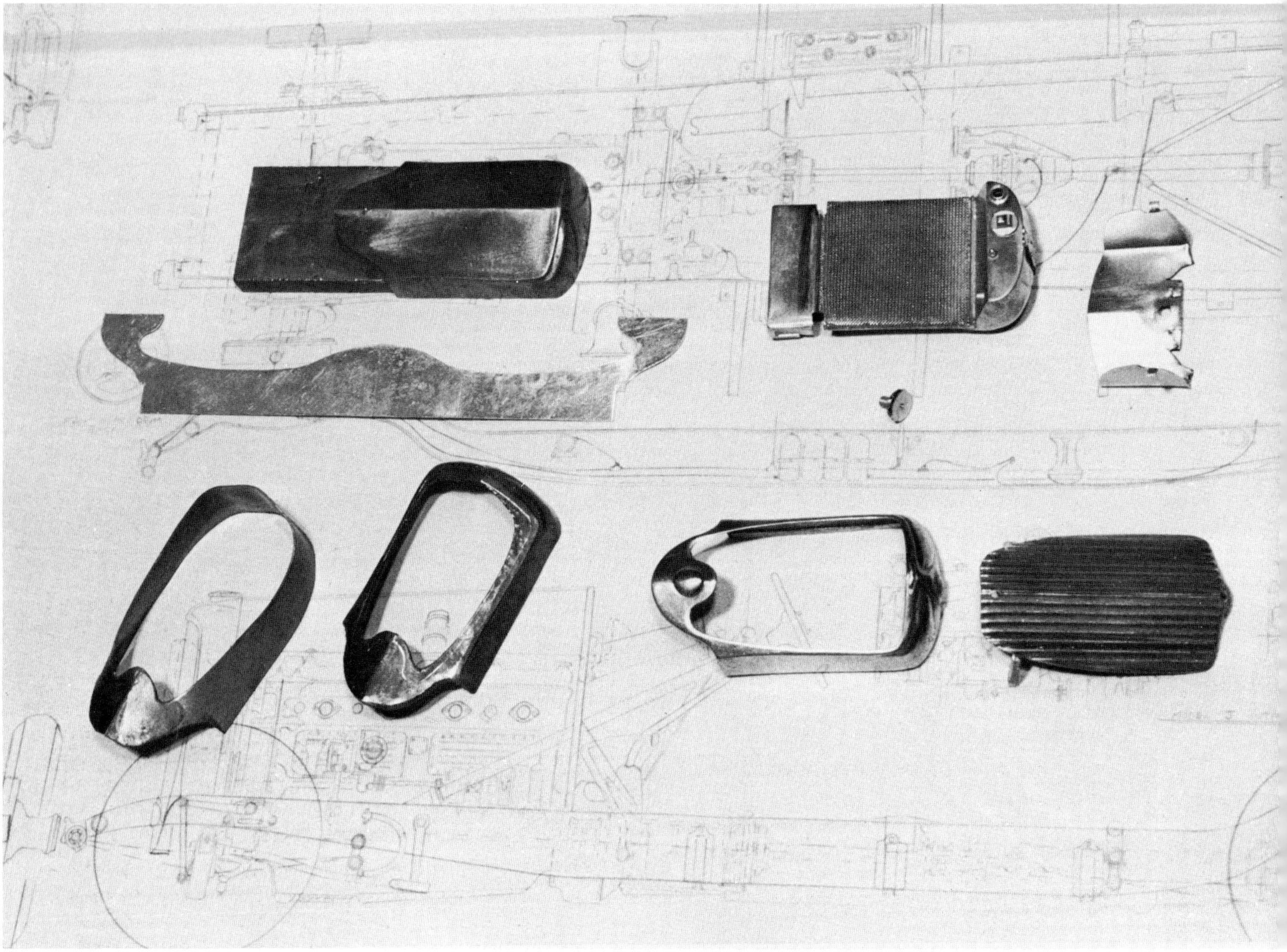

Plate 117.

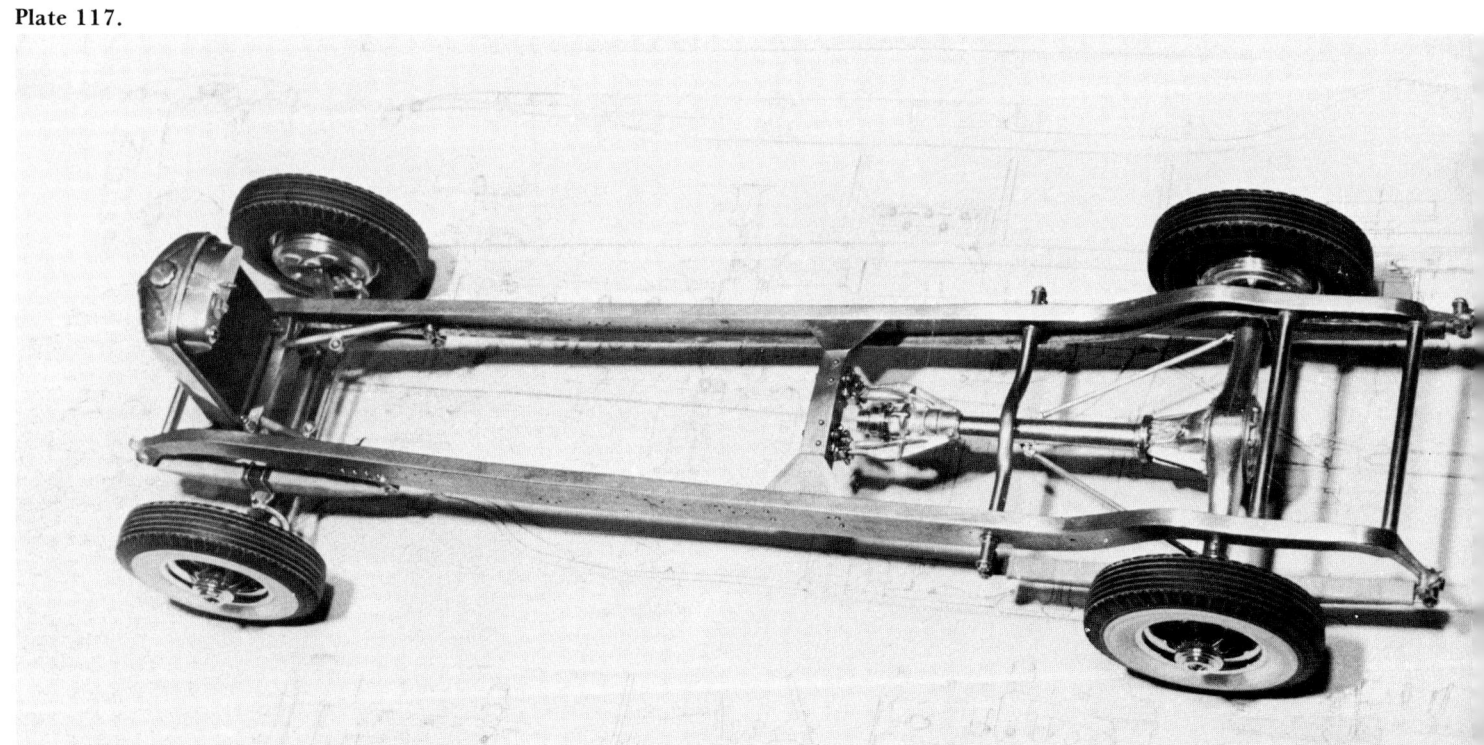

a go at doing it the proper way, beating it out of copper sheet. At the top left of plate 116, will be seen the master pattern, carved to the shape of the radiator shell, less the thickness of the copper sheet, which in this case was .020". Incidentally, below the pattern is the template for marking out the copper sheet and below this, on the left, a cut, bent and silver soldered strip, and on the right a similar strip, which has started to take up the shape of the pattern. In the centre is a finished and polished shell and on the far right, are the simulated radiator shutters that fill the centre of the shell. These shutters can be made quite simply by soldering a number of angled strips of thin brass sheet together.

To get back to the radiator shell, if you can recall to mind the techniques and tools described in Chapter Four to produce both fenders and bodies, you will see that with the exception of the metal, the work is exactly the same. It is a fact that there are very few techniques to master before you can build, from basic materials, a worthwhile automodel. My biggest problem in putting this book together is trying not to repeat myself when dealing with the various parts. It is only when you do something like this, when you have to search your mind and recall how you did do

it, that you suddenly realise just how few basic techniques you did use. With metal, there is turning, milling and soldering. With sheet metal, it is working with hammers. Then there is some woodwork, consisting in the main of squaring up blocks to simple shapes, then rounding off the corners and finally the basic moulding techniques using resin and rubber. I would concede, however, that to be proficient in handling these things, one must have confidence and this can only be acquired with patience, which can be the hardest technique of all to master. Once you have mastered it though, you will find that confidence will follow soon after and a mastery of all these techniques and more, will be at your finger tips before you know it. I am wandering again, so let's get back to the big 'D'. With the radiator made, the chassis frame is now ready for the engine and plates 118 to 129 show what this means.

I think you will agree that the scale of 1/15 produces an engine of just the right size, not too big, yet not too small for every nut and bolt to be represented. The overall length, incidentally, of the completed chassis is about fifteen inches, which in my opinion, is the ideal, if you go much bigger, I think the models can tend to look like toys.

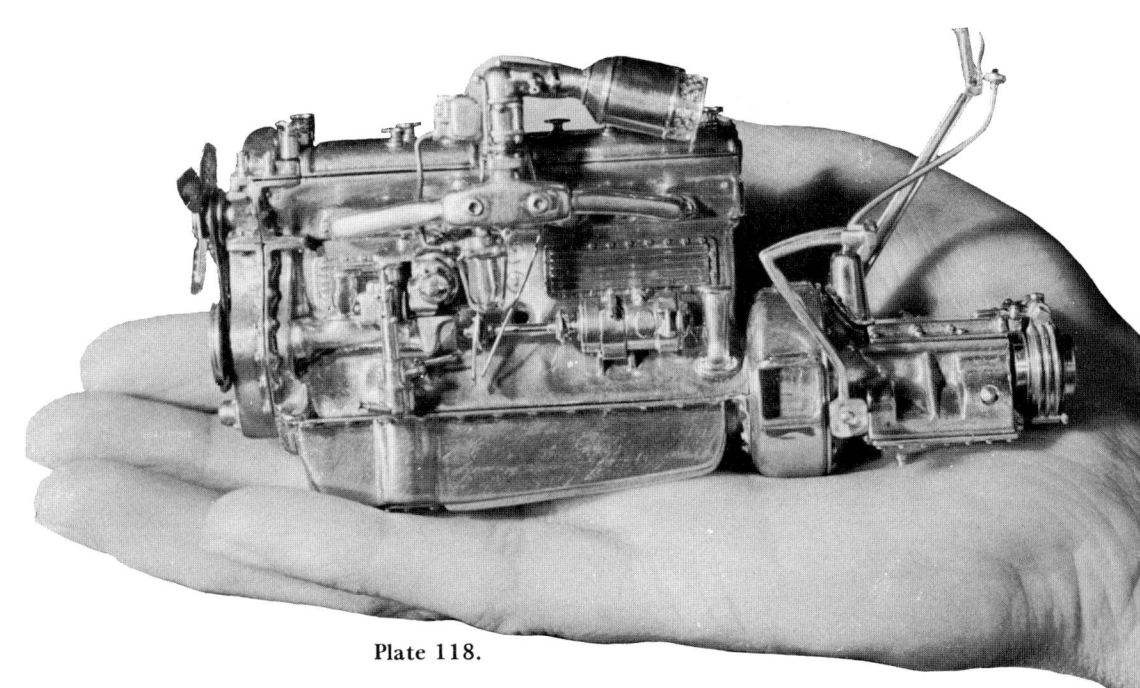

Plate 118.

It would take a book on its own to describe all the in's and out's of building this engine, which I do not think would be much use to anyone, as again it would consist of an endless repetition of the same basic techniques. Of far more value I feel, are the principles to follow, as these will be of value whatever the piece of machinery, and we can illustrate these by taking just one part of it. For this I have chosen the inlet manifold and fittings, including the carburettor and air filter. Plates 121 and 122 show these parts as fitted to the actual car. Plate 123 illustrates the miniature assembly, fabricated in brass and FIG. 35 shows how this was broken down. You will note that we are back with 'squares and rounds!' Any part that cannot be made by either a straight forward turning and/or milling/filing operation is taken apart until it can. This, of course, does not mean you leave anything out or try and simplify it, on the contrary, by concentrating on getting the basic shapes right at the start, you make certain that there is room to get every scrap of detail in.

One might feel, when you look at FIG. 35 and 36, that you would have to spend a month of Sundays with the engine to note all the dimensions necessary, to be able to reproduce this amount of detail. This is not the case, however, as almost all of it can be done by 'related proportion'. By this I mean that if, for example, we had just six measurements of the piece we have been discussing, i.e. the diameter and length of the air filter, the overall distance between top and bottom of the assembly, the overall width of the manifold and the width and depth of the central portion. If you convert the dimensions into their scale equivalent and then plot them out on a plain sheet of paper, you will see exactly how big or small are the missing parts. It is then but a simple matter to sketch in the required amount of detail, within the space allowed, if this is not possible you are drawing it too big, if it looks lost, then you have drawn it too small. It really is as simple, and you will be amazed how accurate the drawing will be. If you are not convinced, go and take a photograph of something, a chair, some cans, a vase or jug, the subject is not important. Now take one or two measurements of it. Convert these to a scale size and mark them out in correct relation one with another, with a small dot or

Plate 119.

Plate 120.

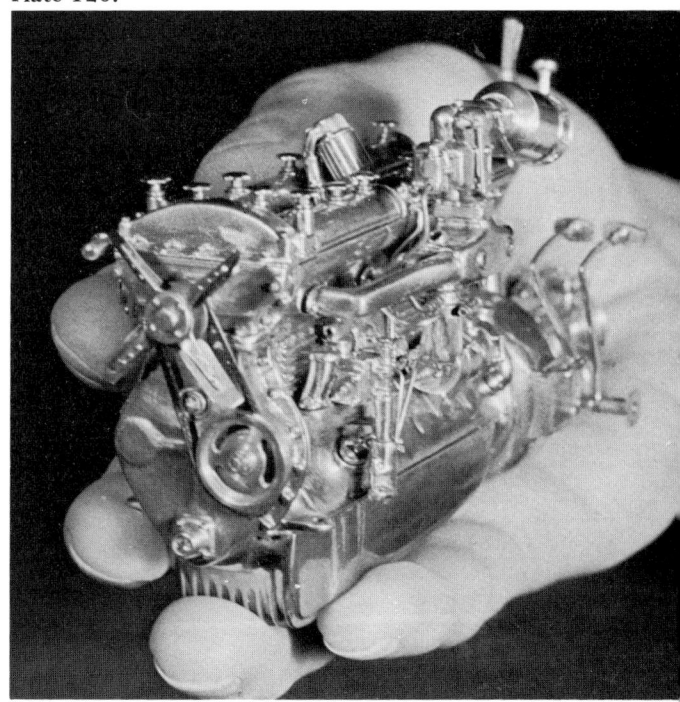

116

Plate 121.

Plate 122.

Plate 123.

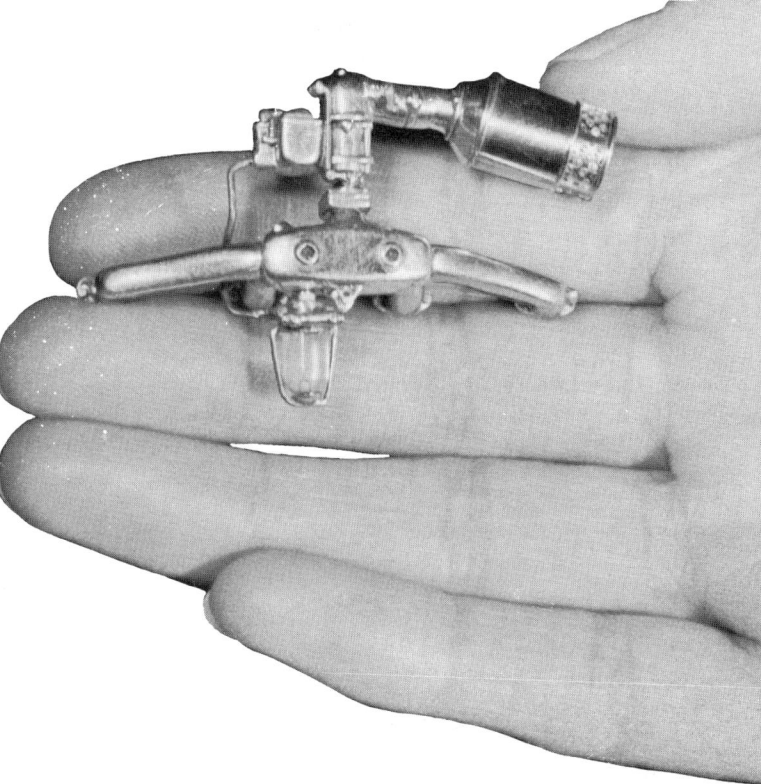

cross on a sheet of paper. Now make a sketch of your subject, using the dots as a guide. If you find you do not have enough measured points to get it right the first time, then do not go back to the original subject for further dimensions, but measure the relative part on the photograph and relate this to another part of the same print that you already know the size of. You may find that the new piece is 7/8ths the length of the part you know the size of, in which case you can work out, with a simple sum, the exact size of your sketch. Do this as many times as you need and when complete, measure your scale drawing, convert back to full size and check with the original. With a little practice, you can do this within less than a quarter of an inch on the full size and even smaller on very fine detailing. The only thing to watch out for, is to avoid taking measurements of any part that is not photographed square on. Parts photographed on

an angle will appear shorter in relation to the height, when relating parts on the same print that are at differing distances from the camera. Those closer to the lens will appear bigger than those further away even though they may be the same size.

You will find that the more detail there is on a part, the easier it is to work out the relative sizes, so that a piece like the mechanical fuel pump and automatic lubricator FIG. 36, to be seen on the lower left of plate 121, is not nearly as bad as it looks. Plate 124, showing the finished scale part. Being a mass of bolt heads and odd shapes, just one or two measurements of this piece and a photograph of it fitted to the engine, would be all that was needed to get it all but identical with the original.

Moving on to plate 126, we come to the hood, or bonnet, which in this case is not provided with

117

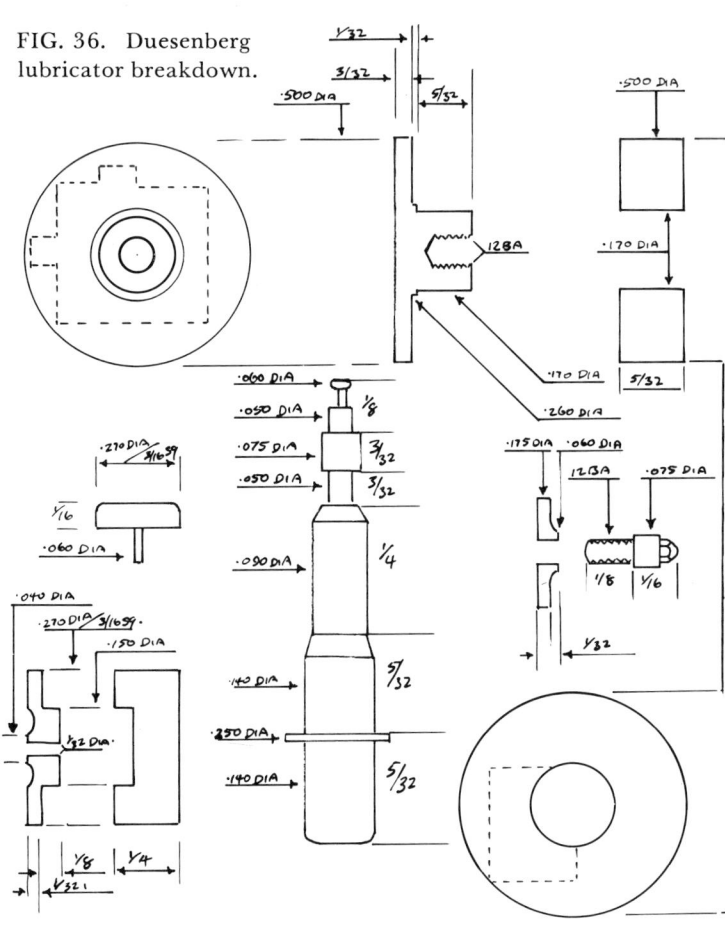

FIG. 36. Duesenberg lubricator breakdown.

louvres, but has in their place chromed wire mesh panels. These are very simply made with a 'T' section brass moulding formed around a small sheet metal pattern, which is then used to mark out the opening in the side of the hood, and also to mark out and cut the mesh to solder into the 'T' section frame. The biggest problem with the opening hood is the piano hinge. There are several ways of making these, and all will take a lot of time and patience.

One way is to take a length of thin sheet brass, about .010" thick by 1/2" wide and double the length of the hood. This is then marked along one edge at

FIG. 35. Duesenberg inlet manifold parts.

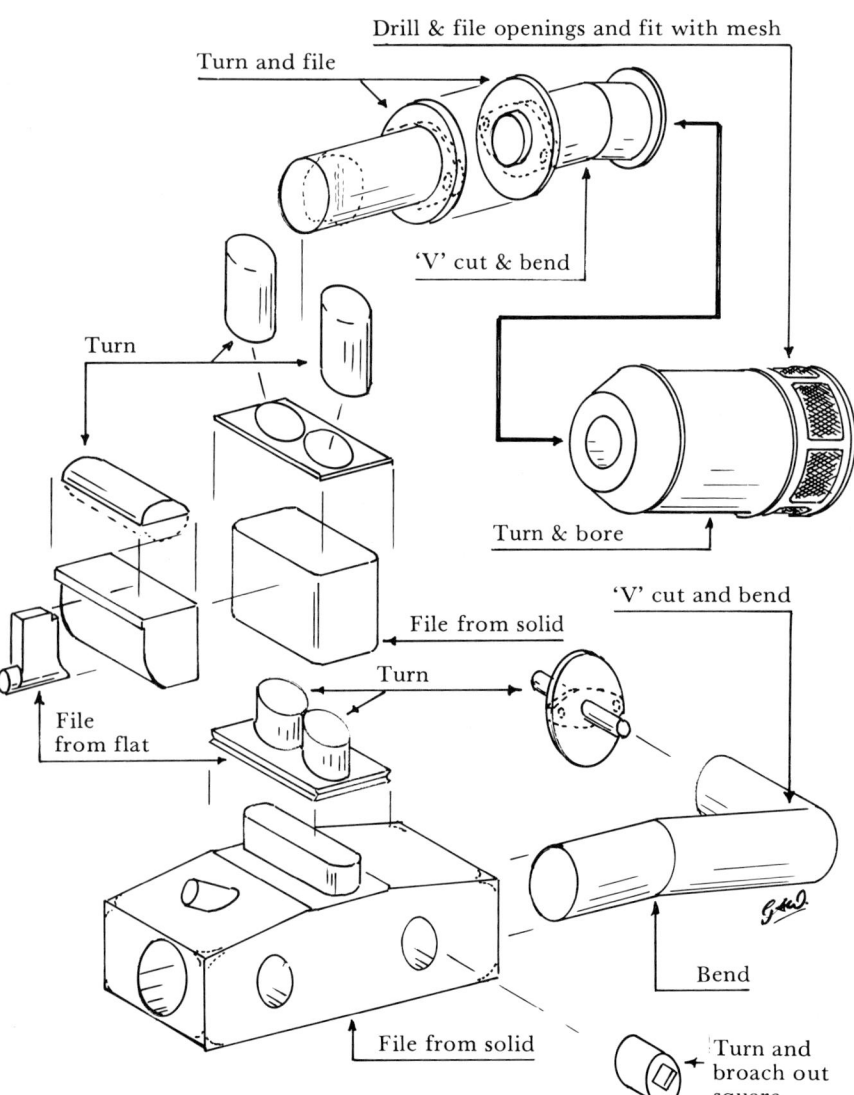

Turn and file

Drill & file openings and fit with mesh

'V' cut & bend

Turn

Turn & bore

Turn

File from solid

'V' cut and bend

File from flat

File from solid

Bend

Turn and broach out square

Plate 124.

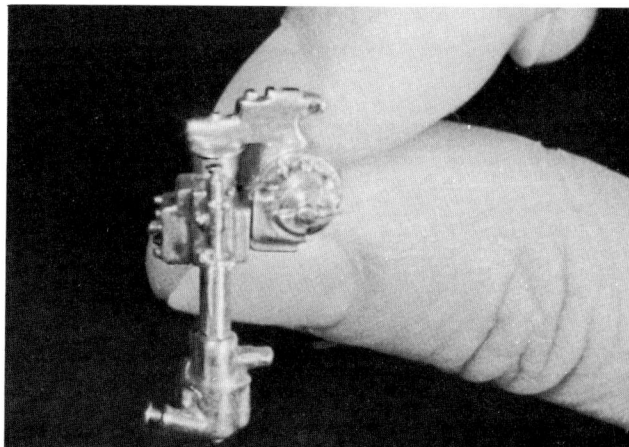

Plate 125.

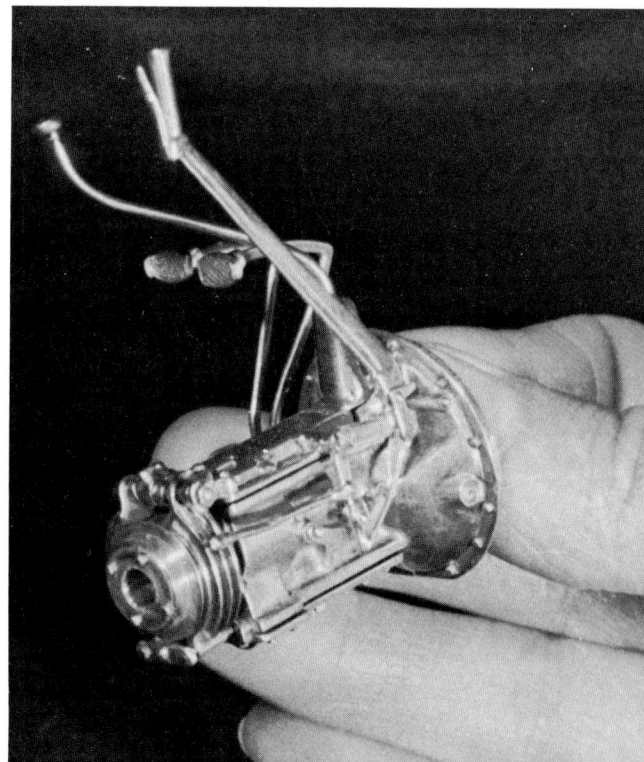

118

1/8" inch intervals. The strip is now held firmly in a vice and each alternate 1/8" is removed with a file to a depth of about 3/32". With this done, each remaining 1/8" is now rolled over a suitable length of wire to form a tube, after which the strip is cut in half, mated together and the wire threaded through both, to form the hinge pin.

A much simpler and neater way of making this type of hinge, and the one I favour, is to make use of the fine brass tube known as capillary tube. I have obtained this material with a bore of only .009", although one really needs to go to one of the larger stockists to get it. However, fine brass tube with a bore of between 1/64" and 1/32" should be readily available at most model shops and the smaller of these will be suitable for making hood (bonnet) hinges. All that is involved, is to silver solder a length of tube, about a quarter inch longer than the hood, to one edge of a quarter-inch-wide strip of brass sheet of the same length. Two of these are required to make up each hinge. The two strips, with tubes in place, are now placed back to back in a vice with the two tubes uppermost and resting on the top of the vice jaws. A 1/8" square needle file is now used to put grooves across these two pieces of brass, in such a way that the amount and placing of the pieces that

Plate 126.

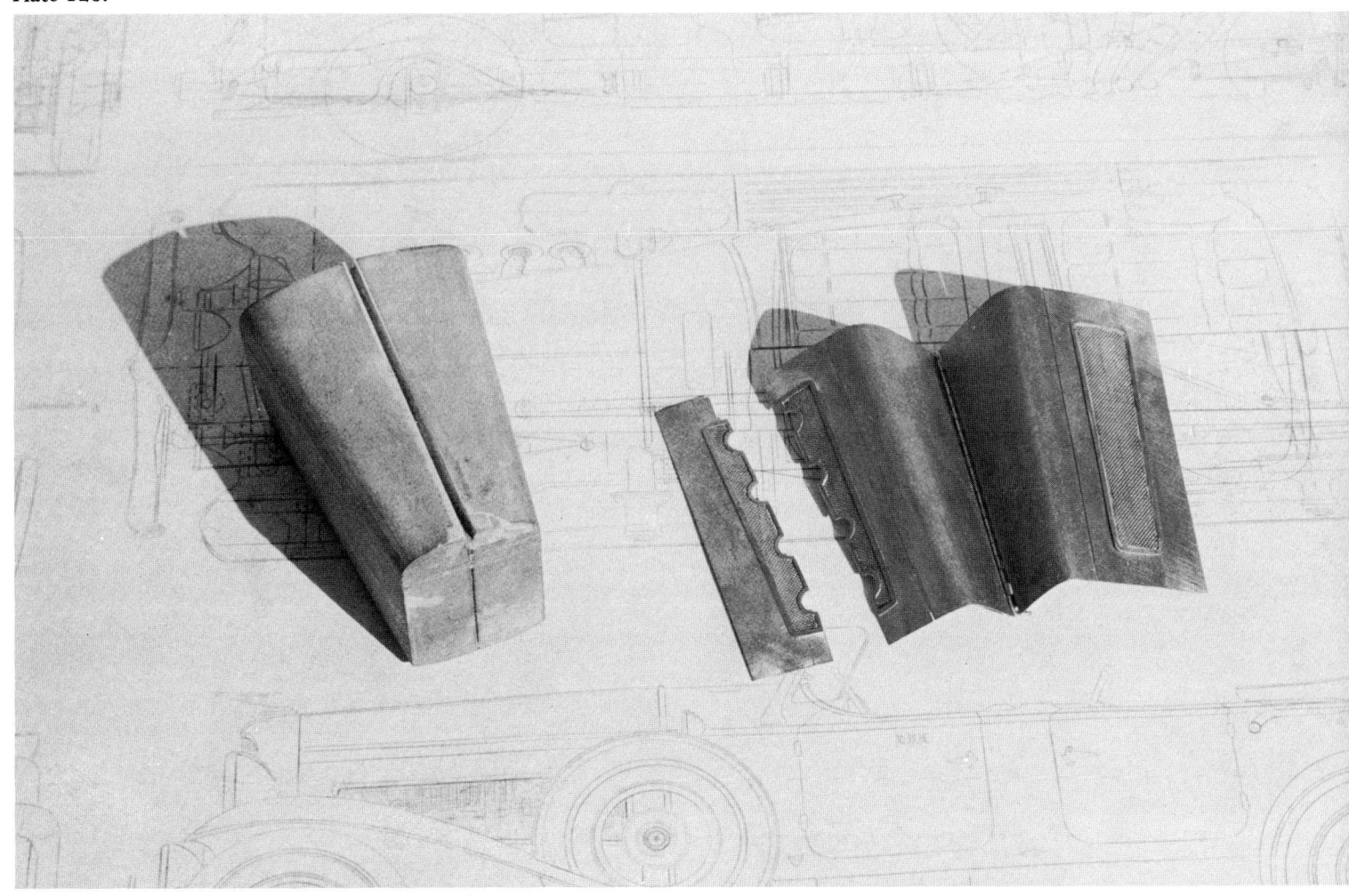

are left, exactly match the spacing between, say a 1/8" length of tube, followed by a 1/8" gap, followed by another 1/8" length of tube and so on, across the whole length. With a little practice, a very neat hinge can be made in this way and it does really need to be neat, because the centre hinge leading back, directly from the chromed or gold plated radiator, is in a very prominent position. Two other hinges, made in the same way, will also be required, one for each side to complete the hood, but these are not quite so important as regards looks, as the actual hinge is fitted to the inside in both cases and is, therefore, hidden from view, even when the hood is folded in the open position. The shaping of the hood parts, particularly the two top ones, are worked over a wooden pattern block, however, I prefer to do this after they have been attached to the centre hinge, which is done with the aid of soft solder. The hinge is first cut to the correct length, less one 1/8" segment at each end. These are compensated for by taking two 1/8" lengths of tube and silver soldering a small pin to the centre of each. Holes are provided in both the top of the fire wall and radiator shell to take these pins, as they are the means of holding each end of the hinge and consequently the hood, in place, on the model. Holes are also drilled at each end of the hood pattern block to take the pins, so that the hinge can be accurately located in the centre. With the hinge so placed, the two flat strips are tinned with soft solder, together with the inside edges of the two pieces of sheet brass, that are to form the hood top. To 'tin' a piece of metal, the area is first cleaned with an abrasive paper, then flux and solder are applied with a soldering iron, so that a thin film of solder (tin) covers the area.

Each of the hood top pieces, which have been cut on the large size, are now, in turn, presented to the hinge, so that the two tinned surfaces are in contact. When these have been correctly located, a hot soldering iron is applied along each side of the hinge, melting the solders and firmly attaching it to the hood/bonnet top. The outer edges of the hood will now need to be wrapped around and taken down the sides of the pattern and finally marked out and trimmed up with snips, to exactly match it. The two side panels are worked in place in precisely the same way.

In plate 130 we can see the full set of body and fender patterns, which are the same as those covered in Part One, except that they are larger and more

Plate 127.

detailed. The next plate, plate 131, illustrates one of the front fenders, together with the well section, to take the fender-mounted, spare wheel. This was made as a separate item and soldered to the underside of the fender later.

Plate 132 shows us examples of the headlamps and fog lamps, fitted to this particular Duesenberg. Underneath these, are arrayed the various parts, that make up each set of lamps. As can be seen, we are again dealing with straightforward turning operations.

Plates 135-6-7 bring us to the painting stage. You may recall that when we dealt with this in Chapter Five, I made the point that before starting any of the painting operations, one should spend some time and thought on providing each piece, or number of pieces, with a handle. In the first two of these plates, we can see examples of these. In the first, the car body has had two small holes drilled and tapped to take two short lengths of a fine threaded rod. These are, of course, placed where they cannot be seen, when the body is eventually fitted to the chassis. Nuts are then threaded on, followed by a length of wood for

Plate 128.

Plate 129.

Plate 130.

Plate 131.

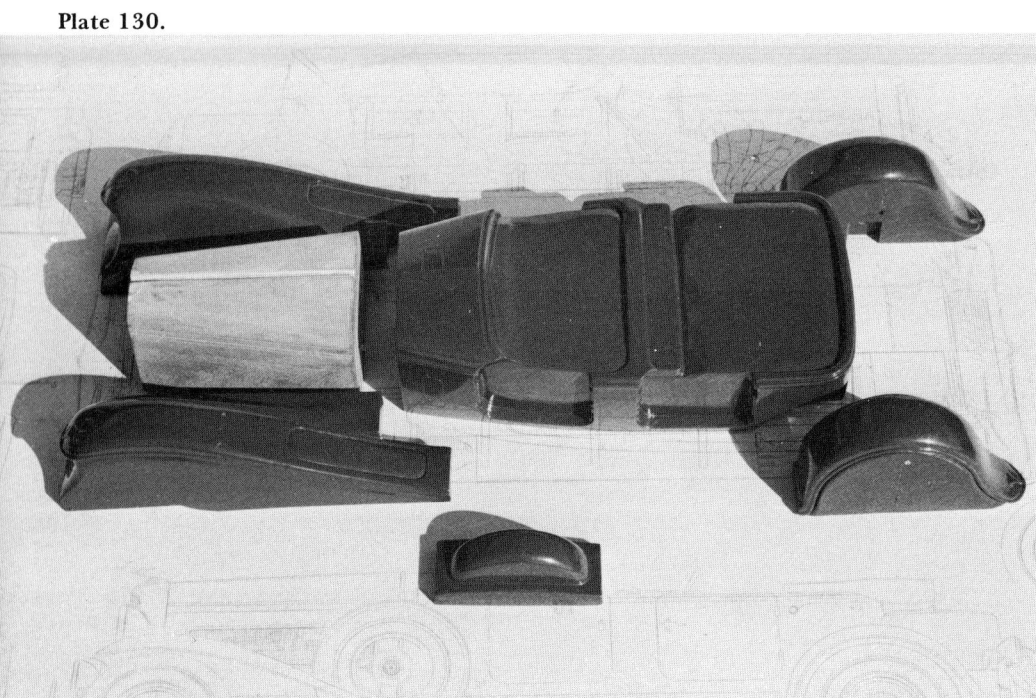

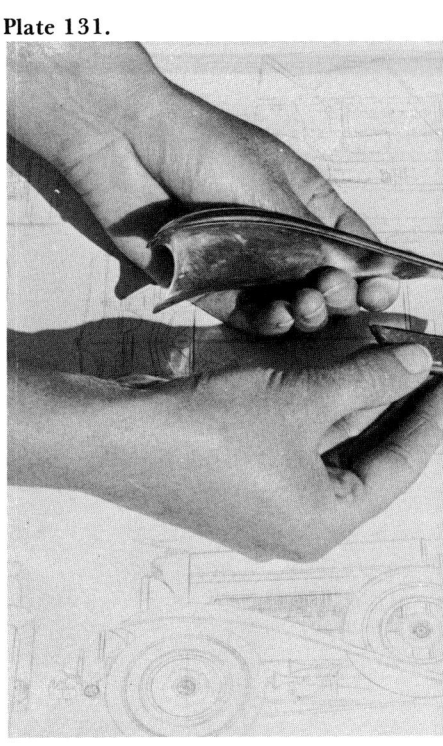

the handle, which is locked in place by two further nuts. In this way, the piece of wood is not fitted directly to the body, as this could tend to mask areas in the spraying stage, but is held off leaving a gap of about half an inch.

In plate 136 we have the fenders. As can be seen, I decided to treat all four, together with the sheet metal work between them, as a single unit. It was much easier to work these in this way, as being on the outside, they tend to be used as handles when picking

up the model, so it is vital that they are secured firmly to the chassis. As there are not too many obvious places where individual fenders can be bolted to the frame, it is much more convenient to solder them all firmly together and then secure them in one piece.

The bar across the front, to which the wire handle is attached, is a temporary fitting, taking advantage of the holes in each fender, to take the spare wheel bracket. As can clearly be seen it does not, in any way, interfere with the spraying. My spray gun, it will be

Plate 133.

Plate 132.

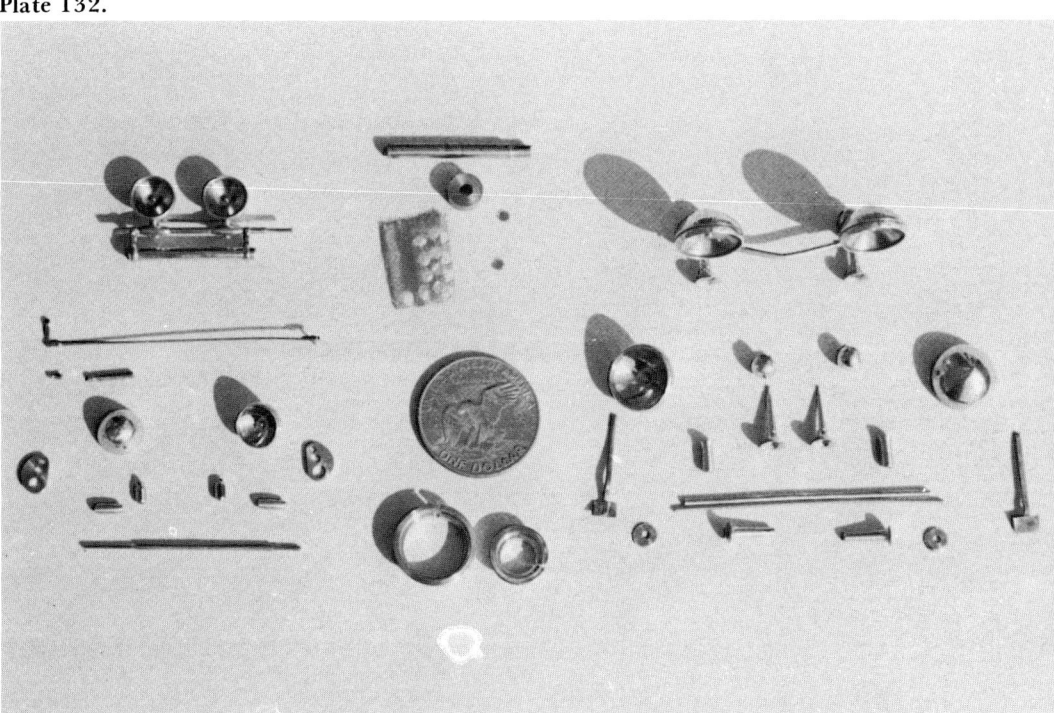

seen from this plate, is in fact an 'air brush', in this case a Paasche model 'H'. This, I feel, is ideal for this size of model, as it is infinitely adjustable and can get into the smallest corners. However, as I stated in the earlier chapters, make use of the spray can in your early stages and only progress to the more precision, and expensive equipment as your techniques develop. This advice should apply to all things in model making. The most expensive tools and equipment in the world, are only as good as their operator.

One feature of our subject was the two-tone colour scheme on the fenders, the underside of which was a pale green, while the main colour was dark green. As there was less of the light green, this was sprayed first, and when fully hardened was masked with a new product to come my way called Maskol. Although I believe there are several products of this sort on the market, they are all more or less the same, in that they look like paint and are applied with a brush or spray. When dry, they form into a flexible skin that

Plate 134.

Plate 135.

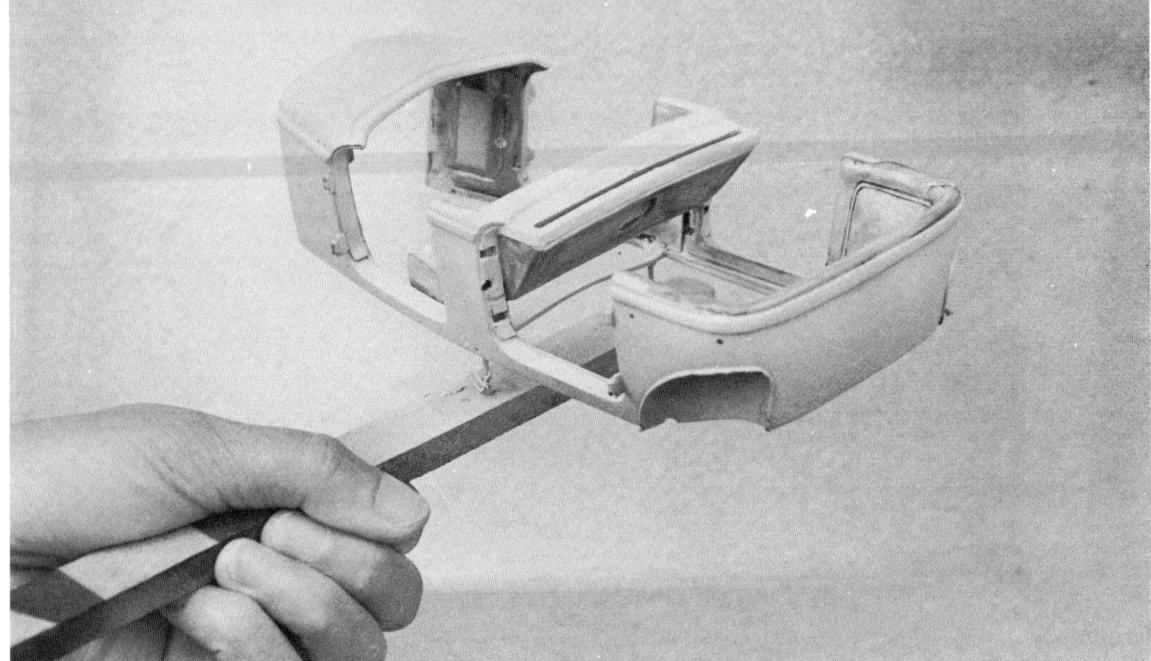

Plate 136.

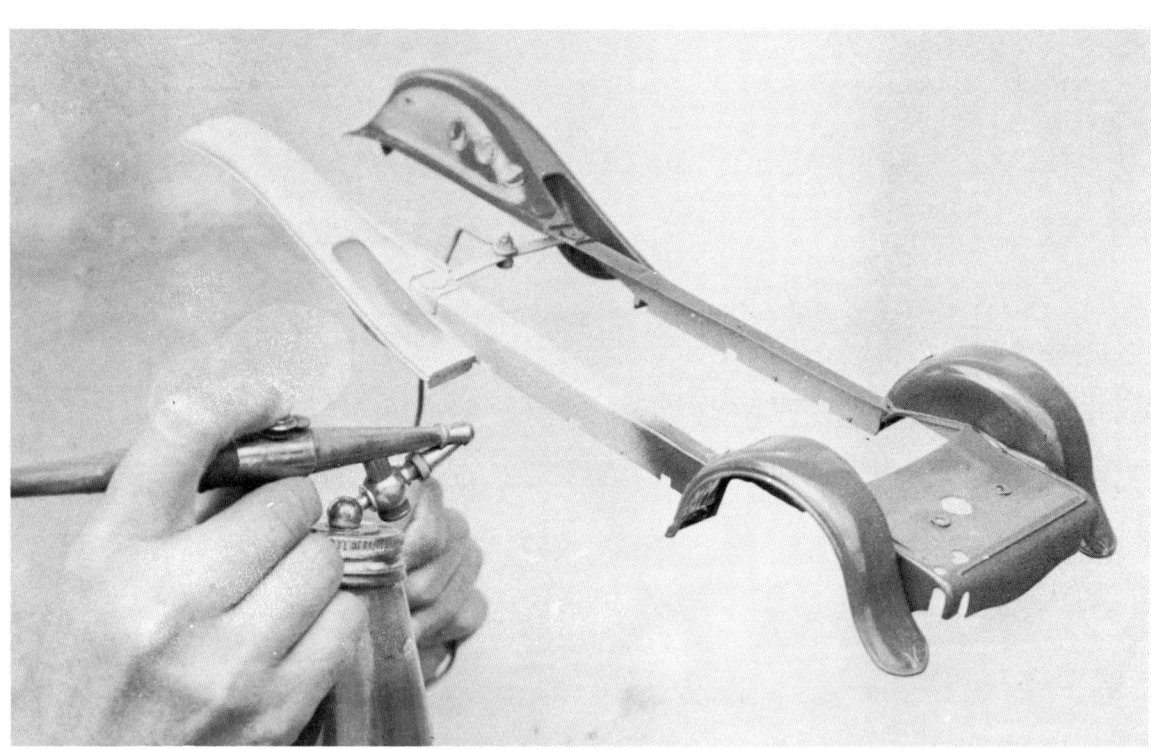

Plate 137.

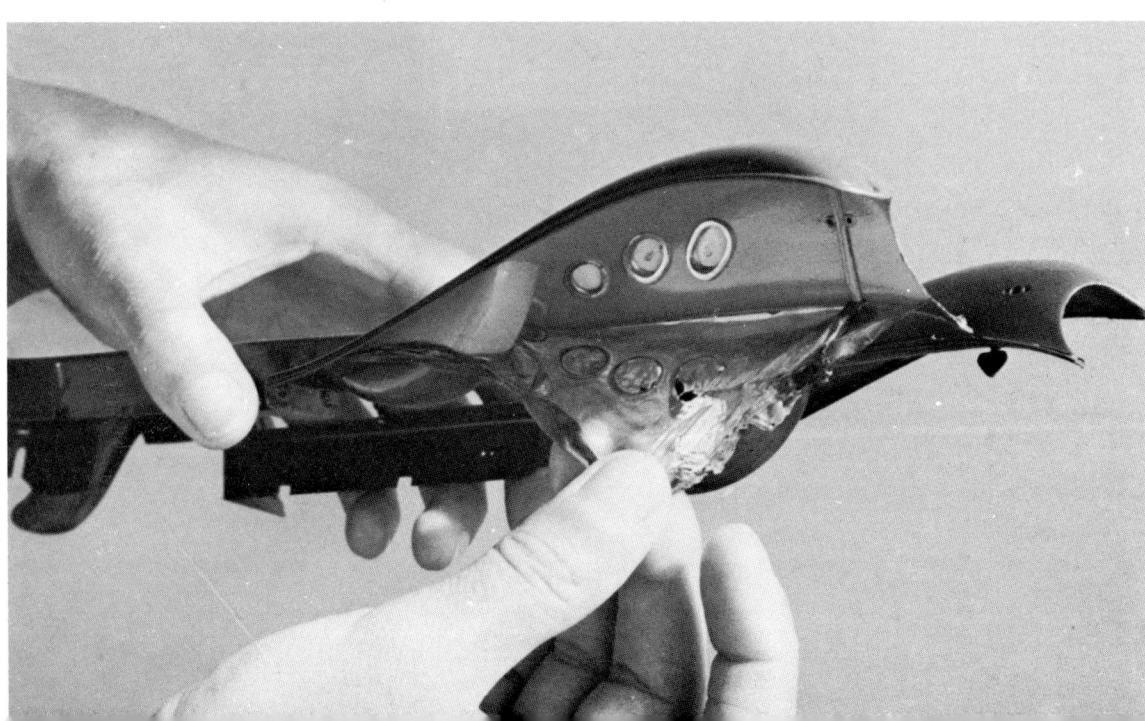

is impervious to paints of any sort, although it is always wise to try them out on a test piece first, to make sure of this under your own particular conditions. They are ideal where large areas have to be masked and where the edge of the masked area corresponds with the edge of the work piece, as with the fenders shown in plate 137. If a fine crisp line or edge is called for, then it is better to get this with masking tape, using liquid masking for the bulk of the remainder. When all the painting is finished, it only remains to lift a corner of the masking, to be able to remove it in almost one piece.

We have now come to the end, or rather I have come to the end and you hopefully are just about to start. I have tried to avoid being too dogmatic on any aspect, as this I feel tends to blank off the mind and discourage it from solving the problems in its own way. It is only when the mind is given a free run through a selection of ideas, techniques and personal experiences, that it is best able to guide the craftsman's hand. What I have tried to do, in the first place is to show that it can be done, in the second, methods of doing it, and in the third place and probably of most importance, the reasoning behind the method.

What you now have to do, if I have whetted your appetite for autominiatures, is to relate this to your own experiences with tools and materials. If you have used them all before, but in another context, then the foregoing chapters will help assist you, if only on the automotive side. All but the very first timer will have had some experience with at least one of the techniques, or materials, and it is at this point that my reader should start. If it be in wood, then make as much as you can of that material and finish the rest off with parts from plastic kits. The important thing is to complete something, only then can you stand back from it and see your weak points and only when you have found these, can you start to perfect your craftsmanship.

Good Luck.

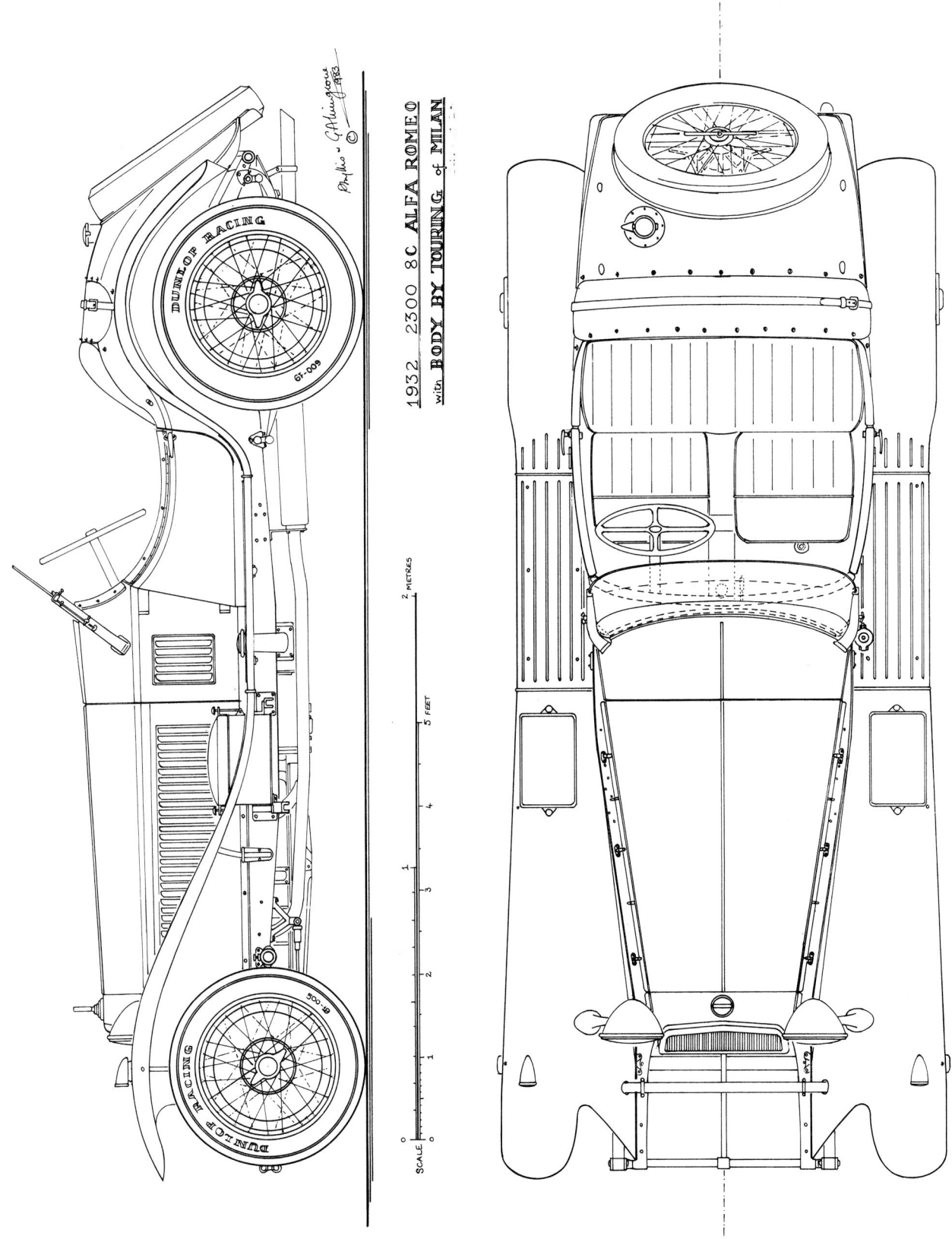

1932   2300 8C ALFA ROMEO

with **BODY BY TOURING** of MILAN

DUNLOP RACING

DUNLOP RACING

SCALE

METRES

FEET

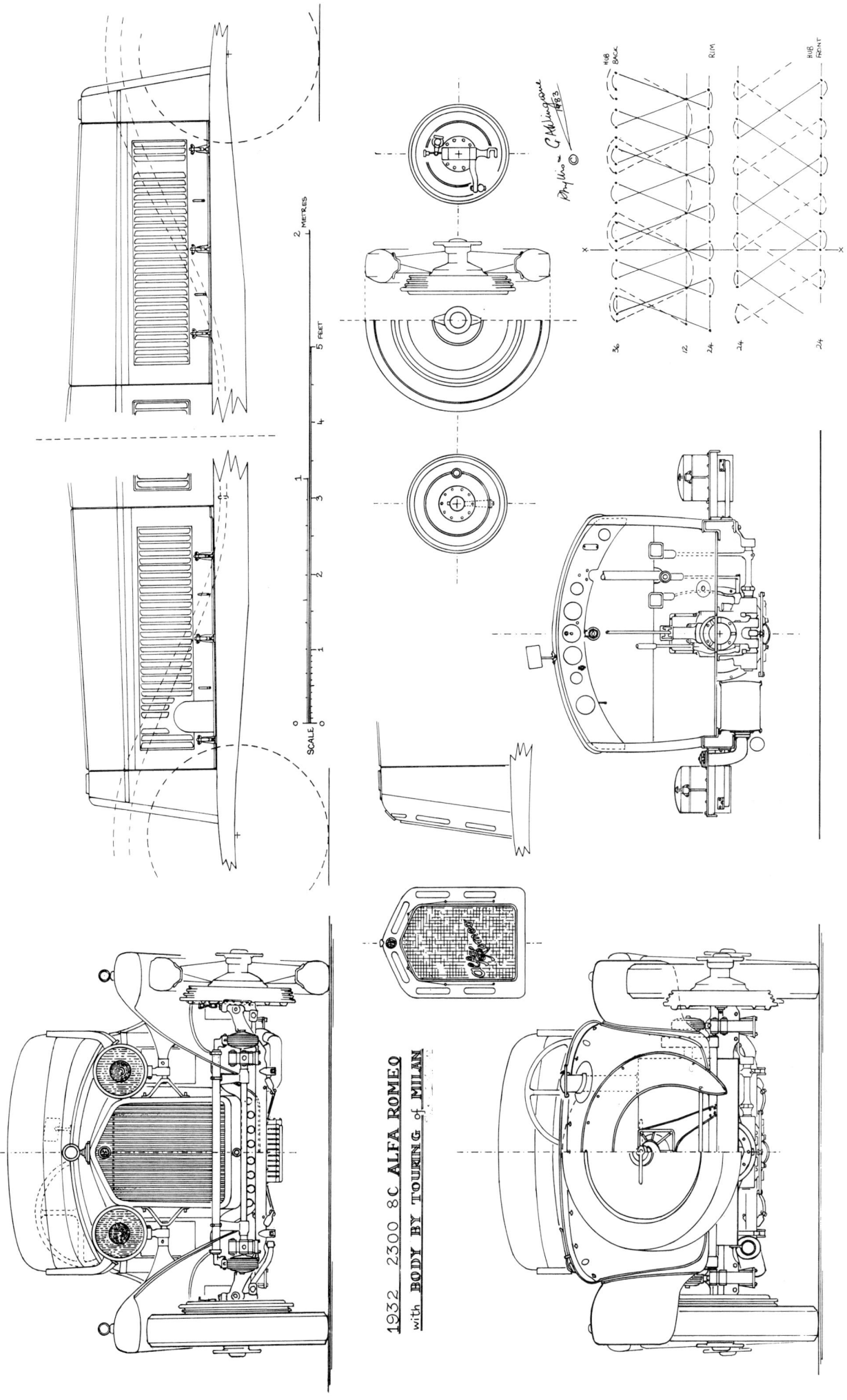

1932   2300 8C ALFA ROMEO
with BODY BY TOURING of MILAN

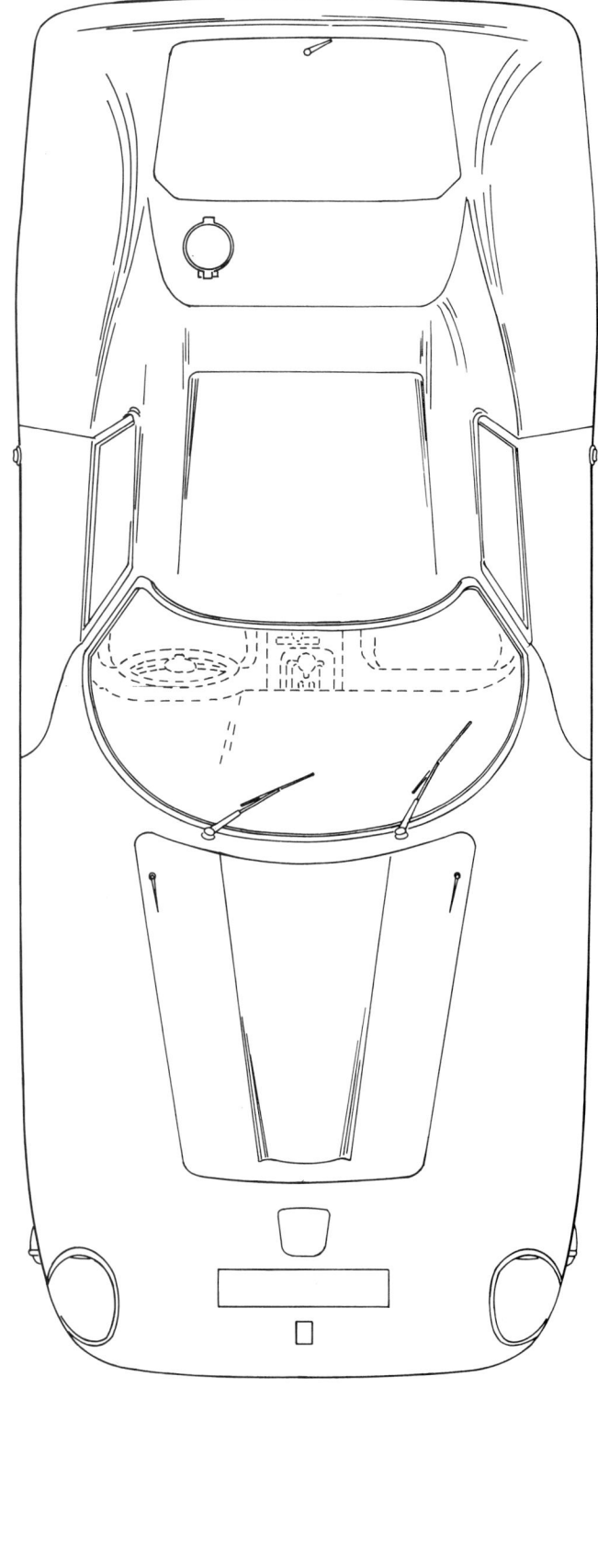

SCALE

METRES

FEET

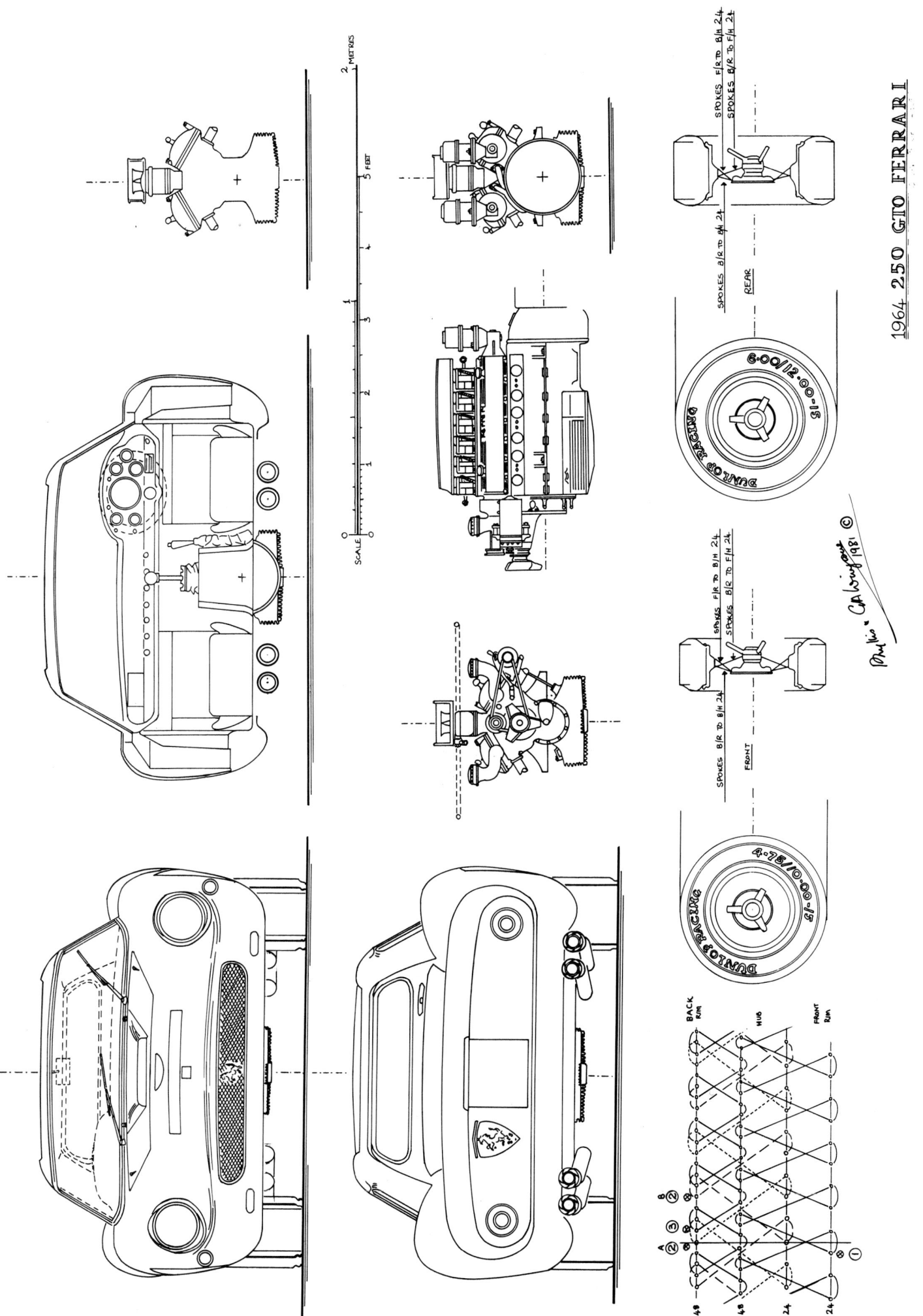

1964 250 GTO FERRARI

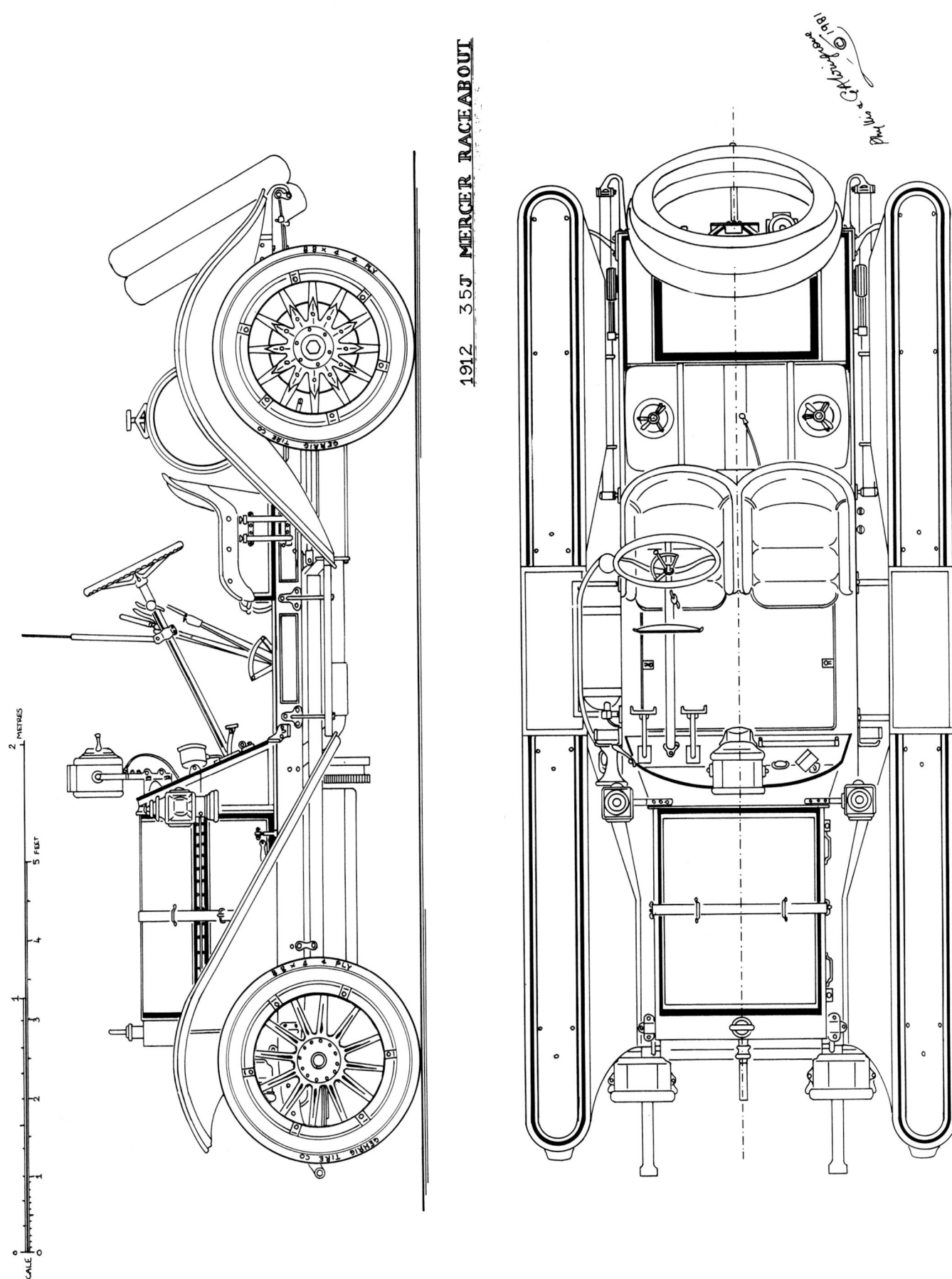

1912 35J MERCER RACEABOUT

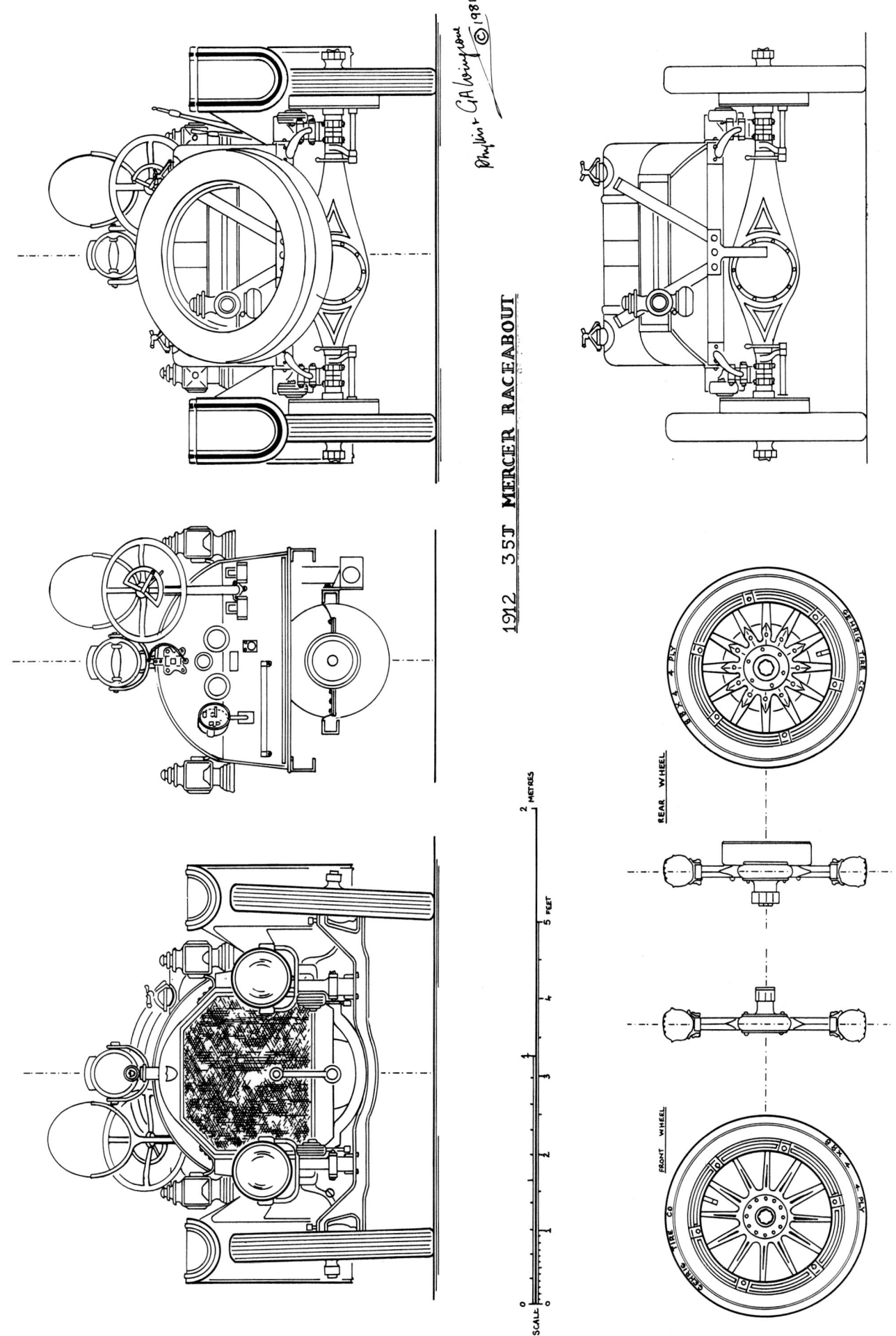

1912 35J MERCER RACEABOUT

REAR WHEEL

FRONT WHEEL

SCALE

METRES

FEET

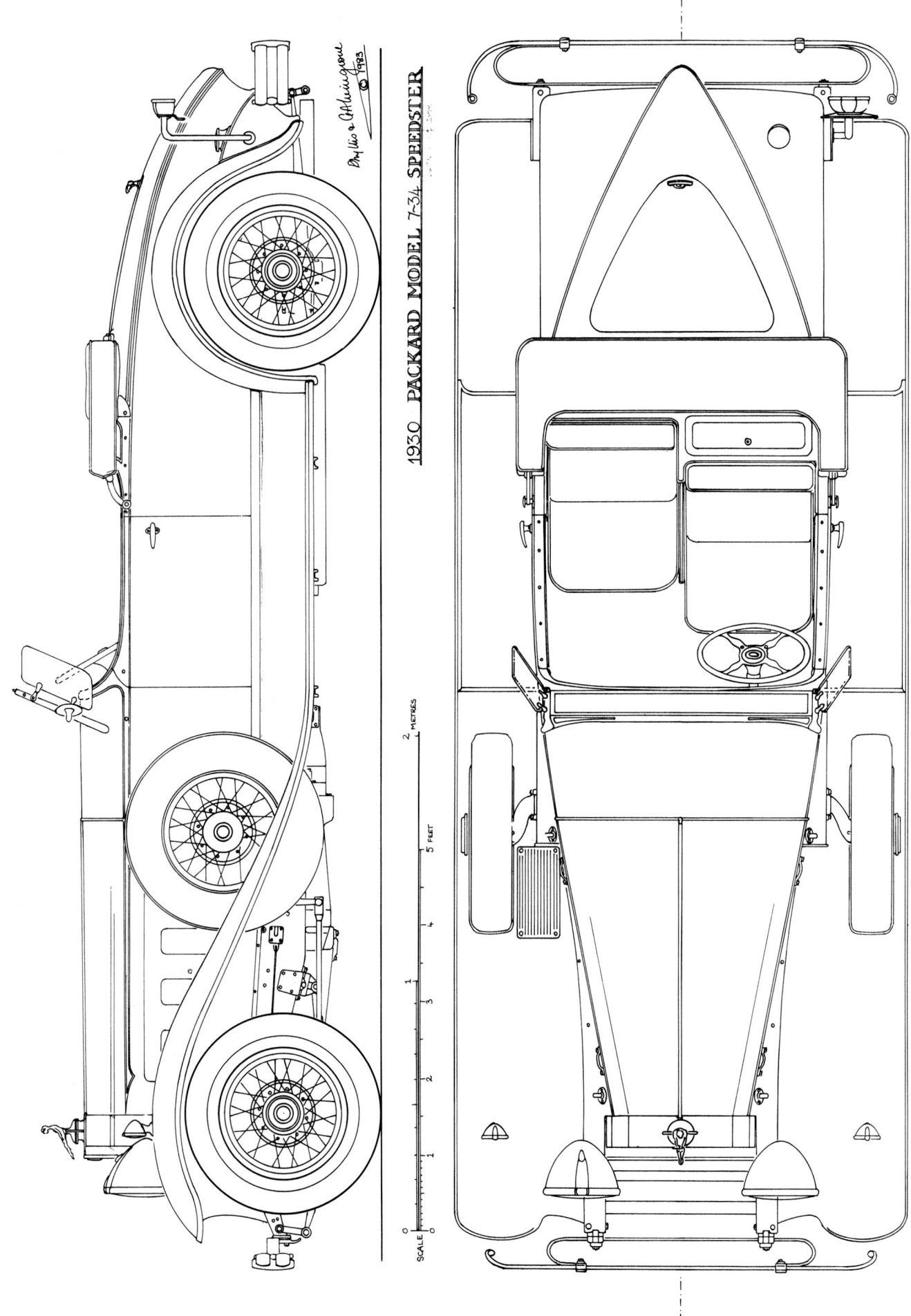

1930 *PACKARD MODEL 7-34 SPEEDSTER*

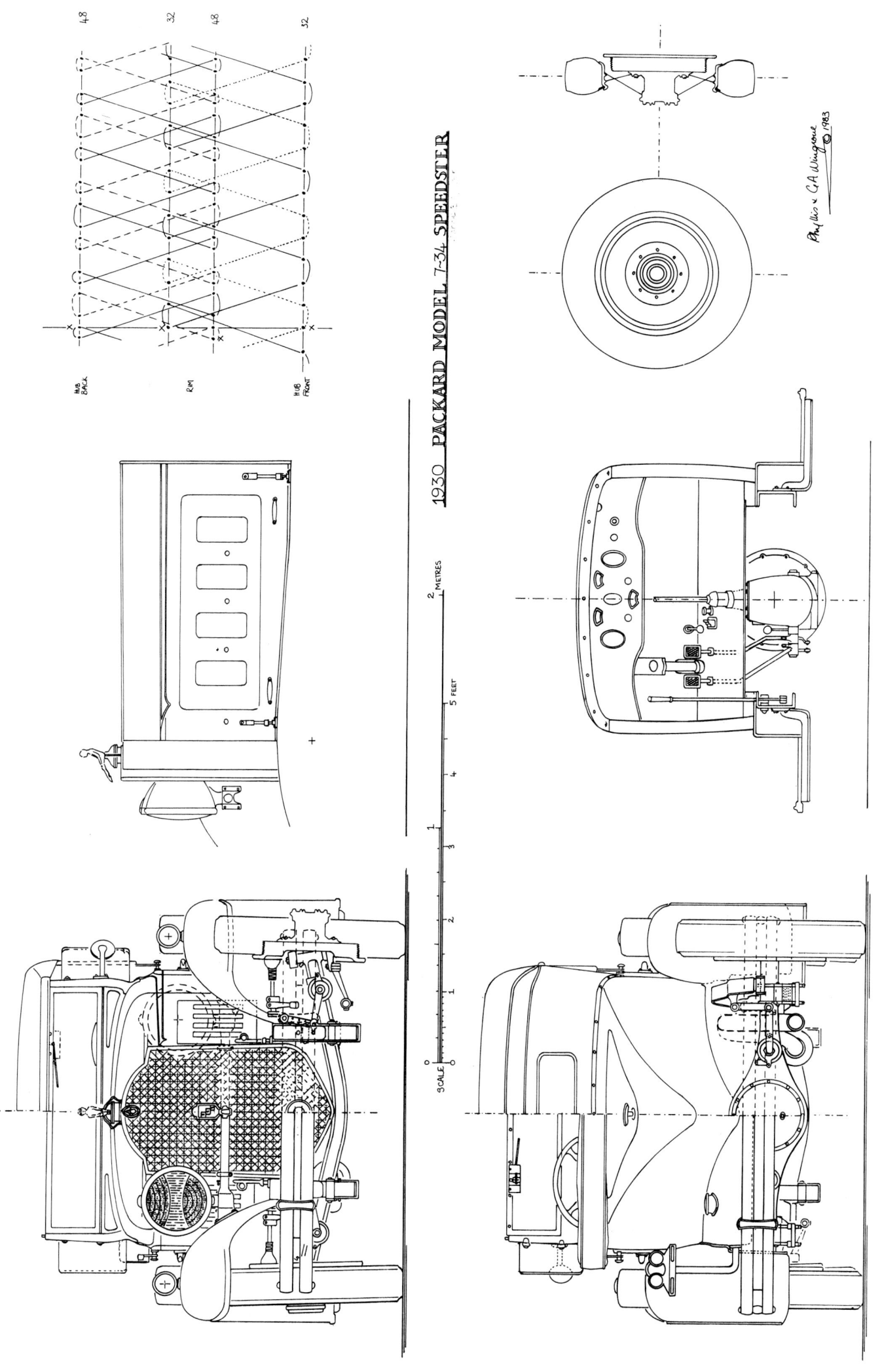

1930 PACKARD MODEL 7-34 SPEEDSTER

INDEX